Three Human Rights
in the Constitution

Three Human Rights
in the Constitution
of 1787

by

Zechariah Chafee, Jr.

with a Foreword by Arthur E. Sutherland

The University Press of Kansas, Lawrence and London

©, 1956, by the University of Kansas Press
First Kansas Paperback edition 1968

Library of Congress Card Catalog Number 56-9451

PRINTED IN THE UNITED STATES OF AMERICA

TO MY FRIEND IN TOIL, TROUBLE, AND HAPPINESS

CARL S. STERN

LONG ON THE FIRING LINE OF FREEDOM

WHO BEYOND STATUTES AND DECISIONS

SEES MEN AND WOMEN

Foreword

Surely Zechariah Chafee exemplified for all scholar-teachers the joy of their calling. Hours spent with him are good to remember. On his seventieth birthday he came to my room in Langdell Hall, asked me if I had any plans for lunch, and took me to the Tavern Club in Boston. We talked all afternoon over a bottle of red wine, scanning the curious follies and greatnesses of mankind. Chafee was a historian, a libertarian, a classicist, a lawyer; his grace, the charm of his slightly raucous wit, made his real greatness rest lightly on him. He taught gladly. The principal theme of his life was man's freedom, but its scarceness in the world never turned him morose. He went on his way rejoicing; we shall not again see his like.

Chafee was born in Providence in 1885, took an A.B. at Brown in 1907, and then for three years worked in his family's long-established iron-foundry. In 1910 he turned to the law, studied three years at Harvard where he distinguished himself by his brilliance and by his refusal of an invitation to join that conventional Valhalla, the Board of Editors of the *Law Review*. He took his degree in 1913 and practiced three years at the Rhode Island bar. In 1916 he accepted Harvard's invitation to join its faculty of law, and remained a member until his death forty years later.[1]

From his first teaching years Zechariah Chafee was deeply concerned with man's liberty. In 1950 he wrote of the Wilsonian humanitarianism still alive in America in 1916:

forward-looking men and women were still engaged in rethinking our traditional political, economic, and social conceptions and considering how they could be best altered to meet the new needs of an industrial and highly developed country. All possibilities were open to examination, under the guiding principle, "Prove

---

[1] The June, 1957, *Harvard Law Review* carried essays in memory of Zechariah Chafee written by Erwin Griswold, Ernest Angell, Benjamin Kaplan, and Austin Scott. They draw a vivid portrait of a profoundly civilized man.

all things; hold fast that which is good." Men's minds moved with a freedom which is now incomprehensible, for thinking had not yet been hardened into queer shapes by the emotions aroused by war and conflicting reactions to the Russian Revolution.[2]

War and tolerant freedom can never coexist. Our war with Germany in 1917 brought the federal Espionage Act of 1917, which the Congress reinforced with amendments in 1918. Despite its title this legislation went far beyond spying. The 1917 Act forbade attempts to cause insubordination in the armed forces or obstruction of recruiting; the 1918 amendment penalized obstruction of the sale of United States bonds "except by way of bona fide and not disloyal advice," and made criminal any language intended to bring into contempt or disrepute the form of government of the United States, the Constitution, the flag, or United States military uniforms. It penalized speech urging curtailment of war-production and the like. It authorized for violation penalties as great as a $10,000 fine, or twenty years in prison, or both.[3]

In 1918 one Jacob Abrams and some of his associates were convicted, under this legislation, in the United States District Court for the Southern District of New York, for distributing pamphlets which protested American intervention in Russia and deplored "Liberty Loans" and production of munitions which might be used to oppose the revolutionary régime in that country. Chafee was aroused by what he considered the injustice of this conviction and its affirmance by the United States Supreme Court.[4] He published two vigorous protests in the *Harvard Law Review*, articles which he developed into his 1920 book *Free-*

---

[2] Quoted from Chafee's paper "Harold Laski and the Harvard Law Review," 63 *Harv. L. Rev.* 1398 (1950).

[3] Act of June 15, 1917, 40 Stat. at L. 217; Act of May 16, 1918, 40 Stat. at L. 553.

[4] *Abrams* v. *United States* 250 U.S. 616 (1919). Holmes dissented from this Supreme Court affirmance. He wrote ". . . I regret that I can not put into more impressive words my belief that in their conviction upon this indictment the defendants were deprived of their rights under the Constitution of the United States." Brandeis joined in Holmes' dissent.

dom of Speech.[5] A committee of the Harvard Board of Overseers in 1921 called Chafee to account for some inaccuracies in the *Law Review* papers; President Lowell vigorously supported Chafee, and the committee recommended that no further action be taken. In November, 1921, Chafee published in the *Review* a list of corrections; they all referred to minor and inconsequential slips having nothing to do with the substance of Chafee's criticisms.

Throughout the rest of his life Chafee was identified with the cause of human liberty. His family background, his associations, his tastes, all bespoke a New England conservatism which added strength and stubborn independence to his concern for freedom. In 1929-1931 he was a consultant to President Hoover's National Commission on Law Observance and Enforcement; characteristically, he wrote part of that commission's report on lawlessness in law enforcement. He was an active member of the American Bar Association's Bill of Rights Committee, and in 1939 took an active part in drafting that committee's *amicus* brief in *Hague* v. *C.I.O.*[6] He served on the United Nations subcommission on Freedom of Information and of the Press. In 1941 he published a revised version of his earlier work on free speech, calling it "Free Speech in the United States."[7]

His industry was prodigious; despite everything else, he found time to teach, write, and promote reform of the law of civil procedure and of commerce. Equity and equitable remedies, evidence, commercial paper, copyright and trademark, unfair competition, communications, legal history—he taught in all of these fields and in many of them brought out brilliant casebooks for law students. But the infinitely diverse quality of the man comes out

---

[5] See "Freedom of Speech in War Time," 32 *Harv. L. Rev.* 932 (1919); "A Contemporary State Trial—the United States versus Jacob Abrams et al." 33 *Harv. L. Rev.* 748 (1920); and *Freedom of Speech* (New York, Harcourt Brace & Howe, 1920).

[6] 307 U.S. 496.

[7] Cambridge, Harv. U. Press (1942).

best in his philosophical writings, in which he seems to sit back and tolerantly view the curiosities of character of his fellow men. Some of the essays in his *Inquiring Mind,* which appeared in 1928,[8] are charming processes of his lambent intellect. Chafee's *Government and Mass Communications,* published in 1947,[9] was a study which he made for the Commission on Freedom of the Press, a nongovernment independent group, functioning under the aegis of the University of Chicago, and containing no members of the press, radio, or motion-picture industries. He continually wrote for periodicals, always wisely in substance, with his sensitive dramatic style. A bibliography of all his publications would expand this Foreword to inordinate length. He knew how to get things done; his drafting work on the federal interpleader act, and his success in bringing about its adoption in 1936, gave him particular satisfaction all the rest of his life.

In 1950, when he was sixty-five years old, Harvard made him one of her select group of University Professors, not attached to any department of the University, chartered to work "in such a way as to cross the conventional boundaries of the specialties."[10] He instituted a new course in Fundamental Human Rights, for which he prepared in 1951 and 1952 a collection of documents published in three thick pamphlets by the Harvard University Press. This was the beginning of a series of books which occupied his remaining years.

In the preface of his *Documents on Fundamental Human Rights* he explained his method—". . . to start with the United States Constitution and next teach history backward, asking what previous experience led the draftsmen to put a particular provision in the Constitution, and then in an earlier document, and then in something still earlier . . . ."

[8] New York, Harcourt Brace (1928).
[9] Chicago, University of Chicago Press (1947).
[10] See "University Professorships" in the Harvard University Catalogue, 1965-66.

In 1951 Boston University invited him to give its Gaspar G. Bacon Lectures; he expanded and rewrote them as his book *How Human Rights Got Into the Constitution,* which the Boston University Press published in 1952. In 1954 he revised a number of his papers published in various periodicals during the 1940s and 1950s, and so made his volume *The Blessings of Liberty,* which Lippincott brought out in 1956. In the latter year the University of Kansas Press published his *Three Human Rights in the Constitution of 1787,* rewritten and greatly expanded from his Stephens Lectures delivered in March and April, 1952, at the University of Kansas School of Law. This was his last book. He chose to become University Professor *emeritus* in June, 1956, though the University immediately appointed him one of its first television lecturers, and throughout the following autumn and winter he broadcasted a series of lectures on human rights under the Constitution. He finished the series a week before his death in February, 1957.

Republication of *Three Human Rights* in 1968 is most welcome. The book is Chafee at his best. The ease and elegance of his historical scholarship, the infinite variety of his literacy, his tolerant passion for a free society, all these are here. Zechariah Chafee never ran down. His choice of three aspirations of man is thought-provoking. He wrote of freedom of debate in Congress, of the constitutional prohibition of bills of attainder, and of freedom of movement. Characteristically, Chafee's first two essays treat two antithetical freedoms. A parliament must be a place where elected representatives can debate anything, argue anything, subject only to their own internal discipline; yet a legislature which votes a man guilty of crime, which enacts a "bill of attainder" or the like, goes beyond the appropriate orbit of legislation. The urges of popular politics are too strong for the just determination of guilt. Conflict between two excellent aspirations was a recurring theme with Chafee. He wrote in 1943,[11] "Anybody knows how to choose between Virtue and Vice. What worries us is the constant necessity of choosing between two nearly right courses of action."

Today, in the United States, few of us worry about any curbs on debate in the national legislature. Constitutionally our Senators and Congressmen may not be and are not "questioned in any other place"—in any place, that is, but their "respective Houses," for "any Speech or Debate in either House." Indeed our Supreme Court in 1951 carried this national restriction into the States and construed the Fourteenth Amendment to allow an extraordinary immunity to California legislators who were members of that State's Senate Fact-Finding Committee on Un-American Activities.[12] But in 1966 the Supreme Court held that the Fourteenth Amendment forbade the Georgia legislature to refuse a seat to an elected member who had during his electoral campaign sharply criticized the policy of the United States in its Viet Nam military hostilities.[13]

Actions of legislatures may cause even greater concern when resentful majorities penalize the political affiliations of hated minorities. In 1959 the federal Labor-Management Reporting and Disclosure Act made it a crime for a member of the Communist Party to serve as an officer of a labor union. In 1966 the Supreme Court of the United States held that this Act of Congress was void as a bill of attainder.[14] Chief Justice Warren wrote for the Court in the Chafee spirit.

While history thus provides some guidelines, the wide variation in form, purpose and effect of ante-constitutional bills of attainder indicates that the proper scope of the Bills of Attainder Clause, and its relevance to contemporary problems must ultimately be sought

---

[11] In a review of Cozzens' *The Just and the Unjust*, in 56 *Harv. L. Rev.* 833, at 835-6 (1943).

[12] *Tenney* v. *Brandhove*, 341 U.S. 367 (1951).

[13] *Bond* v. *Floyd*, 385 U.S. 116 (1966).

[14] *United States* v. *Brown*, 381 U.S. 437 (1966).

by attempting to discern the reasons for its inclusion in the Constitution, and the evils it was designed to eliminate. The best available evidence, the writings of the architects of our constitutional system, indicates that the Bill of Attainder Clause was intended not as a narrow, technical (and therefore soon to be outmoded) prohibition, but rather as an implementation of the separation of powers, a general safeguard against legislative exercise of the judicial function, or more simply—trial by legislature.

Evidently there is still life in the 1787 prohibition against bills of attainder. The Constitution allows free play to our legislatures, national and state—but not too much free play.[15]

Perhaps for 1968 the saddest overtones in Zechariah Chafee's *Three Human Rights* echo in his third chapter, on Freedom of Movement. He wrote at page 174, "The plain truth is that so far as the law is concerned, there was much more freedom of movement between the British Isles and our eastern seaboard at any time between 1607 and 1776 than exists in 1956." Maybe so. Those quantitative comparisons are hard to make. The crowding of the world, the shrinking of oceans by incredibly swift transportation-devices, the rivalry among nations for natural resources, the suspicion felt by one nation or set of nations of the motives of another, the reorientation of our national attention from Europe to the Far East—all these build up increasingly high barriers not only to the mass migration of peoples but to mere visits to see what is going on. China is the most populous nation on earth; how much do our people know of what takes place within her borders?

The Supreme Court is doing what it can, which is little enough. A recent federal statute makes it a crime for

---

[15] On December 11, 1967, the Supreme Court in an opinion by Chief Justice Warren held that a section of the Subversive Activities Control Act making it unlawful for a member of a Communist-action organization to work for a "defense facility" is unconstitutional in that it sought to bar employment indiscriminately for association which is constitutionally proscribable despite the First Amendment, and for association which that Amendment protects. *United States* v. *Robel*, 389 U.S. 258 (1967).

an American citizen to leave or enter the United States "unless he bears a valid passport." In 1967 the Court held that citizens who went to Cuba carrying passports generally valid did not violate that statute by their failure to obtain a State Department endorsement specifically allowing a visit to Cuba.[16] A State Department regulation required such an endorsement, but Congress had not penalized a visit made without it. In 1964 the Court held constitutionally invalid a 1950 federal law forbidding a member of a Communist organization to apply for or use a U.S. passport. Justice Goldberg wrote for the Court, "We hold . . . that §6 of the Control Act too broadly and indiscriminately restricts the right to travel and thereby abridges the liberty guaranteed by the Fifth Amendment."[17]

But ultimately mankind must find its optimal freedom in its own wishes. Chafee wrote in the Introduction to *Three Human Rights*—

The immediate future of human rights in the United States depends less on our experiences in the immediate past than on the fullness or the emptiness of our devotion to the achievements of the remote past. The eight years since the cold war began with the Communist seizure of Czechoslovakia are perhaps more interesting than the seven centuries since Magna Carta. Still, my chief concern is with the seven centuries and what they gave us today. The boughs of the Tree of Liberty may be swayed this way and that by recent gales, but their strength to withstand the wind comes from "the depth and toughness of their roots in the past." The greatest danger to the American people is that they themselves may erode these roots by forgetfulness and indifference— "the slow smokeless burning of decay." In the long run the public gets just as much freedom as it wants.

Here Chafee stated the best reason for reprinting this last book of his. Holmes wisely said in 1913, "For most of the things that properly can be called evils in the pres-

---

[16] *United States* v. *Laub*, 385 U.S. 475.
[17] *Aptheker* v. *Secretary of State* 378 U.S. 500 (1964).

ent state of the law I think the main remedy, as for the evils of public opinion, is for us to grow more civilized."[18] To grow more civilized, men must come to know more civilized men, and of these Zechariah Chafee was one of the rarest and best, one of the wisest, the most unarrogantly learned, the most tolerant. *Three Human Rights* will help the present generation, a little, to know him, to savor his quality, and through him to know the degree of civilization to which man can aspire.

ARTHUR E. SUTHERLAND

Cambridge
January 1968

---

[18] "The Law and the Court," Collected Legal Papers, p. 296 (1952).

Contents

Publisher's Note

In the following book Professor Chafee has revised and greatly expanded material used in the third series of the Judge Nelson Timothy Stephens Lectures, delivered on March 31 and April 1 and 2, 1952, under the auspices of the School of Law at the University of Kansas. The lectures in memory of Judge Stephens were established by his daughter, Miss Kate Stephens, and are provided for by funds administered by the New York Community Trust.

Finally, the record of the past in which all battles are decided and many pains forgotten whereas the most distinguished characters, actions, and works stand out more clearly and in a more final form than they did in their own time, may lull us into a false security and indolence in view of the pains we have to suffer, the decisions we have to make, the actions we have to accomplish, without yet knowing the outcome.—PAUL OSKAR KRISTELLER, *The Classics and Renaissance Thought.*

Introduction

Considerably more than half of the fifty-five men who passed the long summer of 1787 in the Assembly Room of the old Statehouse in Philadelphia were probably no abler than political leaders today. What made them different was, first, their intense concentration upon the tasks in hand. There was no filibustering, no eloquence, no appeal to the folks back home. Fortunately, the press galleries were kept empty. Each day the delegates knew exactly what concrete issues were before them and they directed their attention solely to those issues. The second reason for their great achievements is that they rose throughout to the full extent of their intellectual powers. Every time I go back to the Philadephia Debates, my admiration for these men grows.

One of their main purposes set forth in their noble Preamble was to "secure the Blessings of Liberty to ourselves and to our Posterity." No doubt, they knew that the whole framework of government which they were creating would help to preserve fundamental freedoms, but my concern is narrower. I have long been seeking to learn the meaning and origins of the various liberties which they safeguarded directly by specific provisions, and of those other liberties which were enshrined by later men in Amendments.[1] Therefore, my inquiry can pretty much ignore long passages in the Constitution which deal with political rights, such as the structure of national government, the relation between the nation and the states, and the election or appointment of legislators and officials. It has been my desire to try and clarify the rights of men as men.

Whenever a citizen thinks about human rights in this restricted sense, as they appear in the Constitution, his first impulse is to confine his attention to the Bill of Rights

—the ten Amendments adopted in 1791. The human rights there set forth are, of course, of the utmost importance. Still, there are other human rights of equal value in the original Constitution. Hamilton skillfully pointed this out in the next to the last issue of *The Federalist* (No. 84) and argued that several clauses, taken together, were equivalent to a Bill of Rights, even though this name was not expressly used in the Constitution. In this book I shall speak only of human rights which were secured by the work of the Philadelphia Convention.

The most valuable human right in the Constitution is the writ of habeas corpus, which is protected against suspension except in very limited situations. This I have dealt with at length in my preceding book, *How Human Rights Got into the Constitution.*[2] In the three chapters of the present book, I shall go on to speak of three other human rights in the original Constitution: first, freedom of debate in Congress; second, the prohibition against bills of attainder and, more incidentally, ex post facto laws; and finally freedom of movement.

In each instance something will be said about the way the right has developed in our country since 1787 and about current problems as to its proper scope. Still, the main emphasis will be placed upon the reasons why the right was so precious to the framers that they put it into the Constitution.

The immediate future of human rights in the United States depends less on our experiences in the immediate past than on the fullness or the emptiness of our devotion to the achievements of the remote past. The eight years since the cold war began with the Communist seizure of Czechoslovakia are perhaps more interesting than the seven centuries since Magna Carta. Still, my chief concern is with the seven centuries and what they gave us today. The boughs of the Tree of Liberty may be swayed this

2

INTRODUCTION

way and that by recent gales, but their strength to withstand the wind comes from "the depth and toughness of their roots in the past."[3] The greatest danger to the American people is that they themselves may erode these roots by forgetfulness and indifference—"the slow smokeless burning of decay."[4] In the long run the public gets just as much freedom as it wants.

Therefore, this book has been written in the hope of helping men and women to remember how the human rights in our Constitution grew strong before they gained a place there. These things were not found under a gooseberry bush. They were shaped and achieved through centuries of struggle, through the willingness of men to languish in prison and die there, through long thinking and endless tedious work. Others have labored and we have entered into their labors. Generations gave these human rights to us, and it is for us in turn to "secure the Blessings of Liberty to ourselves and our Posterity," strengthened and enriched while in our hands.[5]

3

Freedom of Debate in Congress

One of my law school professors wisely advised us to read through the whole Constitution once a year. Just as Koussevitzky said, "Every time I go over the score of the Eroica I find something new," so a lawyer is constantly surprised to discover in the Constitution some hitherto unappreciated evidence of the wisdom and foresight of its framers.

The Provisions in the Constitution

In the course of such a continuous perusal of the Constitution, almost the first clause about human rights which will appear is: ". . . and for any Speech or Debate in either House they [the Senators and Representatives] shall not be questioned in any other Place."

Those words in Article I, section 6, are the subject of my first chapter.[1] The objection might indeed be raised that the clause embodies a political right rather than a human right. At most it protects only 531 men and women seated in the Senate and the House. It does nothing directly for the liberties of the other 150,000,000 inhabitants of the United States. Morever, the most obvious purpose of the clause is to enable Senators and Representatives to carry on the government more efficiently and not to benefit them as human beings. Nevertheless, I feel sure that it is fruitful to put this clause in the forefront of my discussion of human rights in the Constitution.

One reason is the very close connection between freedom of debate in the legislature and freedom of discussion by citizens at large, which is now protected by the First Amendment to some extent though not completely. My examination of the history of freedom of debate will show that much the same arguments for limiting it were used by the English sovereigns as are now used by those

4

who want to cut down distasteful expressions of opinion by ordinary citizens.

Secondly, freedom of debate resembles many other individual rights, in this respect: the bigger the right of A, the smaller the right of B. One of my favorite stories concerns a man who was arrested for swinging his arms and hitting a passer-by in the nose. The accused remonstrated in court, "Hasn't a man a right to swing his arms in a free country?" The judge replied, "Your right to swing your arms stops just where the other man's nose begins." For the ordinary citizen, the right of free speech stops just where the law of slander and libel begins. Not so for Senators and Representatives. Still, the more freedom these public servants have to talk, the smaller is the security of plain people against having their reputations ruined by reckless charges and perhaps losing their jobs in consequence. The many citizens who are defamed have human rights as well as the few legislators who do the defaming. Here, however, the regular law of libel and slander does not work. The Constitution takes the whole matter away from the courts.

This is commonly supposed to end the problem. Because a suit for slander or libel will surely fail, it is often assumed that a Senator or a Representative has an unlimited constitutional right to utter falsehoods and vituperation about anybody outside Congress. The Constitution says no such thing. It merely declares that the Senator or Representative cannot be called to account "in any *other* place." But he can be called to account in the very place where he does the slandering. The words in section 6 of Article I ought not to be read in isolation. They are inextricably linked with a provision of section 5, a few lines above: "Each House may . . . punish its Members for Disorderly Behavior, and with the Concurrence of two thirds, expel a Member."

5

As yet, neither the House of Representatives nor the Senate has exercised this power to discourage its members from defaming and insulting private citizens and government officials, no matter how well they have served their country. Nevertheless, this unused power to restrain abuses is an indispensable companion to the privilege of freedom of debate, which is constantly remembered. The relationship between these two clauses of the Constitution is a very important aspect of our subject. We shall have to keep in mind both the rights of legislators and the rights of those who are harmed by legislative speech.

Now we come to our basic problem. How did the clause about freedom of debate get into the Constitution? What did the framers of this provision have in mind when they wrote it?

The Articles of Confederation and Early State Constitutions

The debates at Philadelphia show that freedom of debate was accepted as a matter of course, without any discussion or opposition. The plain reason for such acquiescence was the fact that Congress was already enjoying this privilege. The Articles of Confederation, which were mainly drafted in the early summer of 1776 by John Dickinson, had substantially the same language: "Freedom of speech and debate in Congress shall not be impeached or questioned in any court or place out of Congress. . . ." The privilege was also familiar in state legislatures. It was expressly embodied in the early constitutions of Maryland, Massachusetts, and New Hampshire, and virtually recognized by that of New York.[2]

All this throws our investigation one step farther back. Why did Americans during our Revolution think it important to put freedom of debate into the documents just mentioned? What were the influences upon them from their knowledge and experience?

The Bill of Rights of 1688/9

Again the answer is plain. They were well aware of the similar provision in the English Bill of Rights: "That the freedom of speech, and debates or proceedings in parliament, ought not to be impeached or questioned in any court or place out of parliament."

Three great documents established comprehensive liberties for Englishmen, whether at home or on our own shores. Magna Carta in June, 1215, and the Petition of Right in June, 1628, were granted by reigning sovereigns. The acceptance of the Bill of Rights brought a new King and Queen to the throne. That was the closing scene of the Revolution of 1688. We would call it February 13, 1689, but the New Year then began on March 25th.

An understanding of the Bill of Rights requires a short account of the events which brought it about. Nearly twenty-nine years earlier, in 1660, the English people, weary of republican experiments and military dictatorships since the beheading of Charles I, recalled his eldest son from exile to reign as Charles II. With him returned his brother James, Duke of York, who was to be the next King, since Charles had no legitimate offspring. James had two children, Mary and Anne by his first wife, daughter of Charles' chief minister for several years after the Restoration—Edward Hyde, Earl of Clarendon, the masterly historian of the Civil War whom we shall subsequently encounter at the start and the finish of his political career. James soon became a Roman Catholic, but his two girls were brought up in the Protestant faith. Through the efforts of a later chief minister, the Earl of Danby, who plays a leading part in my next chapter, Mary, the heir

7

after James, was married while not yet sixteen, to William Prince of Orange, the nearest male in the line of succession, since his mother was a daughter of Charles I.

The Prince was a sort of hereditary President of the Dutch Republic. His great-grandfather William the Silent freed the Netherlands from the tyranny of Spain and the Dutch remember him as we remember Washington. The House of Orange is among humankind what the stock of Man of War is among horses. In generation after generation ability and courage never fail. Through terrible disasters like the ceaseless attacks by Louis XIV in the seventeenth century and the Nazi invasion in the twentieth, the ruling family of Holland lives up to the motto on the arms of William the Silent, JE MAINTIENDRAI.

A year after this marriage England was visited by an emotional plague, the Popish Plot. Hysterical terror of Roman Catholics spread by lying informers, as my next chapter will narrate, sent Danby to the Tower, caused many innocent men to be hanged or beheaded, and brought about a powerful effort in Parliament to banish James and exclude him from ever becoming King. Fortunately for him, his bitterest enemies made the mistake of passing over his Protestant daughter, Mary, and seeking to bestow the right to succeed Charles II on Charles' illegitimate son the Duke of Monmouth, a young man of great charm.

> Whate'er he did was done with so much ease,
> In him alone 'twas natural to please. . . .

So Dryden described him as Absalom, the errant son of the Merry Monarch, King David. Bewitched by Monmouth, the credulous crowd accepted a cock-and-bull story how his mother and Charles made a secret marriage-contract which was kept in a black box. Still, many doubters about Monmouth supported the Exclusion Bill, which

8

swept through the House of Commons and almost passed in the House of Lords. One of the few speeches in history which are known to have changed votes was made by George Savile, Marquis of Halifax.[3] He was the most penetrating thinker of the time in politics, but, as a contemporary wrote, "He went backwards and forwards and changed sides so often, that in conclusion no side trusted him." Unlike some other politicians, however, Halifax usually shifted to the party which appeared to be losing. He wanted to balance the boat and was neither a Tory nor a Whig, but (in his own phrase) a "Trimmer."

This victory of the King and James was followed by a loyal reaction. Monmouth and his supporters were exiled. Charles strengthened his power greatly by clever manipulations and might perhaps have become as absolute a ruler as his father desired to be, had not death stepped in the way.

When James II succeeded his brother in February, 1685, he was the first avowed Roman Catholic to occupy the throne for over 125 years.[4] During the same period of time, the English people had become overwhelmingly Protestant, members either of the Church of England, directed by bishops like Episcopalians among us, or of the various dissenting sects which correspond roughly to the Congregationalists, Presbyterians, Baptists, and Quakers in the American colonies. Yet James was their lawful King, whatever his religion. Moreover, his expected heir was his Protestant daughter Mary, whose husband had now made himself the leader of the nations which were resisting the great power of Louis XIV of France. Although James was married again to a Catholic princess from Italy, her infants had soon died and several years had passed without sign of a child. So most Englishmen were ready to give loyal devotion to a Roman Catholic King in his fifty-second year, believing that his reign

9

would only be a short interlude in their long and otherwise unbroken allegiance to rulers of their own faith.

The loyalty of Parliament and most of his subjects to the new King stood the test well in June, 1685, four months after his accession, when the Duke of Monmouth landed on the southwest coast of England and had himself proclaimed king. Multitudes of humble men joined him in the last of the great popular uprisings in England, which began with Wat Tyler and Jack Cade. Both Houses of Parliament promptly passed a bill of attainder without bothering about a trial:[5] "That James duke of Monmouth stand and be convicted and attainted of high treason, and that he suffer pains of death, and incur all forfeitures as a traitor convicted and attainted of high treason." The pains of death came swiftly to Monmouth in the Tower of London after his defeat at the Battle of Sedgemoor.

Unhappily, James II did not stop with the chief culprits. He sent Chief Justice Jeffreys into the west country to wreak a terrible vengeance upon Monmouth's credulous supporters. The King was determined to teach his people a lasting lesson that rebellion does not pay. But does extreme severity pay? The lesson lasted only three and a half years until a very different Protestant leader landed on the Devon coast.

This triumph appears to have made James think he could accomplish anything he wished. He possessed none of Charles II's skill in sensing when he had gone too far, in trying something else, in dodging around opposition or manipulating his opponents. Instead, he plunged straight ahead with all sorts of personal acts to undo the Reformation and increase the royal power. Nobody could persuade him to give up a project or at least go slowly. James had always been fond of saying that "all who opposed the King were rebels in their hearts." When Halifax and other Protestant ministers advised against his measures he dismissed them, and in their place he appointed Roman Catholics—not members of the old families who had long been loyal to both faith and freedom, but adventurers and men whose recent conversions were actuated by ambition rather than devotion. He mainly officered with Catholics the large standing army he was building up on the outskirts of London, not to fight foreigners but to cow Englishmen. When his first Parliament, though unusually subservient in most matters, remonstrated at this, the King dissolved it and never called another. Not even the Pope could dissuade James.

[Innocent XI] was too wise a man to believe that a nation, so bold and stubborn, could be brought back to the Church of Rome by the violent and unconstitutional exercise of royal authority. It was not difficult to foresee that, if James attempted to promote the interests of his religion by illegal and unpopular means, the attempt would fail; the hatred with which the heretical islanders regarded the true faith would become fiercer and stronger than ever; and an indissoluble association would be created in their minds between Protestantism and civil freedom, between Popery and arbitrary power . . . .[6]

"This is precisely what happened," says a writer in the *Catholic Encyclopedia*[7] after quoting these sentences from Macaulay. "And indeed it is not too much to say that British Catholics have, in great measure, to thank the last two Catholic sovereigns [Mary I and James II] for the strong feeling which so long existed against them through the nation. . . ."

Every arbitrary act by James multiplied the number of Englishmen who feared him. The various Protestant denominations stopped quarreling among themselves in their alarm that they might soon undergo the persecutions which the Huguenots were then suffering in France when the Catholic Louis XIV revoked the Edict of Nantes. The Dissenters who hated arbitrary power under Charles I and hated it equally under his son suddenly

11

found themselves united with Churchmen who had been saying for decades that it was wrong to resist a king, no matter how wicked. The families who had always remained Catholic—some of the best blood in England—kept aloof from James, although he restored freedom of worship which had long been cruelly denied them. They were reluctant to stake everything on the life of one man who recklessly disrupted established English institutions and brushed aside the law of the land, instead of patiently persuading Parliament to embody in a lasting statute the spirit of toleration which was growing fast in the latter half of the seventeenth century.[8] Insofar as history has any lessons, it teaches that rulers do not live forever; and that when one of them forces great changes on an unwilling country, the successor who is bound to replace him may go immediately in the opposite direction.

We Americans can get some notion of the consternation which James II was spreading among Englishmen if we recall the detestation our colonial ancestors had for his agent Sir Edmund Andros. Yet the servant did far less than his master, for Andros did not threaten religious liberty. It was enough that he was duplicating the King's policy of wiping out cherished forms of government.

As the prospects of English liberty grew steadily darker, men looked more and more across the North Sea to the one man who might be their deliverer. The Prince of Orange was constantly in touch with his friends Halifax and Danby, and with other members of the Opposition. This is not evidence that he had long and deliberately planned to invade England. Surely, it was sensible for him to want to know as much as possible about the country where his wife would some day be Queen and where, as things went in those times, a husband of William's force would be much more than a ceremonial companion for the ruling lady, like Prince Bernhard or the Duke of

12

Edinburgh today. For all practical purposes the Prince of
Orange would then head both Holland and Great Britain.
To try to accelerate the inevitable by starting another
English civil war might be the height of folly. Attacking
and ruining your father-in-law is not ordinarily the way
to help your wife's chances of inheriting property. Moreover, the Prince of Orange was the last man on earth to
imitate the Duke of Monmouth. He was not going to set
out to rescue the English people, only to find after landing
that the English people did not want to be rescued. True,
he could not afford to have Britain become a mere satel-
lite of France, whose army and navy would be thrown
against Holland by Louis XIV along with his own great
forces. On the contrary, William needed her in the coali-
tion which he was forming against that insatiable French
king. Still, if the British Crown was going to come peacefully to Mary in due course, the wisest policy for her husband was watchful waiting.

Matters were brought to a head in June, 1688, by a
rapid series of events. Mostly I shall let them be told by
Narcissus Luttrell, an indefatigable gatherer of items of
interest in the days before there were hardly any newspapers; these gleanings he sent to his numerous customers
in a sort of Kiplinger *Newsletter*.[9] Imagine the amazement of a Yorkshire squire with broad acres, a zealous
supporter of Church and King who slept in his pew
every Sunday, on reading that on June 8th the King had
put the Archbishop of Canterbury and six other Bishops
in prison. They were charged with sedition for presenting
to James in his palace at Whitehall their respectful petition questioning the lawfulness and propriety of decrees
of his which greatly affected the Church of England:
"As they were carried to the Tower, which was by water,
at their goeing into the barge, and their landing, thou-

13

sands of people knelt down and had their lordships blessings, and acclamation on the water, and prayers for their deliverance." James had made it plain that he would stop at nothing, that nobody was safe.

Luttrell's next item, of two days later, was equally momentous: "The 10th, between 9 and 10 in the morning, the queen was delivered of a prince at St. James, by Mrs. Wilkins the midwife, to whom the king gave 500 guineas for her pains: 'tis said the queen was very quick, so that few persons were by."

A son to James would come ahead of his Protestant half-sisters Mary and Anne, and put England under a Catholic dynasty. Still, one way to dispose of bad news is to disbelieve it. Rumors were credited, especially as reliable counter-evidence was lacking. It was the custom for high ministers of state to attend royal accouchements until a few years ago, when Queen Elizabeth II decided that the genuineness of Prince Charles could be adequately proved by eminent obstetricians. James unwisely invited only councillors who had earned the deep distrust of the public. So suspicions spread fast that the baby was produced by sleight-of-hand. One favorite story had him smuggled into the Queen's bed in a warming-pan. There have been plenty of scandals about who really fathered royal children, but this was the only baby in history to have doubts cast upon his maternity. The rumors were preposterous. Mary of Modena had another boy who became a cardinal. Yet this gossip about her sterility had a good deal to do with preventing her oldest son from becoming king and in bringing about the Bill of Rights.

While England was terrorized by the headlong measures of James, people released by song the emotions they dared not put into plain speech. Support for one of the imprisoned bishops who came from Cornwall was given by the chorus:

And shall Trelawney die?
There's thirty thousand Cornishmen will know the reason why.

Everybody ridiculed the Irish troops whom James was bringing over for his big army by whistling Purcell's tune of "Lilliburlero, bullen-a-la!" Popular disbelief in the baby in St. James Palace took form in the nursery-rhyme, "Rock-a-bye baby on the tree-top," with its foreboding last line, "And down comes baby and cradle and all."

On June 29th came the trial of the Seven Bishops. The court sat in Westminster Hall, one of the oldest buildings in England, built by the son of William the Conqueror and still standing after all the bombings of London. The great hall and all the neighboring court-yards and streets for a long way were thronged with people. The Bishops had several able lawyers, but the strongest argument on their behalf was made by a pre-viously undistinguished barrister of thirty-seven, John Somers. For the outcome I go again to Luttrell:

> So the tryal held till 6 in the evening; and the jury went away, and lay together till 6 the next morning, when they agreed; . . . they . . . came into court, and being called, they found all the defendants Not guilty; at which there was a most mighty huzzah and shouting in the hall, which was very full of people; and all the way they [the Bishops] came down people askt their blessing on their knees: there was continued shoutings for ½ an hour, so that no business could be done. . . . And at night was mighty rejoyceing, in ringing of bells, discharging of guns, lighting of candles, and bonefires in several places, tho forbid. . . .

On that last night of June, when the English people had plainly shown themselves to be solidly against James, a small group of nobles sent a letter by a secret messenger to the Prince of Orange. Halifax had declined to join them; although he had thrown up his hat from his seat in Westminster Hall on hearing the jury's verdict, he was made for thought, not action. Danby, however, was hardened to the risk of death, as my next chapter will tell.

15

He signed, and so did six other peers including Whigs and Tories. Their letters asked the Prince to appear on the island at the head of troops with as little delay as possible; tens of thousands would rally to his standard.

William of Orange knew that now he could intervene without fear of starting another great Civil War in England. In late October he sent over his Declaration that he was coming to end the gross and systematic violation of laws. His sole object was to have a free and legal Parliament assembled, and he solemnly pledged himself to leave all questions to its decision. On November 1st his fleet of six hundred vessels put to sea before "the Protestant wind," and he was close to the cliffs of the Isle of Wight on the 4th, his thirty-eighth birthday. The next afternoon, he landed at Torbay in Devonshire and began marching toward London. The King's army faded away after a little fighting. James was rapidly deserted by everybody who mattered. After sending his wife and child ahead, he fled to France on the 23rd of December and took refuge with Louis XIV at St. Germains.

Anarchy might have ensued if the English had not displayed characteristic resourcefulness in an unprecedented situation. It was impossible to hold a regular Parliament, because the King had gone and nobody else had legal power to order elections. Nevertheless, a practical government was soon devised. The Prince of Orange came to London. All the peers who were on hand assembled, with Halifax presiding; and everybody who had served in the House of Commons under Charles II came together with officers of the City of London. These two bodies were wholly without legal sanction, but very efficient. They requested the Prince to take provisional charge of the administration of affairs and to invite all the usual constituencies to send representatives to Westminster just as if they were choosing an ordinary House of Commons. At the same time the Lords would meet in their own House as usual.

The resulting Convention of Lords and Commoners was equally efficient. Its dominant policy of disregarding historic precedents in order to face immediate needs was expressed by a lawyer ninety years old, Sir John Maynard. Endeared to lawyers as the first editor of the Year Books, an invaluable record of court proceedings under the Plantagenets, Maynard had sat in the Long Parliament and been one of Strafford's accusers in 1641. Now he spoke out of his long wisdom:

> We are at the moment out of the beaten path. If therefore we are determined to move only in that path, we cannot move at all. A man in a revolution resolving to do nothing which is not strictly according to established form resembles a man who has lost himself in the wilderness, and who stands crying "Where is the king's highway? I will walk nowhere but on the king's highway." In a wilderness a man should take the track which will carry him home. In a revolution we must have recourse to the highest law, the safety of the state.

The first question was what to do with the throne. After prolonged discussions of various plans, during which Halifax and Danby were outstanding among the Lords, the Convention decided that the throne was vacant, that the dubious baby should be ignored, and that William and Mary should reign together. They were to be offered the Crown on condition that they accepted a Declaration of Rights which would make law and liberty safe from future royal aggressions.

The next step was to decide what should go into this Declaration of Rights. The initial impulse was to include, not only the great and long-established principles of freedom which had been violated by James II, but also many new laws to purify the administration of justice and cure all sorts of evils of government. To do such a job well

17

might take years of discussion. At last, it was wisely decided to postpone all reforms until the ancient constitution had been restored. Several important safeguards of freedom which greatly influenced the Constitution of the United States were left for Parliament to enact within a few years, like periodic legislative checks on the army, life-tenure for judges, the conduct of trials for treason, and freedom of worship.[10] Only fundamental principles were to be set forth in the Declaration, in most distinct and solemn manner.

The desired document was then prepared by a committee of which the chairman was John Somers. One day he would be Lord Chancellor, but then it was remarkable to have this task done by a young barrister of lowly birth only ten days after he had spoken in the House of Commons for the first time. From what Somers and his associates wrote are derived many of the rights later embodied in our Constitution. Thus, in addition to asserting freedom of debate, the Lords and Commons "for the vindicating and asserting their ancient rights and liberties, declare" that all law-making powers are vested in the legislature and nowise in the executive (see Article I, section 1, of the Constitution); that taxes are to be imposed by the legislature (see Article I, section 8, clause 1); the right of petition (see the First Amendment); the right to bear arms (see the Second Amendment); "that excessive bail ought not to be required, nor excessive fines imposed, nor cruel and unusual punishments inflicted" (almost the exact words of the Eighth Amendment); trial by jury (see Article III, section 2, and the Sixth and Seventh Amendments); and that the legislature ought to meet frequently (see Article I, section 4, clause 2).

All these and others the Lords and Commons did "claim, demand, and insist upon . . . as their undoubted rights and liberties" and, expressing entire confidence

18

that the Prince of Orange would preserve them from violation, their Declaration went on to declare William and Mary King and Queen and prayed them to accept the Crown accordingly.

The great decisions had now been made, and by February 12th, when the Princess Mary landed from Holland, all was ready.

On the morning of Wednesday, the 13th of February, the magnificent Banqueting House at Whitehall, designed by Inigo Jones and all that is left to us of this palace, was thronged for a great ceremony which Macaulay describes:[11]

The walls were lined by the yeomen of the guard. Near the northern door, on the right hand, a large number of Peers had assembled. On the left were the Commons with their speaker [Powle], attended by the mace. The southern door opened; and the Prince and Princess of Orange, side by side, entered, and took their place under the canopy of state.

Both Houses aproached bowing low. William and Mary advanced a few steps. Halifax on the right and Powle on the left, stood forth; and Halifax spoke. The Convention, he said, had agreed to a resolution which he prayed Their Highnesses to hear. They signified their assent; and the clerk of the House of Lords read, in a loud voice, the Declaration of Right. When he had concluded, Halifax, in the name of all the Estates of the Realm, requested the Prince and Princess to accept the crown.

William in his own name and in that of his wife, answered, "We thankfully accept what you have offered us." [His] words were received with a shout of joy which was heard in the streets below, and was instantly answered by huzzahs from many thousands of voices. The Lords and Commons then reverently retired from the Banqueting House and went in procession to the great gate of Whitehall, where the heralds and pursuivants were waiting in their gorgeous tabards. All the space as far as Charing Cross was one sea of heads. The kettle drums struck up; the trumpets pealed: and Garter King at arms, in a loud voice, proclaimed the Prince and Princess of Orange King and Queen of England.

19

The Convention was afterwards turned into a regular Parliament. Next December the whole proceeding was formally written into "An act for declaring the rights and liberties of the subject," which was "to stand, remain, and be the law of this realm forever." In 1690, a duly elected Parliament confirmed all the legislation of the Convention Parliament, including the Bill of Rights. Thus freedom of debate was established in English law.

Once more we have to look backward, through the eyes of Somers, and ask why he selected freedom of debate as one of the few fundamental rights to go into the Declaration of Rights. There is a peculiarity about its presence there. The document opens with a recital of several specific violations of constitutional rights by James II, such as keeping a standing army without consent of Parliament, disarming Protestants while Papists were armed, and persecuting the bishops for petitioning the Crown. The ensuing assertion of the rights and liberties which William and Mary would promise to observe exhibits, in large measure, a point-to-point correspondence with the previous list of violations by James II. Not so freedom of debate. It is among the recognized rights without being in the earlier list of violated rights. And in fact James II did not interfere with discussions in the House of Commons during his single short Parliament, so far as I can ascertain. He had already rendered it subservient by shaping town governments which chose the Burgesses and by intimidating many private citizens who elected the representatives of the counties. The only punishment of an outspoken member in this reign was by the House of Commons itself.

Nor had Charles II imprisoned members of Parliament for what they said in debate. He relied on more subtle methods of getting his way, like intrigues, corruption, manipulating the constituencies, and, in the case of a bitter

20

critic of the profligacy of the court, by sending a gang of bullies to slit the member's nose.[12] It does indeed seem probable that a Joint Resolution of both Houses in 1667 did influence the meaning attached twenty years later to "freedom of speech" in the Bill of Rights. Still, there was no sharp menace to the safety of members in 1667. Only an abstract discussion took place (as I shall show[13]), and that is not enough to get a clause into a fundamental document. The words have to be hammered into it by hard facts.

My surmise is that when freedom of debate was ensured by Somers and his associates in January, 1689, they were not concerned with anything recent. Their minds went back forty-seven years to January 4, 1642, one of the most momentous days in English history. Then, for the first and last time, a sovereign entered the House of Commons. Serjeant Maynard was probably the only man who saw Charles I on that day and lived to see William and Mary accept the Crown.

In describing the long struggle which culminated in the drastic events of January 4, 1642, and was brought to an end by the Bill of Rights, I shall follow the course recommended by the King of Hearts to the White Rabbit, "Begin at the beginning and go on till you come to the end: then stop." Flying back from 1689 over nearly five centuries, let us land in the time when Ivanhoe was living unenthusiastically with Rowena, and King John had never heard of Magna Carta.

Freedom of Debate in the Medieval House of Commons

The subject of freedom of debate in the Middle Ages is a good deal like the book Dr. Johnson read about Iceland, in which the chapter entitled "Concerning Snakes" said only, "There are no snakes to be met with throughout the whole island."

The early history of the House of Commons offered little opportunity for any sort of debate. Edward I did not suddenly get a brilliant inspiration and say, "I am going to establish a House of Lords and a House of Commons, and they and the King will make laws for England henceforth." It was a much more mixed-up affair. Knights had been occasionally summoned from the counties to speak with the King concerning affairs of the kingdom at least since 1213 in the reign of John, and the towns had been directed to send burgesses by Simon De Montfort in 1265 during his contests with Henry III. Yet we should beware of thinking of such gatherings as anything like the separate House of Commons of later days. The whole nature of society and government was different. Landholding was inextricably entangled with the settlement of private disputes. Commoners were not eager to be chosen to go to Parliament. True, they were well paid, getting the price of a cow for each week's work. However, the money had to be found by the counties and towns which sent delegates, and these often economized by disregarding the summons and sending nobody. In any event, the knights and burgesses had no idea that they were going to Parliament to take part in governing England. If they went, it was because the King ordered them to come, little as they liked it.

There was indeed a solid beginning for the House of Lords in the great councils of nobles and bishops and those who held land directly from the King, even though the name of House of Lords would not be used until after the Wars of the Roses. But the commoners were neither a separate nor a co-ordinate body. At first they met in the same room as the nobles and bishops, but were unrespected and disunited. Morever, the knights and burgesses

22

were long distinct from each other. And they were not summoned by the king to be part of the Council, but to appear "before our Council." So subordinated were they that *Quia emptores,* the medieval statute which most plagues law students, was promulgated by the King to the peers a week before the knights and burgesses arrived. When the commoners did begin sitting together in a room by themselves, this was not in the Palace of Westminster where the peers met, but in part of Westminster Abbey. There they were more like a mass meeting than a legislative body. The real Parliament was in the Palace, where the King was deliberating with nobles and bishops, but the only person from the knights and burgesses who could talk there was their Speaker. That is just what his name literally means. His important function as the presiding officer of the House of Commons came later.

Nothing was settled in the way it is today. The counties and towns which sent representatives varied tremendously from Parliament to Parliament, and so did the number to be sent by a given county or town. Often whole regions of England were left out. Plainly, the King each time asked only for those commoners who could tell him something he wanted to know or do something he wanted done. And the purposes for which the knights and burgesses came extended far beyond the enactment of statutes. The King might wish to be informed about a case decided by a particular county court, or to know who could afford to pay taxes in a particular town, or to learn whether a proposed royal regulation would be unpopular, or to gain support from merchants and landowners in his latest struggle with the barons. In short, the word "Parliament" still meant the talking done by the Council—a confabulation and not a governing body. The commoners were there to give help for use in this talking, but not to take part in it.

Morever, the name "High Court of Parliament" corresponded to the fact that at least half the work of Parliament was judicial rather than legislative. Each time a Parliament sat, it received an enormous mass of petitions from all over England. These asked for all sorts of things—the reversal of a judgment in a local court, the redress of an individual grievance, relief from taxation. Whoever knows how the Court of Chancery developed, will readily understand how something of the same sort was going on in Parliament. The great bundle of petitions were sorted out. Many of them were sent to the courts of law for treatment in the regular way. Others went to the King and his smaller Council for extraordinary relief; later they would go to the Chancellor. About many petitions nothing whatever was done. After all this, some still remained upon which Parliament might still take action. Whatever the petition, the King had knights and burgesses there to give any help he might ask for. They were more like jurymen than legislators, especially when we remember that originally jurymen played the part of witnesses rather than impartial deciders of questions of fact.

Gradually things got blocked out. When a new Parliament was to be called, it was easier to send writs to the same counties and towns as the last time and to summon the same number of knights and burgesses as before. And something happened to transform the petitions. They started as statements of grievances by individuals, or by localities like the *cahiers* sent to the States-General in 1789. Perhaps it would turn out that a good many petitions recited the same grievance. Then it became natural for the knights and burgesses to combine them in a single petition. That was really a Bill in Parliament. The Speaker could carry the blanket petition from Westminster Abbey across to the King and the peers in the Palace, with the

24

hope that they would grant the petition by enacting a statute.

Thus there was an imperceptible transition from what has usually been done into what has always been done; and what has always been done shaded into what ought to be done. The counties and towns which were ordered to send men to give the King information for him to do whatever he liked with it, eventually insisted on their right to send men to give him advice about whatever they felt needed advice. Finally they could make sure their advice was followed. But all this took many centuries.

When we search for a modern parallel to what was going on under the Plantagenets in these meetings of knights and burgesses, we ought to look at something very different from the United States Senate and the House of Representatives. There is a resemblance, I think, to an occasional gathering which the head of a business might convoke in his factory office on Saturday afternoons. The heads of the various departments would be there, as a matter of course. Sometimes, he would ask some of the foremen to come too. Another week he might summon the salesmen. It would depend on whose information would be useful for the questions on the agenda of this particular Saturday afternoon. Nobody would like coming, because they would much rather be at home or fishing or playing golf. And it would be well understood by the foremen and the salesmen that they were not to speak except when they were spoken to. If, at a conference to discuss a proposed increase in prices, a salesman should suddenly jump up and suggest that the dividend-rate was much too high and ought to be reduced, the head of the business would sternly tell him, "This isn't what you are here for." He might end by going home without a job just as the indiscreet member of the House of Commons used to find himself in the Tower of London.

25

With such analogy in mind, an incident under Edward I in 1301 becomes easier to understand.[14] When Parliament met, the King told the bishops and nobles that he wanted their approval for certain measures, including a higher tax. They sent a message enumerating various reforms as urgent, and added that if these things were done, the people of the realm would grant the requested tax. Otherwise nothing would be levied. This petition has been called the first real Parliamentary Bill. What is significant is that the bishops and nobles maneuvered to get it presented by a knight from Lancashire. Hence it was impossible for the King to regard the list of grievances as a mere declaration of ill-will among the barons. Consequently, Edward I had to consent to the blanket petition as expressing the unanimous wish of the nation. But what happened then? Several months later he had the Lancashire knight imprisoned in the Tower, and did not pardon him until the knight had taken a solemn engagement never again to oppose the royal authority.

Although Parliament as a whole acquired more power under later Plantagenet Kings, it is not clear that the House of Commons shared in this increased authority or was free to talk. When we come to bills of attainder, we shall see in the next chapter[15] how Thomas Haxey had an even worse time than the unfortunate Lancashire knight a century earlier.

To sum up, the amount of freedom of debate in the House of Commons depended greatly upon the extent of the matters about which its members were able to reach decisions. So long as the knights and burgesses were only suppliers of information on matters submitted to them, they might enjoy considerable liberty while discussing those matters, but whatever they said about anything else was sure to be most unwelcome to the King. He would do his best to make them stick to the point.

Freedom of Debate under Henry VIII

The position of the House of Commons changed very much during Henry VIII's reign. He was engaged in a fight to the death with a very formidable opponent, the Roman Catholic Church, and he needed all the help he could get wherever he could find it. By having the delegates from the counties and towns take a larger part in government, he could build up a strong support for himself to counteract not only the bishops but also those nobles who sympathized with the old faith. Although one may doubt whether members of Parliament exercised much individual judgment in passing the numerous statutes between 1531 and 1539 which confiscated the property of the monasteries and severed the Church of England from Rome, the fact remains that the King acted through legislation and not by royal decree. Men who give great help to a master become more important in their own eyes. And the discussion of many momentous questions gave the knights and burgesses new experience in great issues of state. It was to Henry's interest to foster this sense of importance and competence, and freedom of debate was a natural means to strength.

Even before the Reformation, the widening scope of freedom of debate had been significantly illustrated by Strode's Case in 1512. Richard Strode, a member of Parliament from a borough in Devonshire, had agreed with other members to get through some bills regulating tin-mines in his county. He happened to be a tinner himself, and an influential competitor haled Strode before the Stannary Court, which was a regional tribunal with power over mining disputes. This court fined Strode £160 for trying in Parliament to destroy all the liberties, privileges, and franchises concerning tin-miners. When he did not pay the fine, several of the rival tinners caused him to be imprisoned in a dungeon in a deep pit under the ground in a castle, where he stayed for three weeks in irons with nothing to eat except bread and water. At the next session, Strode humbly prayed Parliament to wipe out his fine and condemnation. It accords with the judicial aspects of Parliament, of which I have already spoken, that this reversal of a local court decision was accomplished by a statute.[16] Not only did this declare the pending prosecution of Strode to be utterly void, but also it nullified all future proceedings against him "for any bill, speaking, reasoning, or declaring of any matter or matters, . . . communed and treated of" in Parliament.

In the ensuing century and a half of bitter debate over freedom of debate, one side would brush away the statute in Strode's Case as an isolated incident, while the other side hailed it as a solid rule of law protecting every speaker in Parliament from outside penalties.

The Speaker's Requests

When Henry's daughter Elizabeth I, the greatest of English sovereigns, came to the throne in 1558, the procedure of the House of Commons was crystallizing. What had been usually done was becoming what had to be done. The Commons were no longer holding a more or less secret debating assembly in Westminster Abbey and taking a less active part in Parliament than the audience does in a public meeting of today. In the preceding brief reign of Edward VI they had moved back into the Palace of Westminster, where they occupied Saint Stephen's Chapel, close to Westminster Hall. They were separated from the room where the House of Lords met only by the Long Gallery and the Painted Chamber. Thus the House of Commons could now be definitely considered one of the two houses of Parliament. Yet then as now, its members did not come into the presence of the King or Queen, except when they were called into the House of Lords for some notable ceremony like the opening of a new Parliament.

The procedure when Elizabeth's first Parliament met on January 25, 1559, will show what customarily happened. The knights and burgesses remained sitting in their own House, until notice was brought them that her Majesty and the Lords Spiritual and Temporal were expecting them in the upper House. They went there immediately and listened to an address from the Lord Keeper, father of Francis Bacon, who, on behalf of the Queen, gave a general description of the matters and causes upon which this Parliament was to consult. Specific royal proposals for debate and examination would be given later.

Thereupon, the knights and burgesses departed to their own House and took their several places.

One of the Queen's chief ministers reminded the Commons of her desire that they should choose a Speaker, and he suggested Sir Thomas Gargrave as worthy of their consideration, although he did not intend to debar any others present for uttering their free opinions and nominating anybody else whom they thought to be more fitting. With common consent Sir Thomas Gargrave was then elected as Prolocutor or Speaker. He stood up uncovered, and in all humility disabled himself as being unfurnished with that experience and other qualities which were required for so great a charge. So he requested the House to proceed to the election of some worthier member amongst them. This customary modesty always had to be displayed by a new Speaker and was always disregarded. Two royal ministers rose from their places and going to Sir Thomas' seat took him, one by the right arm and the other by the left, and led him to the chair at the upper end of the House of Commons, and there placed him. Having sat awhile covered, he arose, stood bareheaded, returned hum-

29

ble thanks to the whole House for their good opinion of him, and promised to do his best for the faithful discharge of that weighty place to which they had elected him.

Three days later, after the members of the House of Commons had again received notice that their attendance was expected in the Upper House, they repaired immediately thither with their Speaker-elect. Sir Thomas was led to the rail at the lower end of the House of Lords, where, after three reverences made to the Queen, he modestly excused himself as being unable to undergo the many and great difficulties of the place to which he had been chosen. Notwithstanding, the Lord Keeper assured him of the Queen's acceptance of him as Speaker. Whereupon the Speaker made a customary "discreet and submissive answer" full of hopes for the good success of the Parliament.

Then, in accordance with the usual form, the Speaker made four requests. First, that the House of Commons might have liberty of access to the Queen's presence upon all urgent and necessary occasions; this actually meant access for the Speaker himself. Second, if he should ever mistakenly report anything that the House of Commons wanted him to declare, that this might be corrected without prejudice to the House and his error be pardoned. Thirdly, and this is what chiefly concerns us, the Speaker requested "that they might have liberty and freedom of speech in whatsoever they treated of, or had occasion to propound and debate in the House." The fourth request was for the privilege of the members from being arrested during the continuance of the Parliament and during their journeys to and fro, "as in former times hath always been a custom." Thus the privilege from arrest was closely linked with the privilege of debate, just as they are linked in section 6 of Article I of our Constitution.

It will be observed that both the second and third requests concern freedom of speech. The second is for the Speaker to be able to speak without danger. In medieval days the only freedom which the Speaker asked was this, on his own behalf. In the reign of Henry VIII, however, whom A. F. Pollard calls "that great architect of Parliament," the third request was added, with its entirely different claim to freedom of speech on behalf of individual members in the House of Commons.

After the requests of the Speaker, the Lord Keeper, without any long pausing, gave the customary reply. The Queen was "right well content" to grant these petitions "as largely, as amply, and as liberally as ever they were granted by any of her noble progenitors. . . . Marry with these conditions and cautions." Access of the Speaker to the Queen was to be confined to needful matters and convenient times. His mistakes in conveying messages from the Commons were to be as rare as possible. The privilege from arrest was not to be sought solely for defrauding creditors and carrying out wrongs. As for the third request, for liberty of speech, "therewith her Highness is right well content, but so as to be neither unmindful or uncareful of their duties, reverence, and obedience to the sovereign."

This oft-repeated ceremonial opened three serious possibilities of trouble, so far as freedom of debate was concerned.

In the first place, although the freedom was claimed and granted, not as a matter of right, but only out of the sovereign's gracious kindness, this ritual might in time come to be, at least to the House of Commons, as much a meaningless form as the Speaker's modest disclaimer of fitness for his task or as the allegation in the action of ejectment that the entry on another man's land was made with "knives, swords, and staves." What was still grace for the King might turn into a right for the House and the people.

Next, the qualification of the grant of freedom might not mean the same thing to the two parties involved. Members of the House of Commons might think it part of their "duties" to the sovereign to give very unwelcome advice.

Finally, the House might fail to respect the sovereign's desire to limit debate to proposals which had been submitted to the Commons by royal authority. Members and the people would perhaps come to think that some other issues were of tremendous importance and ought to be aired on the floor. The truth was that the English people had been going through a revolution since the abolition of the monasteries. One of the numerous objections to revolutions is that they are likely to go much farther than was originally intended. The only revolution I know of which did not run such a course is our own. It stopped exactly where most of those who started it, like George Washington and John Adams, wanted it to stop, although this was hardly what Sam Adams and Tom Paine wished. Henry VIII began the English Reformation to sever the Church of England from the Universal Church, but he thought that substituting himself for the Pope would pretty much end the change. Instead, once the tie was cut, everything began to slide—theological doctrines, the organization of the clergy and the subordination to bishops, ceremonies, the wording of church services. The pull of Geneva, where lived one of the most powerful personalities in history, John Calvin, brought about a tug of war in which the sovereign and the bishops found themselves getting dragged over the ground, no matter how hard they dug in their heels. Religious questions had ceased to be merely the concern of a great institution and had become causes of intense anxiety for individuals. Salvation was as personal as marriage, and all over England men were wrestling with their own consciences about the right way to attain it. Was Parliament to be the only place where these matters of everlasting import were passed over in silence? The very fact that Henry VIII and his successors had asked the House of Commons to participate actively in many chief religious measures whetted the appetites of the members to take up other religious changes which seemed to them equally imperative. The House of Commons had come to feel that it was a place where big issues were discussed.

The drive of a large number of Englishmen toward Puritanism had an additional effect on the House of Commons. Loose gatherings in favor of church reform were taking place and dissenting groups were conducting their own kinds of religious services. Consequently, men were getting trained outside Parliament how to organize and how to manage troublesome affairs. The new abilities thus acquired were bound to show themselves eventually in the House of Commons. Politics was becoming a matter of skilled group action. We have seen something similar in our own time when workmen learned how to deal with controversial matters at their trade union meetings and later put this practical education to use in legislatures and national campaigns for the treatment of public issues.

The First Crisis in Freedom of Debate— Queen Elizabeth and Peter Wentworth

There were two questions of great importance to the whole of England which Queen Elizabeth I was very anxious not to have debated in Parliament—reforms in church government and who was to be her successor. These were the very two questions which one member of the House of Commons, Peter Wentworth, felt that God had called him to discuss. He began talking about them in 1571 and went on doing so for twenty-one years.

33

Peter Wentworth, born about 1524 in Buckingham-shire,[17] was a distant member of the Yorkshire family which would later produce Thomas Wentworth, Earl of Strafford. According to the fashion of his day, he rounded off his education by legal training at Lincoln's Inn. At the advanced age of forty-seven he was prompted to enter Parliament, not so much by a desire for public life and experience as by an urgent sense of duty. For several years past he had been much interested in the succession question, being first stirred up to deal with it, he writes, "by godes good motion." Queen Elizabeth had been taken very ill only four years after she began reigning, which made the problem acute, and of course marriage has been a matter of interest to everybody since the world began.

A baby for the Queen was pretty much out of the question by 1571, when Wentworth first sat in the House of Commons, but ecclesiastical agitation was always timely. A zealous and intemperate relative of Wentworth's, also in the House, disregarded the warning of the Lord Keeper at the opening of the session that the Commons should "meddle with no matters of state save such as should be propounded unto them." He got a committee appointed to consider some bills for church reform, which the House tactfully held up until the bishops should be consulted. Wentworth and others went for a conference with the Archbishop of Canterbury. Wentworth raised the question whether some of the Thirty-nine Articles agreed with the word of God, and the Archbishop said this was a matter to be referred wholly to the bishops. Wentworth retorted, "That were but to make you bishops Popes."

The Queen quietly managed to smother these bills, but Wentworth was not silent for long. A private member introduced a subsidy bill, although such measures were usually brought in by a Privy Councillor. The member suggested that the House of Commons should not wait for the sovereign thus to take the initiative, but should hasten to proffer the added revenue itself. This was resented as polishing an apple for the teacher. One opponent, a prominent lawyer, sought to link the supply of money to the Queen with redress of grievances, which he proceeded to specify. The lawyer was sent for by the Council and dealt with so hardly, according to Wentworth, that he came back to the House with an amazed countenance which daunted all in such sort that for more than ten days nobody in the House durst deal in any matter of importance. Consequently rumors ran around the House, as Wentworth put it: "Sirs, you may not speak [of these grievances], the Queen's Majesty will be angry. The Council will be angry." Subsequently, on the last day before a recess, Sir Humphrey Gilbert, who afterwards was a pioneer in colonizing America (as my last chapter will tell), attacked the lawyer's proposal as a violation of the royal prerogative. Gilbert's speech was disliked, but immediate adjournment stopped members from answering it.

On the day after the recess, Peter Wentworth hit out vigorously at Gilbert, noting his disposition to flatter and fawn on the Queen and comparing him to the chameleon, which can change himself into all colors except white. Even so, Sir Humphrey could change himself to all fashions but honesty: "[Wentworth showed Gilbert's] speech to tend to no other end than to inculcate fear into those which should be free. He requested care for the credit of the House and for the maintenance of free Speech (the only means of ordinary proceeding), and to preserve the Liberties of the House, to reprove Lyers [for David said in the Psalms], 'Thou, O Lord, shalt destroy Lyers.'"

Although the Speaker tried to pour the royal oil of flattery on the troubled waters, a stormy debate followed, including remonstrances against the confinement of Wentworth's relative to his home for presuming to introduce bills on religion. The Council prudently sent the relative back to his seat in the House, and this troublesome Parliament was soon dissolved by the Queen. Speaking on her behalf, the Lord Keeper Bacon gave unalloyed thanks to the Lords, but he condemned those few members of the House of Commons who "have showed themselves audacious, arrogant and presumptuous, calling her Majesty's Prerogatives in question, contrary to their Duty and place that they be called unto."

Nowise discouraged by this denunciation, Wentworth came back to the next Parliament in 1572. Elizabeth had just been very ill again from "a great tortion of the stomach after eating fish." Hence there was a powerful attack in the House of Commons on her lawful successor, Mary Queen of Scots, who was shut up in an English castle. Many members agreed to bring pressure on Queen Elizabeth to attaint Mary or at least deprive her of her right to succession. Although materials on this Parliament are meager, somebody ransacking an English country house a few years ago discovered Wentworth's summary of a speech he delivered: "Did I not publish Mary openly to be the most notorious whore in all the world?" In spite of Wentworth, the campaign against Mary failed, and this Parliament was adjourned, not to meet again until 1576.

During the quiet of four years Wentworth brooded over the coercion he had witnessed in his two sessions of Parliament. He decided he ought to do something about it. So he prepared a speech, taking as his text some verses from the Book of Job: "Behold, I am as the new Wine which hath no vent and bursteth the new Vessels in sunder, therefore I will speake that I may have a vent. . . . I will regard no manner of Person, no man will I spare." The speech indicted the Queen, the Council, and Parlia-

36

ment, and he meant to speak it whenever he should be back in the House of Commons. "Twenty times and more as he walked in his grounds, his own fearful conceit warned him that the speech would surely lead him into prison"; but his conscience outcried his fears.

Hardly had the new session begun when Wentworth rose and astounded the House with this speech. He argued that freedom of debate was granted to Parliament by a special law, because without it the Prince and State could not be preserved or maintained, and therefore even the Queen was subject to it. "[The] Queens Majesty is the Head of the Law, and must of necessity maintain the Law . . .: hereunto agreeth the most excellent words of Bracton, who saith, 'The King ought not to be under man, but under God and under the Law.'"[18] Wentworth attacked those who spread rumors around the House of Commons: "Take heed what you do, the Queens Majesty liketh not such a matter; whosoever preferreth it, she will be offended with him—Her majesty liketh of such a matter; whosoever speaketh against it, she will be much offended with him."

All this commanding and inhibiting was very injurious to the freedom of speech and consultation, Wentworth said. He must spare none, for the higher place a person had, the more harm he might do. Some of the Councillors had stifled the bill against Mary Queen of Scots in the last session. They were traitors and underminers of the Queen's life. "None is without fault, no not our Noble Queen—"

Here Peter Wentworth paused at the amazement on the faces of his hearers. The House of Commons stopped him, committed him to custody, and appointed a committee to examine him "for the extenuating of his fault." In the amusing account of the investigation that followed, the committee was evidently anxious to let Wentworth off, but he did not help them out. He would never say that he was sorry for anything he had said, and insisted instead that his whole speech should be shown to the Queen. Then the Queen intervened and the House released him after he had craved her pardon.

Thereupon the Chancellor of the Exchequer, Sir Walter Mildmay, preached a sermon to the House of Commons on their duty toward the Queen. The fact that Lady Mildmay and Mrs. Peter Wentworth were sisters may have brought some glimmerings of the viewpoint of his fiery brother-in-law into the courtier's speech:

> True it is, that nothing can be well concluded in a Councel where there is not allowed in debating of Causes brought in deliberation, Liberty and Freedom of Speech; otherwise if in Consultation men be either interrupted or terrified so as they cannot, nor dare not speak their Opinions freely . . .; even so all the Proceedings therein shall be rather to satisfie the wills of a few, than to determine that which shall be just and reasonable.
>
> But herein we may not forget to put a difference between liberty of Speech, and licentious Speech; for by the one men deliver their opinions freely, and with this caution, that all be spoken pertinently, modestly, reverently and discreetly; the other contrariwise uttereth all impertinently, rashly, arrogantly and irreverently; without respect of person, time, or place: and though freedom of Speech hath always been used in this great Councel of Parliament, and is a thing most necessary to be preserved amongst us; yet the same was never nor ought to be extended so far, as though a man in this House may speak what and of whom he list.

In short, when you oppose the government, you can speak freely so long as you speak politely. Then, as usually in our own day, no such qualification is imposed on the speech of those who side with the government.

During the five years before the last session of the same Parliament, Wentworth was again in hot water. A bishop informed the Privy Council that a great crowd of people had come to Wentworth's house to receive Communion according to Puritan rites, and he was summoned before the Council. We do not know what happened to him there, but so far as the records show, he kept very quiet when he got back to the House of Commons in 1581. And for some reason he did not go to the next Parliament in 1585.

In October, 1586, however, Wentworth was back in a new Parliament where normal business was completely subordinated to urgent demands for the death of Mary Queen of Scots. She was executed during the Christmas recess. Then a fresh campaign began for reformation of the Church of England on a Presbyterian basis. Although the Speaker reminded the House of the Queen's prohibitions against considering this matter, members persisted in supporting it. One of them said: "He had been at strife with himself, whether to speak or to hold his peace; but considering his duty to God, loyalty to the queen, and love to his country he could not be silent, but in a place of free speech must be willing and ready to deliver his conscience. Whatever the cost, they must not turn God out of doors."

When the Queen stifled all attempts to discuss abuses in the Church, Peter Wentworth resolved to act. He regarded her interference as a derogation from the rights of Parliament. Encouraged by the refractory spirit manifest in the Commons he determined to strike at the root of all their troubles and obtain from the House rulings on its privileges. He believed that the members should not leave it to the Queen to define freedom of speech, but confront her with a definition of their own. Accordingly on March 1, 1587, he handed to Serjeant Puckering, the Speaker, a series of written questions, intending that the replies to these should stand as rulings of the House of Commons. Some of Wentworth's questions touching the liberties of the House ran as follows:

Whether this Council be not a place for any Member of the same here assembled, freely and without controllment of any

39

person or danger of Laws, by Bill or speech to utter any of the griefs of this Commonwealth whatsoever touching the service of God, the safety of the Prince and this Noble Realm.

Whether that great honour may be done unto God, and benefit the service unto the Prince and State without free speech in this Council, which may be done with it.

Whether the Speaker or any other may interrupt any Member of this Council in his Speech used in this House, tending to any of the forenamed high services.

Whether the Prince and State can continue, stand, and be maintained without this Council of Parliament. . . .

The Speaker prudently pocketed Wentworth's paper and cut the debate short. Afterwards he showed Wentworth's questions to one of Elizabeth's ministers, who so handled the matter that Wentworth went to the Tower and the questions were not at all moved. The next day several other church reformers in the House were sent to join him.

J. E. Neale, in his articles on Wentworth in the *English Historical Review,* makes a convincing argument that these imprisonments were not just for speeches delivered in Parliament. The reason, he thinks, may have been that these persons incurred the wrath of the government because they had conferred before Parliament met and prepared their bill concerning church rites. Consequently, they had discussed matters of state outside Parliament, where there could be no question of privilege. So the problem concerns liberty of speech for the general public. Neale goes on: "This, which may seem a quibble, is really an important distinction. Ultimately the wider freedom had to reveal itself as a necessary corollary to the narrower . . .; but though it be assumed that the real object of the imprisonment of these members was to frustrate their agitation in parliament, yet the choice of the ground of attack was a tacit acknowledgement that it was inadvisable—we cannot say illegal—to imprison members for speeches in parliament, even when they were upon forbidden topics."

I should like to push Neale's interpretation even farther. It looks to me as if these gatherings of Puritan members in advance of the session marked the beginning of caucuses. Queen Elizabeth and her Council did not relish this new device, which has subsequently developed into an essential instrument of political action.

We do not know how long Wentworth and his fellow prisoners stayed in the Tower, but apparently they did not return to the House of Commons that session.

From this time on Wentworth's mind became absorbed in another forbidden problem, the succession to the throne. Mary's execution allayed the fears of most men about it, and they were content to let time work out its own solution. Some Englishmen were still anxious about it, but they were easily cowed into silence by the well-known opposition of the Queen. Except in their secret thoughts, the cause was dead. Not so with Peter Wentworth. He dared to breathe new life into it.

During 1587 he wrote a pamphlet, *A Pithie Exhortation to Her Majestie for Establishing her Succession to the Crown.* This gave a harrowing picture of the condition of England if Elizabeth should die and no successor be already selected:[19] "The strong will be slain in the field, children and infants murdered in every town, religion will be lain in the dust, and neither God or man will be regarded." Elizabeth was then fifty-four years old and could not have enjoyed this vivid anticipation of her approaching end:

Whensoever it shall please God to touch you with the pangs of death (as die most certainly you shall) we beseech your Majesty to consider, whether your noble person is like to come to that honorable burial, that your honorable progenitors have had, if your successor be not settled before your death. We do assure ourselves, that the breath shall be no sooner out of your body, but that all

41

your nobility, counsellors, and whole people will be up in arms, and then it is to be feared that your noble person shall lie upon the earth unburied, as a doleful spectacle to the world.

A year or so later, after the defeat of the Armada and just before a new Parliament was to meet, Wentworth got a schoolmaster to write out his pamphlet in a fair hand and carried it to London with him, with the audacious intention of having it presented to the Queen. He had a friend send it to a tailor's shop to have more duplicates made. Copies got abroad and the Privy Council sent for Wentworth in August, 1591. He was committed a close prisoner to the Gate-house and his lodgings were ordered to be searched for any letters or papers, especially if they touched on the succession. Nevertheless he kept writing Lord Burghley to get him to persuade the Queen to choose her successor. After six months he was lucky to be released. Burghley wrote Wentworth that he had read his pamphlet three times and was sure his arguments were true, but that the Queen had determined that the question should be suppressed so long as ever she lived.

Unwisely drawing encouragement from this brush-off, Wentworth went up to his last Parliament in February, 1592, determined to lose no time in bringing the succession out on the floor. His pockets were stuffed with a fresh copy of his pamphlet of advice to the Queen, a speech which he was going to make in the House of Commons on the succession, and a bill all drafted except for blanks to be filled in after Parliament had decided who was to be the next King.

Parliament was opened on Monday and adjourned to Thursday. Wentworth thought up the idea of a caucus in Lincoln's Inn on Wednesday, inviting some other members and also private persons who were interested in the succession. The group spent the morning in reading and discussing some of Wentworth's papers, and after dinner, which was early in those days, they sat over the papers for two hours more. Several of those present were more timid than Wentworth. But at any rate they would have another conference on Friday in different London rooms. That was never held, because the whole scheme leaked out, and on Thursday morning Wentworth was summoned before a number of Privy Councillors, who sent him to prison, where several of his associates soon went too. During his subsequent examination before the Council, Wentworth refused to give up the draft of his speech, since, so he said, "It was to have been delivered in Parliament where speech was free," and he claimed the privilege of Parliament in refusing to show it.

So Peter Wentworth was in the Tower. He refused to purchase his liberty at the price of confessing his fault and renouncing all desire to hasten a settlement of the succession. There he stayed for five years, and there in 1597, just as arrangements were afoot to free him, on strict conditions, which he insisted on seeing before he consented, he died at the age of seventy-three.

It is not quite accurate to regard Wentworth's long final imprisonment as a restriction of freedom of debate. He went to the Tower before he had any chance to say anything in the House of Commons. The trouble was that he had written and conferred outside the House, in any convenient room he could find. His last offense, then, was not outspokenness in debate but anticipation of the political caucus.

Still, both the question whether laying political plans outside the walls of Parliament was an offense and the prolonged controversy with Queen Elizabeth and her ministers about freedom of debate belong together as aspects of a deeper and constantly recurring conflict between the few who governed England and the many who were governed.

The Queen and her Council knew about governing, and thought that it was their business alone.[20] All important laws ought to be initiated by the Council and not by Parliament. The great legislation of Henry VIII's reign came from above. For example, Thomas Cromwell probably had a large share in drafting the famous Statute of Uses. Very likely the outstanding statutes of Elizabeth's reign from the Act of Supremacy in 1559 to the Poor Relief Act in 1601 were merely submitted to Parliament for approval. Indeed, the infrequency of Parliaments and the shortness of their sessions made it impossible for them to do much of the law-making work of a modern legislature. Competence in drafting documents, for instance, is usually the product of long experience. No doubt, just as in the medieval Parliaments already described in this chapter, the Tudor sovereigns occasionally found it helpful to seek the views of Parliaments on some large question of policy, for the sake of a money grant or to get the sense of the representatives as to how great burdens and changes the merchants and the common people would accept willingly. Yet these representatives were not to originate discussions of big issues—what could they know about them anyway!

In spite of all this, the representatives did feel that they ought to have a larger control over decisions. After all, how is it fair to say that government is not the concern of those who are governed? They fight the wars, they foot the bills, their businesses are dislocated or ruined by laws. If Queen Elizabeth should die without a settled successor, it was the plain people who would suffer the most from the ensuing anarchy. Moreover, in those days their ways of worshipping God were shaped or forbidden by the government. When rulers persecute, they put religion into politics for everybody. Finally, although in Elizabeth's reign the middle and lower classes of Englishmen were still inexperienced in affairs, they were reading, which they had never been able to do till recently, and they were talking among themselves more than ever before.

When just claims to share in power are strongly pressed by men who are not yet capable of exercising power, questions of right and wrong become almost unanswerable. Unless force comes into play, as it did in the middle of the next century, the practical solution is likely to leave power pretty much in the hands of those who have long been accustomed to its use.

As between Queen Elizabeth and her Council on one side and Peter Wentworth on the other, the choice of who ought to rule England is as plain today as it was in the sixteenth century. For that job Wentworth was wholly unfit. He was not a great parliamentarian and was rarely appointed to committees. He was too immoderate, too blind to everything except his few chosen causes. His importance did not lie in what he did or could have done, but in his anticipating what members of Parliament generations later would be able to do well. The time would come when caucuses would promote effective political action, and when the House of Commons, no longer a headless body as it remained long after his time, would choose the real rulers of England and support or guide or restrain them by outspoken speech on or off the floor.

"To Wentworth himself," Neale writes, "his career must have appeared a failure. The church remained unreformed, the succession unsettled, his conception of free speech unrealized. That his mantle had fallen upon the group he had gathered about him, that parliamentary tradition had put on immortality as country gentlemen and lawyers made membership the hobby of a lifetime, and that his own experience and experiments were in consequence not lost, this he could not have known."

45

The Second Crisis—James I and the Parliament of 1621

It is easier to get men to agree with you about concrete things which ought to be done than about formulation of abstract principles. Queen Elizabeth I was well aware of this sound political maxim. She was content to let the boundary between her power and the power of Parliament remain uncharted. When any particular question arose of how far she or Parliament ought to go, this could be worked out in the light of circumstances. She knew that she could rely on her own wisdom and the deep devotion of her subjects to attain a reasonably satisfactory solution of each case as it should arise. Her successor, however, lacked her wisdom and her power to draw the realm to her.

James is to me one of the most puzzling men who ever headed a nation. He is perhaps the first ruler since Marcus Aurelius who might have been a professor, though it would be hard to imagine two professors more unlike. He was often eager to demarcate a precise line between royal and parliamentary power in writings and garrulous harangues which went far beyond the actual requirements of the situation. Such an attitude was bound, sooner or later, to bring about a collision with the new forces which were seething in England.

Trouble might have been less if James had leaned on wise advisers. Unhappily, he united with his pedantry a susceptibility to the influence of favorites, especially handsome young men. Fate threw in his way the Duke of Buckingham. The great affection which the Duke inspired in Anne of Austria and the Three Musketeers of Dumas was not shared by the people of England. His possession of boundless influence over both James and Charles I was one of the greatest calamities which ever hit the English throne. Another favorite, less good-looking but equally baneful, was Gondomar, Ambassador from Spain, the most Catholic country in Europe and the traditional foe of England for decades.

The founder of a new dynasty may fairly ask for quiet years in which to get settled. James, however, was thrown at once into bitter controversies between Puritans and strict members of the church, and was constantly forced to deal with popular demands for a more vigorous enforcement of the penal laws against Roman Catholics. All this was not his fault, but he let himself become steadily in need of large sums of money. He was a great buyer of jewelry and lavished generous gifts on his favorites. As if those troubles were not enough, the Thirty Years' War broke out in 1618 through the folly of his son-in-law, the Elector Palatine. This prince of a fertile and prosperous domain along the Rhine accepted an invitation to become King of Bohemia, which had revolted against the Emperor. Soon embroiled in fighting, he appealed to his father-in-law for help. James, like Neville Chamberlain, had abundant cause to regret that Shakespeare was wrong when he gave Bohemia a seacoast. If only the British Navy could land troops near Prague. Within three years the rash prince was not only hopelessly defeated in his new kingdom, but was also about to lose his old domain, the Rhenish Palatinate, where his German enemies were aided by Spanish soldiers.

Consequently, on November 6, 1620, while our ancestors on the "Mayflower" were nearing Cape Cod, James summoned a new Parliament to meet in January, 1621, after a gap of six years. There was no other way for him to get great sums of money to pay his expenses and help his daughter and her husband save the Palatinate. It was an extraordinary assemblage of able men. John Pym and Sir Thomas Wentworth sat in the House of Commons for the first time. Sir Edward Coke brought an experience drawn from far back in the reign of Elizabeth. We know a great deal about this Parliament, for many members had the happy habit of keeping diaries, which have been assembled and magnificently edited by Wallace Notestein and two colleagues.

At the first meeting for business on February 5, 1621, the House of Commons urged stronger measures against Roman Catholics and then discussed the way several of its members in the previous Parliament had been imprisoned, after it was over, for words said in debate. They proposed to ask the King to accept their right to freedom of speech. They also considered a bill which would make it impossible in the future to punish members for what they said on the floor. The King's chief spokesman in the House was Sir George Calvert, a Secretary of State. Afterwards he became a Roman Catholic, was made Lord Baltimore, and founded Maryland, although it was his son who landed there. Calvert reported gracious messages from the King. James marveled that they troubled themselves so much about the matter. He had already assented to the Speaker's request "for such freedom of speech as had been anciently granted." He hoped that no one would "so far transgress the bounds of duty as to give any cause to be questioned for speaking what becomes him not." If anybody did so, James was sure that the House of Commons would be more ready than the King to censure him. Thus matters were smoothed over for the time being, and the House unanimously granted £160,000 as testimony of their devotion to the King. This was pleasant for him although far less than he wanted.

Then began an activity in the House of Commons unprecedented since the time of Henry VIII, but now the initiative was taken by the House and not by the King. Monopolies which had been granted to numerous favorites were investigated. Impeachments were revived, a matter for my next chapter.

48

As the months went by without passage of a single bill or any further grants of money, James and Buckingham got so annoyed that they could not wait until the end of the session to imprison audacious members. In the middle of June the King arrested Sir Edwin Sandys, one of the founders of Virginia, whom James detested so much that he told the London board of the Virginia Company "to elect the Devil, if they liked, but not Sir Edwin Sandys." The King now insisted that he was punishing Sandys for something connected with Virginia, but "men shrugged their shoulders incredulously." They suspected that Sandys' real fault was in speaking of the perilous situation of Protestantism in Germany. Sandys stayed shut up for a month, and the King gave Parliament a long summer vacation until November 14th.

The King's attitude toward free speech in general is illustrated by a broadside he issued during this summer.[21] In an earlier proclamation just before Christmas, James had strictly commanded his loving subjects, from the highest to the lowest, to take heed "how they did intermeddle by Penne, or Speech, with causes of State, and secrets of Empire, either at home, or abroad," and to "containe themselves within modest and reverent regard, of matters, above their reach and calling. . . ." They were not to give attention or any manner of applause to such discourse, but tell some members of the Privy Council about it within twenty-four hours or else be sent to prison. Although this December proclamation enabled Gondomar to get a preacher punished for cleverly caricaturing him, its threats evidently failed to turn hearers of gossip into telltales. Nay rather, as the King lamented, in his subsequent proclamation on July 26, 1621, "The inordinate liberties of unreverent speech, touching matters of high nature, unfit for vulgar discourse, doth dayly more and more increase." Consequently, James now renewed his

49

order against offending "either by licentious and bold Speaking or Writing, or by applauding, entertaining, covering, or concealing such unfitting Discourse." He charged all his officers and ministers and loving subjects to use "all diligence to discover and bring to Justice" everybody who offended in any of these ways. He would be as severe against those who conceal such talk as against "the boldness of audacious Persons and Tongues, so unrespective of dutie to Government."

No doubt, James was willing to give more leeway than this to speech on the floor of the House of Commons. Whenever he asked the members for something, naturally he had to let them talk about it. But when they strayed into subjects on which he had not sought their advice and especially into the exercise of his royal prerogatives, he inclined to the old Plantagenet attitude of "That's not what you're here for." Members of Parliament who contumaciously talked about such matters which he thought only Privy Councillors should discuss were not much better than impudent gossipers in an alehouse.

In fairness to the King, we ought to realize there was something to be said for his side. The House of Commons did some outrageous things and was eager to suppress and punish publications which expressed views it disliked. Also James was more enlightened about foreign policy than the knights and burgesses. He knew that if he began persecuting English Catholics, as the House kept urging him to do, this might easily stir up much worse treatment of Protestants in Catholic countries. Informed by John Digby, Earl of Bristol, an able ambassador to many capitals who worked for England and no party, James saw that Spain was losing strength. Hence he believed that Continental Protestantism had much more to fear from the Emperor. To fight either the King of Spain or the Emperor vigorously would be enormously

50

expensive. To fight both at once was impossible. For the House of Commons, however, Spain was the hereditary enemy whose great Armada had been destroyed by English seamen. A war with Spain was always popular. Not that they wanted the King to stop there, for it was shameful for England to let the lovely English-born Queen of Bohemia be driven hither and thither by the Emperor. They were eager to fight everybody without raising taxes.

Nevertheless, in spite of James' superior knowledge, he was no statesman and he could not be trusted. It was pushing friendly relations with Spain beyond the bounds of common sense for him to flirt with Gondomar about a marriage of the future Charles I with a princess of the royal family which had tried to conquer England only thirty years before. He told Gondomar not to mind anything that might be said in Parliament, since the King would take good care that nothing was done which would displease the King of Spain. Then James would turn round and encourage the Commons in their zeal for Protestantism, hoping it would bring him a large grant of funds and thinking he would always be able to keep this zeal under control. "But how often," says Ranke, "has a policy been shipwrecked, which has thought to avail itself of great interests and great passions for some end immediately in view!"

On Tuesday, November 20, 1621, the House reconvened. Real or pretended illness detained the King at Newmarket near Cambridge, now a racetrack town. On his behalf, Lord Keeper Williams recommended the Commons "to avoid all long harangues, malicious and cunning diversions," and to postpone all business except the grant of money for aiding the Palatinate until they met again in February. This effort at restriction was not welcomed. An old Parliament man said, "It would be an evil precedent if the King were permitted to assume the right of prescribing the subject of their debates." Other members protested against the recent imprisonment of Sir Edwin Sandys. When Calvert explained that this was not for anything said or done in the House, murmurs of dissatisfaction broke out.

On Monday, November 26th, came a great debate on foreign policy. The Commons mingled devoted patriotism with defective knowledge of the designs of European courts. Members kept saying that Spain was the real enemy. One reminded the House that "there were those at home whose hearts were at the service of the King of Spain"; precautions must be taken against their machinations. A speaker who was gifted with every virtue except discretion proposed that, until the English Catholics were suppressed, all money grants should be refused. Others resembled the Congressman who plagued Abraham Lincoln during his worst anxieties;[22] they wanted to dictate how the war should be conducted, for they would furnish the money. In vain did moderate members point out that it was useless to put the armed forces of England in motion without the good-will of the King.

The day was closed by a speaker who was disgusted with this ineptitude—the new member from Yorkshire, Sir Thomas Wentworth. His policy was purely English. He feared the renewal of religious wars, and though resenting Gondomar's influence shared the Earl of Bristol's belief that Spain would yield to reasonable demands. Wentworth's chief interest, however, was in domestic affairs. He despised the incapacity and corruption of Buckingham and his hangers-on. At the same time, he hated Puritanism and the restlessness of the champions of liberty. Still more, he hated opposition to his own will. Parliamentary discussions he compared to the jawbone of an ass. Gardiner writes, "The clash of thought, the conflict

52

of opinion out of which lasting progress springs was to him an object of detestation." Although possessing a clear and commanding intellect, he "was never one in feeling with those with whom he was politically associated."

So Wentworth's sensible suggestion to adjourn the debate for a few days was rejected, and next morning the discussion of foreign affairs was resumed. Many urged war with Spain and harrying their Catholic fellow-citizens as the chief supporters of Spanish influence in England. Every hour the lack of confidence in the King was becoming plainer. He had placed his supporters at a terrible disadvantage. He got them to ask for a large sum of money without disclosing his policy, and by lingering in Newmarket he made it impossible for them to say with any authority what he did want to do with the money. As sometimes happens, legislative distrust of the Executive and anxieties over real evils threw speakers into tantrums. Even so able a man as Coke lashed out at the Catholics with all the rumors of the past sixty years. The Jesuits had tried to poison Queen Elizabeth. The scab which destroyed so many English sheep came from Spain. Syphilis spread over Europe from Naples, and Naples belonged to the King of Spain.

At last the House was brought back to the business in hand by a speech from John Pym. A great sympathy grew up between him and his audience. "By listening to him," says Gardiner, "they made the discovery that their own opinions were better and wiser than they had ever dreamed." He now revealed the qualities which would, twenty years later, make him the leader of the Long Parliament. After his speech, the House voted unanimously that a subsidy should be granted to the King for troops in the Palatinate. It was characteristic of the intolerance of the age that English Catholics were to pay a double tax, the same tax as was paid by foreigners living in England.

With December, however, the flood-gates were opened again. On Saturday the 1st, a petition to the King was introduced requesting that Prince Charles be "timely and happily married to one of our religion"—let the King lead Protestant Europe—and much more advice about foreign policy. Gondomar got hold of a copy and sent it to James in Newmarket with the most astonishing letter that an English sovereign ever received from a foreign ambassador. He remonstrated against "the seditious insolence of Parliament." Except that he relied on the King to discipline the House of Commons, Gondomar would have broken off relations already by leaving England: "This it would have been my duty to do, as you would have ceased to be a king here, and as I have no army here at present to punish these people myself."

Thereupon, without waiting to get the petition from the House of Commons in the regular way, James wrote from Newmarket to the Speaker on Monday, December 3rd: "We have heard, by divers reports, to our great grief, that our distance from the Houses of Parliament, caused by our Indisposition of health, hath emboldened some of the House of Commons, to argue and debate publickly of the matters far above their reach and capacity, tending to our high dishonour, and breach of Prerogative Royal." The House was to be ordered, in the King's name, "That none therein shall presume henceforth to meddle with any thing concerning our Government, or deep matters of State, and namely not to deal with our dearest Son's Match with the Daughter of Spain, nor to touch the honour of that King. . . ." Finally, he told the Speaker to inform the Commons: "That we think our self very free and able to punish any man's misdemeanors in Parliament, as well during their sitting, as after: which we

54

mean not to spare hereafter, upon any occasion of any man's insolent behaviour there that shall be ministered unto us. . . ." And if any contemplated petition touched on any of those forbidden points, they must be struck out before it came into his hands, or else he would not deign to hear it or answer it.

When this letter was read next day in the House, consternation followed. If James had only had the good sense to explain his foreign policy to the Commons (if he knew what it was himself) and ask them not to embarrass his negotiations by discussions, the House might have retreated gracefully. However, by reopening the question of freedom of debate, he drove the House into its citadel where it had no choice except to die or fight. Everybody agreed to fight, including the staunchest supporters of the government. No member could contribute properly to the deliberations of the House if he knew that soon he might be sent to the Tower for some phrase the court happened to dislike. "Never," said one man, "had any matter of such consequence been before them." "Let us rise," said another; "let us resort to our prayers, and then consider of this great business."

For days the House refused to enter on any other business until their privilege had been defended from further attack. On Saturday the 8th they finished a second and very conciliatory petition to the King. They said they did not insist on any right to decide on peace or war and to choose a wife for his son; but, representing the whole commons of his kingdom, they had resolved out of their cares and fears to lay their views before his Majesty, which might not otherwise come so fully and clearly to his knowledge. They expected no answer on these points. What they did ask was for him to receive and read their petition and reply to a portion of it about the enforcement of the laws against Jesuits, priests, and Catholics who stayed away from parish churches. A final paragraph modestly claimed freedom of debate.

A delegation of twelve members carried this second petition to Newmarket on Tuesday, December 11th. They met with a more cordial reception than they expected. James had recovered his temper and did have a certain kind of humor. As they approached the King, he cried out to his attendants, "Bring stools for the ambassadors to sit down." He treated the delegates with great familiarity and sent them away with a long rambling letter.

When this letter was read to the Commons on the 14th, they received it loyally, but felt considerable anxiety over some final sentences about their privileges. James objected because their petition spoke of these as "their ancient and undoubted right and inheritance." Instead, he said, they got their privileges from the grace and permission of his ancestors. Still, he would be careful as any of his predecessors to protect them as long as members kept within the bounds of their duty. But if they didn't—

Historically, James was probably right. He was borne out by the already quoted ritual of the Speaker's request for freedom of debate and the royal response.[23] The trouble with James' position was his unawareness that what was always done might be passing into what had to be done. His wisest but unheeded advisers realized this. While the House was trying to find a way to maintain freedom of debate without quarreling with the King, Bishop Williams, the Lord Keeper, wrote on Sunday the 16th advising James to be moderate and declare that the privileges of the House were originally granted by the favor of princes, but that they were now inherent in the powers of its members, and that he had no wish to diminish them.

Such prudent counsel came too late. James had let Gondomar and Buckingham make up his mind for him.

On the same day that Lord Keeper Williams wrote his letter, the King sent a letter to Calvert. James complained of the way the Commons were wasting time, and reiterated with unmistakable precision his view that their privileges were not rights but merely given as a favor by his predecessors. So, he concluded, "Let them go on cheerfully in their businesses, rejecting the curious wrangling of lawyers upon words and syllables."

Listening while Calvert read aloud this letter on Monday, the House knew all further correspondence with the King was useless. Both Sir Edward Coke and Sir Thomas Wentworth agreed that the best plan now was to know precisely what their privileges were. Coke said, "If we did set down our privileges and liberties, it would clear us of all those rubs."

And so the Commons spoke out for themselves on Tuesday, the 18th of December, 1621. In the morning they went into a Committee of the Whole to consider the debates on the privileges of the House. One member summed up the matter:[24] "Though the calling of a Parliament and the continuing, prorogation and dissolving of it be in the King's sole power, yet, when we *are* called, we are without limitation, to deal in what business ourselves think best. For otherwise we shall not be able to do the business of those for whom we come hither, which is the business of the country."

A subcommittee was appointed, on Coke's motion, to sit in the afternoon and consider "our Liberty of Speech, and our Power to punish those that speak too lavishly." Among the heads to be considered by this subcommittee on privileges and drawn into "the Form of a Protestation" were these:

1. Concerning Freedom of Speech; and therein to remember that Parliament is to deal with "the arduous and urgent affairs of the realm," according to the words of the Writ of Summons, whether it be concerning the King or otherwise.[25]

57

2. Touching the Liberty of this House to punish the Misdemeanors of any Parliament Man in Parliament, for Things whereof this House hath Cognisance, whether he ought not to be censured here by the House only.

4. Whether our Privileges be not our Right and Inheritance.

Peter Wentworth's questions of 1587 were before the House of Commons at last.

Speed was essential. The King had threatened to send the members home at any moment for a long Christmas vacation. The House knew that this adjournment might very well happen before the Protestation was made, "and so we may endanger the Validity of our Privileges and Liberties, in those Points wherein they seemed to be impeached." Consequently, the subcommittee report was ordered to be ready for action at four o'clock, which is almost darkness in a London December and later than the Commons usually sat in the seventeenth century.

At the hour appointed, the subcommittee brought in its draft with these memorable assertions:[26]

The Commons now assembled in Parliament, being justly occasioned thereto, . . . do make the Protestation following,

That the Liberties, Franchises, Priviledges, and Jurisdictions of Parliament, are the ancient and undoubted Birth-right and Inheritance of the Subjects of England;

And that the arduous and urgent affairs concerning the King, State, and Defence of the Realm, and of the Church of England, and the maintenance and making of Laws, and redress of mischiefs and grievances which daily happen within this Realm, are proper Subjects and matter of Counsel and Debate in Parliament;

And that in the handling and proceeding of those businesses, every Member of the House of Parliament hath, and of right ought to have, freedom of speech, to propound, treat, reason, and bring to conclusion the same;

And that the Commons in Parliament have the liberty and freedom to treat of those matters in such order as in their Judgments shall seem fittest;

And that every such Member of the said House hath like freedom from all Impeachment, Imprisonment, and Molesta-

tion (other than by censure of the House it self) for or concerning any bill, speaking, reasoning, or declaring of any matter
or matters touching the Parliament or Parliament-business. . . .

And then the House of Commons in the Parliament of
1621 took what was to be virtually its final action:[27]

"The Speaker being in the Chair.

"It is ordered, by Question in the House, that this
Protestation shall be here entered forthwith in the Book
of the House, and there to remain, as of Record.

"And accordingly it was here entered, sitting the
House, between Five and Six of the Clock at Night, by
Candle-light."

After Christmas, James in Council sent for the book of
the Commons Journal and tore this page out with his
own hands, not in a fit of temper but with extraordinary
solemnity and deliberation. He hoped now he would hear
no more about liberty of speech. Though no subsidies had
actually been paid and no legislation enacted, the Council
decided to dissolve Parliament. Buckingham hurried off
to congratulate Gondomar, who said: "It is the best thing
that has happened in the interests of Spain and the Catholic religion since Luther began to preach heresy a hundred years ago today." He urged James to punish members for their insolence. James had already done so. Coke
was in the Tower, with his papers seized, and there he
stayed with others for eight months. Pym was confined
to his house. Some members were ordered by the King to
spend the depth of winter investigating the grievances of
Ireland. On January 6th, the King dissolved Parliament[28]
with an outburst against the "evil-affected and discontented persons" who had put through the protestation, so
he said, "in an unseasonable hour of the day and a very
thin house."

But he could not tear it out of men's minds.

These events of 1621 illustrate a problem of great importance. How far is it desirable for discussion to outrun the discusser's power to decide? It is the same problem which arises today with respect to citizens at large. For example, during the First World War men were punished for speeches and pamphlets urging that the war should be financed out of taxes, not Liberty Bonds. The prosecutors said this was a question for Congress to decide, so citizens had no right to talk about it. In 1621 the King alone could decide matters within his prerogative like peace and war, treaties, and royal marriages. Even now in England these can be decided by the Crown as advised by the Cabinet, without any need for a vote by Parliament. James I insisted that the House of Commons must not discuss such questions, because it was plainly unable to decide them.

When men's discussions outrun their power of decision, this tempts them to unwelcome endeavors to expand their control over what they are talking about. In any event, it embarrasses those who do the deciding, and it distracts the talkers from considering matters properly their own, on which their decision is urgently desired. Grants of money, for instance. "Talk about taxes," James kept ordering—"those are your business, while starting wars and marrying Prince Charles are my business."

Still, there are many reasons why the people and their chosen spokesmen in the national legislature ought to be able to discuss matters which will be decided by the executive officers. The whole conception of the right of petition involves statements by many men to influence action by a few men. It is desirable for those few, who alone can act, to know the grievances felt by the multitude. By listening to those whom their decisions will affect, they will learn how far it is safe to go and occasionally they will receive wise advice. Furthermore, the power of the few to decide some matters can never be isolated from the power of the many to decide different matters. The electorate cannot start or stop a war, but it can vote. Parliament could not pick a wife for Prince Charles, but it could refuse to supply revenues to his father. He who pays the piper cannot play a note himself but it is often sensible to give him some say about the tune. James' chief fault was his failure to recognize that, whatever his own prerogatives, Parliament had more control over other essentials of government than it possessed under Edward I, and even more than the majority of the House of Commons were disposed to claim under Elizabeth, because of a reverence for her which did not pass to James with the throne. The Peter Wentworths were multiplying fast. The members of the House no longer resembled foremen on the outskirts of a conference of the department chiefs. Instead, they were like bankers who know that their money is indispensable to the heads of the business and who occasionally use that power to make suggestions and get information about policies which, legally, belong solely to the board of directors. Money reaches farther than law.

To put the matter more broadly, the scope of freedom of speech tends to be a function of the political power of those who want to talk. Rulers are often unconvinced by the arguments of Milton about the social advantages of open discussion, and yet tolerate such discussion out of respect for the multitude who have the final decision on granting or withholding favors which the rulers very much want. It is significant that Parliament acquiesced in the suppression of public discussion of public questions until after the franchise had been greatly extended in the nineteenth century.

Milton's dream of free speech for everybody was only a dream under the early Stuarts. The House of Commons was then the last refuge of free speech. The clergy could be disciplined, judges dismissed, books suppressed, and authors pilloried, deprived of their ears, and thrust into jail. Only in Parliament could unwelcome criticism be spoken. James tried to silence even that, and so did his son. They mostly failed because there was so much Parliament did have the power to decide. And it is more than a coincidence that Parliament attained complete freedom of debate in 1689 by the very same document in which English sovereigns acknowledged Parliament to be the supreme lawmaker, whose control included even the award of the throne itself. Free speech tends to grow as self-government grows.

Thus the quarrel over freedom of debate was, in large measure, an aspect of the main controversy between the early Stuart Kings and Parliament as to which should govern England. That main controversy seems to me one of those frightening political situations in which no right solution is possible until one side or both sides change their whole nature. Neither James I nor Charles I nor their ministers could be trusted; none of them was fit to wield the great power they claimed as rightful. But the House of Commons, on its side, was equally unfit to rule England. It was immature and irresponsible. And no body of hundreds of men, however wise and experienced, can do the actual governing of a nation. The problem was hopeless until some new political device could be worked out to link the King and a few chief advisers and those hundreds of men in mutual confidence and effective co-operation. That would take decades, and hardly anybody was searching for such a solution. On each side, it was everything or nothing.

The Third Crisis—Charles I and Sir John Eliot

Charles I was more likable and less shrewd than his father. With the throne he inherited Buckingham. Instead of husbanding his resources, the new King soon sent Buckingham on a wild expedition to relieve the besieged Huguenots at La Rochelle. Unwilling to go to Parliament for the necessary funds, Charles tried a forced loan and threw into jail those who refused to lend. When five knights whom he had thus locked up sought habeas corpus, the jailer simply told the court that they were imprisoned "by the special command of his majesty." Popular resentment was increased by Buckingham's collapse on the French coast. Parliament met in an uproar in the spring of 1628. Long efforts to end such arbitrary imprisonments were made by the House of Commons under the leadership of Sir Edward Coke, Sir Thomas Wentworth, and Sir John Eliot, a youngish member from a Cornish borough with Puritan beliefs, who though incapable of casting off the religious intolerance of his time possessed courage, selflessness, and nobility of character. Finally, Charles was forced to agree to the Petition of Right, in which he promised not to imprison any subject again unless he was charged with a specific offense. The session closed in a joyous ringing of church-bells and blaze of bonfires.[29]

During the interval before Parliament met again, Charles had the unappreciated good fortune that Buckingham was assassinated. However, the King opened fresh causes for dissension. He subjected the merchants to new and unpopular customs duties on his own authority and allowed Laud to promote high church practices which were detestable to the Puritans. Still, Charles insisted that Parliament had no say in religious questions. Then he obtained the ablest of all his advisers, by winning over Sir Thomas Wentworth from the opposition. The future Earl of Strafford became a viscount and a royal minister. Wentworth's shift was doubtless sincere. He felt that the danger of anarchy and disorder had formerly come from the

63

government, but now it came from the Commons. So he was a powerful supporter of the King's policies about taxation and the Church.

Parliament took a very different view when it reconvened on January 20, 1629. Oliver Cromwell made his maiden speech on a religious issue. John Selden opened a wider problem by urging that it was "a great invasion of the liberty of the subject" to punish printers for issuing a book, and wanted a law against it, but this plea for free speech outside Parliament was unheard by those who were eager to talk inside. Sir John Eliot became the virtual leader of the House of Commons.

Eliot wrote a set of Resolutions, which to Charles I were detestable. They declared, "Whosoever shall bring in innovation of religion . . . shall be reputed a capital enemy to this kingdom. . . ." And so was anybody who counseled the levying of taxes not granted by Parliament, while any merchant who voluntarily paid such taxes was called "a betrayer of the liberties of England."

After a week's adjournment forced by the King, the House met on March 2, 1629. The Speaker, Sir John Finch, declared the King's pleasure that the House should be adjourned again till the 10th. Shouts of "No! No!" rose on every hand. Eliot stood up. Finch tried to check him by saying he had an absolute command from his Majesty instantly to leave the chair if anyone tried to speak. Eliot had expected all this and made up his mind that the time had come for the House to claim the right to adjourn itself.

As the Speaker moved to leave the chair, Denzil Holles and Benjamin Valentine stepped forward, seized him by the arms, and thrust him back into his seat. Several Privy Councillors hurried to his assistance. For a moment Finch broke away from his captors, but crowds barred the way, and Holles and Valentine pushed him back into his chair.

"God's wounds!" cried Holles, "you shall sit till we please to rise." The Speaker made no more effort to escape.

Then Eliot spoke from the highest bench at the back of the House and threw forward his paper for some one to hand it to the clerk to read his Resolutions even if the Speaker refused his consent. Shouts of "Read! read!" broke out in the midst of a confused struggle. The crowd swayed backwards and forwards around the chair. In the midst of the excited throng, one member struck another. The Speaker defended himself, by asserting that the House had never continued to transact business after the sovereign's order to adjourn. Eliot rejoined that they were quite ready to adjourn in obedience to the King after the Resolutions had been read. William Strode insisted that they ought not to be turned out "like scattered sheep."

Some members rose to leave and avoid defying the King's command. The Serjeant-at-Arms was ordered to shut the door. When he hesitated, a member locked the door and put the key in his pocket. The Speaker lamented his official dilemma in serving two masters. "I am not the less the King's servant for being yours." He said he did not dare to put the Resolutions to a vote.

Eliot then lost his head. He made a long speech proposing to impeach the King's chief minister, Lord Weston, as guilty of treason for his share in the hated taxes. Weston's son was a member and rose to defend his father. The discussion threatened to become endless. At some stage Eliot, despairing of getting a formal vote, threw his Resolutions into the fire and so did not act on Selden's suggestion to take the chair and put the question of their adoption.

A knocking on the door was heard. The Usher of the Black Rod brought a message from the King. Charles had sent for his guard to break into the House. Not a moment was to be lost. Holles recited the Resolutions from mem-

65

ory, and put the question himself. After hearty shouts of "Ay! Ay!" the house voted to adjourn. And then, so Gardiner writes: "The door was thrown open at last, and the members poured forth to convey to the outer world the tidings of their high resolve. Eleven years were to pass before the representatives of the country were permitted to cross that threshold again."

Next day, Eliot, Holles, Selden, Strode, and five more members were summoned before the Council and committed to the Tower or other prisons. Eliot replied to every question, "I refuse to answer, because I hold that it is against the privilege of the House of Commons to speak of anything which was done in the House." Charles soon issued a proclamation speaking of Eliot as "an outlawed man, desperate in mind and fortune."

And now we encounter a frequent feature of free-speech cases. Often, it is said that the speakers are not punished for what they said, but for something else—words plus a conspiracy, words plus a breach of the peace, words plus the systematic holding of meetings with associates and formation of plans to do something illegal at some time or other. So here Eliot and the others were not charged with words spoken in debate. Instead, they were accused of a conspiracy during a whole week before the exciting events of March 2nd to publish false statements against Privy Councillors, not for the purpose of questioning them in a legal or Parliamentary way, but to bring them into the hatred of the people and to bring the government into contempt. And secondly, it was urged that as soon as the Speaker had delivered the King's order to adjourn, the House was legally adjourned. The assembly was no longer the House of Commons, and everything happening afterwards was not privileged; it was tumultuously opposing the law and starting a riot. Such offenses, it was contended, were punishable outside Parliament just like the crimes of ordinary citizens.

Habeas corpus was then sought by most of the prisoners. When it was pointed out that the original warrants for imprisonment "at the King's pleasure" violated the Petition of Right, new warrants stated the ground of committal to be notable contempts against the King and his government and the stirring up of sedition in the State. When Charles learned that the judges would probably grant bail for such offenses, he evaded it by refusing to produce the prisoners "because they behaved insolently on a former occasion"; they must wait until "they would make a better demonstration of their modesty and civility." The servile judges acquiesced in this run-around for fear of losing their jobs.

After the summer had gone by, the prisoners were offered bail if they would give surety bonds for their good behavior while at liberty. This meant that they were not to make the government unpopular by recounting their wrongs. Security for future good behavior was hardly ever asked by English courts except from turbulent disturbers of the peace, profligate women, or keepers of disorderly houses. So Eliot and his companions in the Tower regarded this offer as a deadly insult, to be indignantly repelled.

In January, 1630, the government dropped its theory that the House of Commons became like a private home after the first moment of March 2nd when the Speaker read the King's order to adjourn. Now, the crime charged was a conspiracy formed in Parliament to resist that lawful order and to rend asunder the links which bound Charles to his subjects, by calumniating the ministers of the Crown and by assaulting the Speaker. The object of all this (according to Attorney General Heath) was to compel the House to listen while Eliot invited the people to refuse obedience to the King.

A nice question is raised by this line of argument against Eliot and the other prisoners. Is a murder of one member by another on the floor of the House privileged? No, everybody would agree—that is a plain crime. How about treason—say, an exchange of plans among three members to seize the Channel Islands and use them as a base against English naval ports? If we agree to that, how about words spoken "maliciously and seditiously"? This, the defense counsel insisted, is surely going too far. Otherwise, all actions of Parliament men might, "under pretense of malice," be drawn into the ordinary courts.

However, the judges accepted the prosecutor's theory. True, what was done in Parliament by consent of all the House should not be questioned elsewhere, but if any private member of the High Court of Parliament "puts off the person of a judge, and puts on the person of a malefactor, becoming seditious," his immunity vanishes. He has made himself incapable of his privileges.

Of course the prisoners could not concede this. They were well aware of what a moderate adviser of the King observed with common sense: "The object of the trial was to let the world see that Parliament men must be responsible for their words and actions in other courts, and so they will be more moderate and circumspect hereafter, and the King, when he finds good, may meet his people with so much the more assurance that they will never transgress in the point of due respect and obedience."

In February, 1630, Eliot was fined 200 pounds, Holles 1000 pounds, and Valentine 500, since he was less wealthy. None of them was to be released without acknowledging that he was at fault and giving security for his good behavior. The other prisoners made their peace one by one. These three stood their ground. Strode and Valentine

68

stayed in prison for eleven years in all until the Short Parliament met in 1640; both sat in the Long Parliament, where we shall meet Strode again. Eliot, who was only thirty-eight, refused to get back to his wife and children by merely uttering a few words of submission. Before long his health broke and he died in the Tower of illness in 1632.

> Many years [writes Gardiner] were to pass away before Eliot's principles were fully adopted by the nation. The mass of mankind is never moved by the fear of impending evils. To the farmer as he plodded on his daily rounds, to the trader as he looked for customers in his shop, it was nothing that the powers exercised by the King might possibly be put forth at some future time to the detriment of religion or of commerce. Much as the intelligent classes were dissatisfied with the course which Charles had taken, not even they, and still less the bulk of the nation, were as yet prepared to defy the King.
>
> It was impossible for a sovereign to cut himself off from sympathy with his people, and yet to keep free from actual misgovernment. To Eliot belongs the glory of being the first to see plainly that Charles's isolation was a fruitful seed of evil. His countrymen would follow by-and-by through the breach which he had made at the cost of his life.[30]

The Last Crisis of Freedom of Debate—
Charles I and the Five Members

After the day in 1629 when the Speaker was held down in his chair, eleven years went by without a Parliament. Charles levied his own taxes despite the resistance of John Hampden. Wentworth, now Earl of Strafford, carried out the King's policies and Laud ruled the Church. Thousands of our ancestors migrated to New England. The spirit of one youthful Puritan changed from

> Come, and trip it as ye go,
> On the light fantastic toe

to

69

"The hungry sheep look up, and are not fed. . . .
But that two-handed engine at the door
Stands ready to smite once, and smite no more."

At last Charles and Laud provoked the Scotch into invading England. So much money was needed to resist this rebellion that the King had no choice except to summon a Parliament in the spring of 1640. Immediately the House of Commons took up where it left off on the last day it sat. It proposed to discuss innovations in religion, unlawful taxes, and punishing men out of Parliament for things done in Parliament. The King got angry and sent them home after one month. This was long enough to prove that something extraordinary had happened to mature the House of Commons during the eleven years in which it never sat. The intense pamphleteering and talks and ferment in the boroughs and counties throughout those eleven years made the members arrive at Westminster in 1640 with a mastery of organization and procedure, and audacity in legislating.

They had little opportunity to display these newly won abilities in the Short Parliament of that year; but when they came back for the Long Parliament on November 3, 1640, they began at once with a series of astonishing measures which the King did not dare to refuse to sign, not even the Act of Attainder to be discussed in the next chapter, which put to death his devoted minister, the Earl of Strafford.

Down to the end of August, 1641, this Parliament was unanimous. It accomplished reforms which were permanently accepted after the Restoration. Thereafter the church question caused an irreconcilable division between the members who wanted only moderate reforms and the Root-and-Branch men, who desired to abolish bishops, substitute something like Scotch Presbyterianism, and change the Prayer Book completely or abandon it. The

70

moderates turned into Royalists under the leadership of Edward Hyde, who would later become Earl of Clarendon and the vivid historian of the stirring events of which he was a large part. The gulf between the two groups grew still wider when the outbreak of the Irish Rebellion in October called for greater revenues and raised questions whether the army should be controlled by the King or by Parliament. The extremists feared the possibility that Charles would bring his army to London and overawe the House of Commons, and were afraid to supply him with large new forces for Ireland, which he might use in London instead. Besides talking about control of the army and the militia, they proposed that Charles should employ only ministers of whom Parliament approved. Thus the division on religious grounds became also a division on political grounds as to the acquisition of supreme authority by Parliament. This became evident on November 21, 1641, when the Grand Remonstrance, a long statement of the radical reforms just described, was adopted in the House of Commons at the then extraordinary hour of midnight by a bare majority of eleven.

Then came the kind of situation which disheartens thinkers, where force begins to replace reason as the determiner of decisions. The mob was becoming a factor as in the French Revolution—or rather two mobs. By the end of December the London apprentices were gathering at Westminster and scared all the Bishops but four from taking their seats in the House of Lords. The House of Commons was apprehensive of the King's using troops and disbanded soldiers. He placed a debauched ruffian in charge of the Tower of London, which forecast the imprisonment of members. Courtiers with swords formed a guard to repel the apprentices. The names Roundheads and Cavaliers were derisively affixed by each side to the other. Charles set an armed guard of his officers at White-

71

hall, and the City of London offered to send its militia to protect Parliament. Fights broke out. Debates shifted from the merits of measures to the question whether Parliament was "free." The House of Lords voted by a majority of four that it was "free," while the Archbishop of York and eleven Bishops carried a petition to the King that it was not "free" and that Parliamentary action in their absence was void.

On Thursday, December 30th, the House of Commons, which was so zealous for free speech itself, voted to impeach the Bishops for what they said in their petition. Thus the Commons anticipated the folly of Charles' son James II in the summer of 1688. They charged the bishops with high treason by "endeavoring to subvert the fundamental laws of the kingdom." Before night the unlucky Archbishop of York and eleven bishops were in prison. That day an observer wrote in a letter: "I never saw the Court so full of gentlemen; every one comes thither with their swords. This day 500 gentlemen of the Inns of Court came to offer their services to the King. The citizens, for the most part, shut up their shops. Both factions look very big, and it is a wonder there is no more blood yet spilt, seeing how earnest both sides are."

Only the wisest and most courageous leadership could have surmounted this crisis. Charles took no steps to restore confidence. He had let his ablest adviser go to the block. He ignored the best moderate royalists in the House of Commons like Hyde and Falkland, although he had promised to consult them about every important act. His main reliance was on Queen Henrietta Maria, who was anticipating Marie Antoinette's interference with politics, and on Lord George Digby, the eldest son of the Earl of Bristol, who has already been mentioned as the wise ambassador of James I. That Lord George inherited only a lopped-off portion of his father's qualities is brought out by Clarendon:[31]

> The Lord Digby was a man of very Extraordinary parts by Nature and Art. A Graceful and Beautiful Person; of great Eloquence and Becomingness in his discourses and of so Universal a Knowledge, that he never wanted Subject for a discourse: He was equal to a very good part in the greatest Affairs, but the unfittest man alive to conduct them, having a confidence in himself, which sometimes intoxicated, and transported and exposed him.
>
> But his Fatal infirmity was, that he too often thought difficult things very easy; and considered not possible consequences, when the Proposition administred somewhat that was delightful to his Fancy, by pursuing whereof he imagined he should reap some Glory to himself. By this unhappy temper he did often involve himself in very unprosperous Attempts. The King himself was the unfittest Person alive to be served by Such a Councellor, being too easily inclined to sudden Enterprizes, and as easily Startled when they were entred upon.

On Sunday, January 2, 1642, Charles got news that the Parliamentary leaders had resolved to impeach the Queen for conspiring to bring over numerous Irish rebels to aid her husband. There was little doubt that she was guilty. Digby, who had worked with her and was also in danger of imprisonment, urged Charles to impeach the impeachers of the Queen. Whatever the faults of Charles, he adored his wife. For her sake he had sacrificed Strafford and was ready now to stake his throne.

In a regular impeachment like that of Strafford, the House of Commons was accustomed to accuse a King's minister before the House of Lords. Here it was impeachment upside-down, because the King through his minister was seeking to have the Lords try members of the House of Commons.[32] Charles was going back to a procedure of the thirteenth and fourteenth centuries (briefly discussed in my next chapter[33]) when the King haled some great offender before the Lords. Oddly enough, the only victim of this procedure for scores of years was Digby's own father, the illustrious Earl of Bristol; and his trial in the House of Lords in 1626 for high treason, without any action on the part of the House of Commons,[34] was brought about by the very King whom Bristol's son was now egging on to do it again. Strafford had urged this method of impeaching the chiefs of the Parliamentary party, just before they impeached him. It was characteristic of Charles I to ignore advice from Strafford while it had fair prospects of success, and then accept it from Lord George Digby when the sands were running out.

As the leaders to be accused, the King picked out John Pym, the spearhead of the Long Parliament; John Hampden, who had fought Ship-money in the courts; Holles and Strode, outstanding participants in the fracas of 1629 when the Speaker was forced back into his chair; and Sir Arthur Haselrig, "an absurd, bold man" in Clarendon's opinion, who though a newcomer in the House of Commons was in the forefront of the Root-and-Branch men. Charles arranged with his Attorney General to lay charges against the Five Members before the peers the first thing on Monday morning. He and Digby stupidly added a viscount to the list, thus antagonizing the House of Lords, on whom everything depended.

As soon as the Lords met on Monday, January 3rd, the Attorney General appeared in their House to charge these six persons with high treason. They had traitorously endeavored (he said) to subvert the fundamental laws and government, and deprive the King of his legal power, and give subjects a tyrannical power over his Majesty's people. They had endeavored by force and terror to compel Parliament to join with them in their traitorous designs, and to that end had countenanced tumults. They had levied war upon the King. The Lords, unwilling to order the arrest of their fellow-peer, stalled for time by appointing a committee to inquire whether the procedure of the Attorney General was according to law.

The House of Commons soon got news of this impeachment. Pym told how royal officers had sealed up his study and those of Holles and Hampden, in order to make sure of their papers. The Commons resolved that doing this without their leave was a breach of privilege. The Serjeant-at-Arms appeared with orders to arrest the Five Members. The House did not definitely refuse, but named a committee to tell the King they would send a reply as soon as they had given full consideration to their privileges, and that meanwhile the five gentlemen named would be ready to answer any legal accusation. Then the House ordered the Five Members to appear in their places from day to day.

Meanwhile, the King's previous large majority in the Lords dwindled to a bare minority. Because the Lords were accustomed to issue their own orders about the arrest of impeached persons, they resented the King's determination to do the arresting himself. They ordered the sealed-up studies broken open. The Commons arrested the officers who had done the sealing.

That Monday evening Charles took counsel with his intimates at Whitehall. Urged on by Digby and the Queen, he resolved to go himself and arrest the Five Members in the House of Commons. The Tower was filled with artillerymen. The Lord Mayor of London was directed to refuse to obey orders from the Commons; he was to fire on rioters if necessary. The lawyers in the Inns of Court, who were on the King's side, were told to stay indoors and be ready to march at a moment's warning.

If the members were to be arrested at all (Gardiner says), the King should have seized them in their beds that night as Napoleon III seized his Parliamentary opponents in the *coup d'etat* of 1851. Such a course was impossible

75

for Charles. He was eager to preserve the appearance of legality; and always conscious that he was a King, he did not expect a persistent refusal. As Bertrand Russell remarked to Whitehead, in thinking about Charles I we ought not to forget that he lived his entire life without realizing that he lost his head.

Then came Tuesday, January 4, 1642. That morning the Five Members were in their seats and protested their innocence. News came of a great gathering of armed men about Whitehall and of affairs in the Tower. The Commons sent a message to warn their friends in the City. Nothing more had happened when they adjourned for dinner at noon.

Charles ought to have been in the House that morning if he meant to come at all. Instead, he sought out the Queen and gave strong reasons against carrying out the plan. "Go, you coward," replied his wife, "and pull these rogues out by the ears, or never see my face more." Rather than face such taunts, Charles resolved to hang back no longer. Soon afterwards the Queen repeated the secret to one of her ladies-in-waiting, who at once conveyed the news to one of the King's chief opponents in the House of Lords. Before the Five Members had finished their dinner, they got a message from this noble—the King was coming himself to seize them; they had better get out. However, they returned to the House of Commons when it met again at one. Still nothing happened.

About three o'clock Charles hurried down the stairs of Whitehall with his princely nephew, heir to the unhappy Palatinate, and called out, "Let my faithful subjects and soldiers follow me." A coach happened to be near the door. Charles threw himself into it and drove off. Three or four hundred armed men marched behind him.

No great speed was possible for so large a procession. A French bystander pushed through the crowd and ran swiftly to the House of Commons. He got a member he knew to come out and told him what was on the way. The House immediately asked the Five Members to withdraw. Strode wanted to stay and had to be dragged off by his cloak to join Pym, Hampden, Holles, and Haselrig at the river-side. There boats were always waiting, like gondolas at the Ducal Palace today. All five got aboard and were rowed down the Thames to the City of London, where multitudes would give them protection.

The King's fierce retinue was scattering terror while it neared Westminster Hall. Shopkeepers hastily barred their windows. Charles alighted from his coach and strode rapidly through the Hall between the ranks of his armed throng. As he mounted the steps toward the House of Commons, he signaled his followers to await his return there, but about eighty of them pressed after him into the lobby, including many desperate ruffians. Charles, doing his best to maintain a show of decency, sent a message informing the House of his arrival. When he reached the door with the young Elector Palatine at his side, he told his followers to remain behind. One of them leaned against the door to keep it open so that the members might see the men outside, armed with pistols and swords. Many of them had dropped their cloaks in Westminster Hall so as to leave their sword arms free. In their forefront stood one of the greatest scoundrels in England. The entrance of Charles I through the door which none of his predecessors had ever passed was in striking contrast to the meeting of James I in 1621 with the members at Newmarket. Then the House of Commons had gone to the King, but now it was the King who went to the House of Commons. They would no longer come to him.

Charles walked forward between the members standing bareheaded on each side. His glance went to the front seat usually occupied by Pym. It was empty. When he reached the upper end of the House, he said to the Speaker, "I must borrow your chair a little."

"He declared to them," writes Clarendon, who saw it all, "that no King of England had been ever, or should be more careful to maintain their Priviledges, than he would be; but that in Cases of Treason No man had priviledge; and therefore he came to see if any of those persons, whom he had accused, were There; for he was resolved to have them, wheresoever he should find them."

Then, standing in front of the chair, he looked around for the Five Members. "I do not see any of them. I think I should know them." Then the King called each of them by name. No voice replied. He asked the Speaker where they were. Lenthall knelt and told the King, "I have neither eyes to see, nor tongue to speak in this place, but as this House is pleased to direct me, whose servant I am here."

"Well," answered Charles, "I think my eyes are as good as another's." Again he looked carefully along the benches. "Well, I see all the birds are flown." And so he gloomily left the House, amid cries of "Privilege! privilege!" behind him. The House at once adjourned while the King's supporters were proposing to him to attack them. One member went right to his lodgings and immediately made his will.

On Wednesday the 5th the King went to the City with the vain hope of arresting the Five Members there. Instead, he found crowds shouting "Privileges of Parliament!" The rest of the week went by in turmoil. The House put itself under the protection of the government of the City, where a committee of its leaders met every day. On Monday morning, January 10th, the Five Members joined the committee with a hearty welcome, and Charles and his Queen left Whitehall. He did not see it again for seven years, until the afternoon of January 30,

1649, when through the middle window of the Banqueting Hall he stepped out upon the scaffold.

The Long and Winding Track out of the Wilderness

Thus culminated the long series of struggles which wrote the clause on freedom of debate into the Bill of Rights of 1689 and thence into the Constitution of 1787. True, this right was not yet actually won when Charles I walked out of the House of Commons, but henceforth it depended on what happened to the broader problem of who should govern England.

Within a few months that problem was transferred from the Houses of Parliament to the battlefields. War, as is so often the case, destroyed a great deal and solved very little. After the fighting ended, some questions no longer needed to be answered: but they were replaced by new questions which were just as difficult. Our own Civil War wiped out the question of slavery, but merely transformed it into the question of two races of citizens living together in the South. The English Civil War removed the King and still left open the underlying issue, how the few who governed should be controlled by the many who were governed.

When the last Royalist troops surrendered at Stow-on-the Wold, their leader said to his conquerors from the Parliamentary army, "You have now done your work and may go play, unless you will fall out amongst yourselves." At once, the army of 50,000 was divided from Parliament by deep differences in outlook. Cromwell's soldiers, drawn as they were from all ranks of society and from most creeds, were closer to the wishes of the English people than were the predominantly Presbyterian merchants and lawyers and country squires in the House of Commons. The soldiers were more representative of new forces which were again emerging in England. For instance, John Bunyan, who was one of them, could never have written *Pilgrim's Progress* before the Civil War.

"On becoming soldiers," they told the Commons, "we have not ceased to be citizens." Cromwell and many of his officers and men sensed the real needs of England which the outworn Long Parliament was ignoring, especially the need for freedom of worship for all kinds of Protestants, for Jews too, perhaps even for Roman Catholics. Consequently, with all Cromwell's genius and strong desire for "healing and settling," he was never able to get along with Parliament. And yet he was unable to get along without it, for no country will long remain contented to be governed by an army, not even by its own army.

During more than a decade of wrangling and intermittent military dictatorships, freedom of debate was subjected to far worse indignities by the army than by all the Stuart Kings put together. The House of Lords was run out of existence. Pride's Purge expelled 140 of the majority in the House of Commons. "By what right do you act?" asked a member. "By the right of the sword," replied Hugh Peters, a former New England parson.[35] When the Rump of the Long Parliament refused to dissolve itself twelve years after that Parliament was elected in 1640, Cromwell went with a company of musketeers to the door of the House of Commons. He sat down quietly in his place, clad in plain gray clothes and gray worsted stockings. When a bill he detested was about to pass, he strode into the midst of the chamber, clapped his hat on his head, and exclaimed, "Your hour is come, the Lord hath done with you! Come, come, we have had enough of this. I will put an end to your prating!" Cromwell lifted the mace from the table. "What shall we do with this bauble?— Take it away!" And the door of the House was locked.

Fortunately, the Restoration turned into usurpers the men who did these high-handed acts, and they never served as precedents. The privileges of Parliament were reinstated along with as much else as possible. Charles II had no inclination to imitate his father, either in losing his head or in any other respect.

The issue of freedom of debate did get raised by Parliament in 1667, in rather an academic fashion.[36] Some lawyer had just published a volume of reports of old court decisions, including the condemnation of Sir John Eliot, Denzil Holles, and the others for what they said and did in the House of Commons on March 2, 1629, when the Speaker was held in his chair.[37] The Commons accidentally learned of the book, and resented some of Attorney General Heath's narrow statements in it about freedom of debate. The fact that they were then engaged in impeaching Clarendon[38] may have had something to do with their interest. Eliot's Case, they said, "did very much concern this great Privilege of Parliament." They feared that "passing from Hand to Hand amongst the Men of the Long Robe," it might come in time to be regarded as good law and a binding precedent against liberty of speech in Parliament. So the House inquired into precedents, especially Strode's Case under Henry the Eighth.[39] Some writers had contended that this old statute was just a Private Act to keep an individual member of Parliament out of jail, but the House of Commons interpreted it much more broadly.

Thereupon a Resolution was drawn and sent up to the House of Lords for concurrence: "The Act of Parliament . . . commonly entitled 'An Act concerning Richard Strowd,' is a general law, extending to indemnify all and every the Members of Parliament, in all Parliaments, for and touching any Bills, Speaking, Reasoning, or Declaring of any Matters or Matter, in and concerning the Parlia-

81

ment, to be communed and treated of; and is a declaratory Law, of the ancient and necessary Rights and Privileges of Parliament."

The Lords were somewhat puzzled by this sudden interest of the Commons in ancient history. A series of conferences between the two Houses followed, in which the reasons of the Commons were ably presented by Sir John Vaughan. Soon he would become a judge and make a great decision in Bushell's Case, which solidified the constitutional right to trial by jury.[40]

Vaughan began by pointing out that Parliament could not be punished for whatever it enacted, and went on to argue that debates ought to be equally immune, since they were the indispensable first stage of the legislative process:[41] "Nothing can come into an Act of Parliament, but it must be propounded by somebody. . . . The Members must be as free as the Houses. An Act of Parliament cannot disturb the State. Therefore, the Debate that tends to it cannot, for [the Act] must be propounded and debated before it can be enacted."

The Lords were thus persuaded to pass the Joint Resolution, including a final sentence declaring the convictions of Eliot, Holles, and the rest to be illegal and "against the Freedom and Privilege of Parliament." And for good measure, the Lords ordered Holles, who was now a peer, to appeal to their House from the judgments given against him and his friends. Then they reversed the convictions, about forty years too late.[42]

There can be little doubt that the foregoing pronouncements in Parliament about freedom of debate shaped the content of that freedom for John Somers and the other men who wrote it into the Bill of Rights.

It is always pleasant to assume that what we regard as notable steps toward liberty were hailed with equal enthusiasm by men who lived at the time. Yet history rarely works like that. On November 25, 1667, while the House of Commons was framing its Resolution, Samuel Pepys recorded in his diary a conversation with the father of the founder of Pennsylvania:[43] "This morning Sir W. Pen tells me that the House was very hot on Saturday last upon the business of freedom of speech in the House . . .; so that he fears there may be some bad thing which they have a mind to broach which they dare not do without more security than they now have. God keep us, for things look mighty ill!"

After 1667 twenty-one years ran by and nothing more happened to freedom of debate. But the underlying problem of who should share in the government of England was always causing trouble, as I related early in this chapter. At last, a few days over forty years since Charles I walked through Whitehall to his death, the Banqueting House was again astir for a momentous ceremony —this time joyous. The vexatious problem had reached a solution which was almost final. The King and his ministers would still do the governing—anything else had been proved impracticable—but Parliament alone would make the laws. And the few who governed would be constantly subjected to Parliamentary control and unable to infringe fundamental freedoms.

So the Bill of Rights was made law. Freedom of debate and many other liberties became the rights of Englishmen and our rights.

Freedom of Debate under the Constitution

Suppose that the guaranty, thus achieved, of freedom of speech for Senators and Representatives had been whittled down by the Supreme Court like the guaranty in the First Amendment of freedom of speech for everybody. The Justices might have said that freedom of debate is sometimes subordinated to the other purposes of society and does not extend to gross abuses. They might have relied on English history to show that the clause was intended to protect legislators against imprisonment by executive tyranny, and not to deny redress to private citizens who are victims of vituperation. How apt it would have been to quote Justice Holmes, that "a page of history is worth a volume of logic." Fortunately they resisted such intellectual temptations and preserved freedom of debate as one of the few absolute human rights in the Constitution.

Freedom of debate operates in every way which will enable Congress to carry on the business before it, and not merely to guard Congress against the precise kinds of interference which hindered English Parliaments before the Bill of Rights. The only possible limitation ever suggested by the Supreme Court is that Senators or Representatives might not be immune if they imitated the Long Parliament by executing the Chief Magistrate or the French Assembly during the Reign of Terror by becoming a court for imposing capital punishment.[44] Except for such unlikely possibilities, the constitutional clause, as construed, seems judicially and in practice, to cover everything a member does as part of the business of Congress. The "Speech or Debate in either House" need not relate to any specific measure; Senator Couzens of Michigan was held immune when he spontaneously defended himself against rumors of tax-evasion.[45] Even the casual conversation of members in the aisle which was not addressed to the chair and was not about a matter then before the House might perhaps be protected in Congress, although the similar privilege in the Massachusetts constitution has been held not to give any immunity under such circumstances.[46] The "Speech" need not actually be in the "House"; it may be in a committee room in the Office Building of either House.[47] It need not be spoken, but may consist of a printed committee report.[48]

Some problems do remain unsolved. Does the phrase "in either House" cover remarks by a Senator during the hearings of an investigating committee which sits in San Francisco, 3,000 miles away from the Senate chamber? Does it cover what the chairman of such a committee says to newspaper reporters after the committee has adjourned for the day, in order to get big headlines by blasting innocent men? Does it cover an informal conference of the majority members of a committee, who are planning its work for the next session of Congress at a hotel in Bermuda?

Another unsolved problem is whether the constitutional immunity extends to what the member of Congress does with his speech after he has delivered it. Suppose he broadcasts copies of it through the mails to his constituents or the general public.[49] The purpose of the Constitution was to enable him to participate in the business of the House. Building up support for his re-election is something else. Perhaps the only defense he then has is like the common-law privilege of newspapers to circulate a fair report of legislative proceedings, but (as I point out later) that defense does not do either a newspaper or a member of Congress any good if the report be garbled or if it be sent out for the deliberate purpose of injuring the victim of lies and insults.

Is it valid for the member of Congress to waive the privilege of freedom of debate? Such a course was tried by Senator William Benton of Connecticut when another Senator sued him for a million dollars for defamatory statements made by Benton in the course of Senate business. I submit that the Constitution requires every court to refuse flatly to have anything to do with such a case. The privilege of freedom of debate is not a personal favor to the individual Senator or Representative. It exists for the protection of Congress in its work. This is plain from a statement by James Wilson, a member of the Philadelphia Convention who had much to do with putting this clause into the Constitution:[50] "In order to enable and encourage a representative of the public to discharge his public trust with firmness and success, it is indispensably necessary, that he should enjoy the fullest liberty of speech, and that he should be protected from the resentment of every one, however powerful, to whom the exercise of that liberty may occasion offence." Inasmuch as the privilege thus rests on "the public necessity for untrammeled freedom of legislative activity" within the powers of Congress,[51] no member of either House possesses any authority to give up the right of that House to his uninterrupted and uncoerced services in aiding its work. Only the Senate or the House of Representatives can waive the privilege, if it can be waived at all.

What is frequently forgotten is that the Constitution protects only Senators or Representatives, and not third persons who hand on what they say. True, newspapers and their editors, columnists, etc., who paraphrase or quote from Congressional debates or hearings before investigating committees can, if sued for libel, seek safety in the defense of Fair Report which has been built up by judges as part of the common law. My point is that this defense for private persons is more restricted than the constitutional immunity of members of Congress.

The common-law defense of Fair Report has been carefully formulated:[52] "The publication of a report of . . . proceedings of a legislative body . . . is privileged, although it contains matter which is false and defamatory, if it is (a) accurate and complete or a fair abridgement of such proceedings, and (b) not made solely for the purpose of causing harm to the person defamed." The two qualifications at the end have much bearing on what I have just been saying. They show that garbled extracts may be actionable. If the reporter or columnist adds any comments or inferences of his own, these get no benefit from the defense of Fair Report.

Take a concrete case where the application of this defense is problematical. A columnist keeps repeating snippets defaming a government official from a Senate committee report long after it ceases to be news. He does so with the deliberate intention of injuring the official. The columnist says nothing about strong language exculpating the official in the minority report in the same pamphlet. He knows that the harmful statements by the majority have been decisively disproved since they were uttered. It is by no means certain that the derogatory words are immune from a damage action merely because they were printed by Senators. Keeping libels alive in the press for months and years is quite different from the normal endeavor of newspapers to give the public an adequate account of what happened in Congress yesterday.

Abuses of freedom of debate have been so conspicuous in recent years that proposals have been made to by-pass the constitutional immunity by various devices. For example, Senator Humphrey of Minnesota has suggested that we taxpayers should reimburse the victim of Senatorial defamation. A fund would be set up out of public revenues, and any person who thought himself injured could claim against the fund and be paid if he proved regular slander or libel. With due deference, I am opposed to all such proposals. Not only is it important that a Senator or Representative should be able to say what he believes without fear that a court will make him sacrifice a substantial slice of his savings, but also he ought not to be distracted from his Congressional duties by the need to appear as a witness to defend either himself or a fund against all-comers who think they are defamed. If Senator Humphrey's plan were adopted, any member of Congress worth his salt would feel an obligation to spend time and effort to protect the taxpayers' money against unjust claims.

No new remedy is necessary to stop abuses of freedom of debate. The remedy has been right there in the Constitution since 1787. A Senator or Representative can be punished or expelled by his own House. The real issue before each House of Congress is whether it regards itself as a club with no concern for private citizens who are injured with gross injustice. What kind of club would that be where members could with impunity sit in the window and pour dirty water over pedestrians on the sidewalk below?

Congress, however, has never expelled such a member of the club or even reprimanded him. Claude M. Fuess remarks, "A legislative body which in times past has not been too much concerned when its members have been maimed, like Senator Sumner [by Representative Brooks on the floor of the Senate], or killed [by another Congressman in a duel] like Representative Cilley, is unlikely to be very much disturbed over ordinary vituperation, especially when the victim is an outsider." Mr. Fuess in 1951 and one of my law students in the spring of 1954 examined all the reported cases in which either House was asked to exercise its constitutional power (under Article I, section 5) to "punish its Members for Disorderly Behavior."[53] Neither investigation turned up a single case in which a Senator or a Representative was actually disciplined for saying anything about anybody. Subsequently, in the autumn of 1954, the Senate did condemn one of its members for insulting language about fellow-members. The carefully chosen bipartisan committee which considered the charges also recommended that the same Senator be censured for grossly insulting a distinguished gen-

88

eral.[54] The Senate did not bother to take a vote on this question of protecting an outsider.[55] Thus the practice of the Senate allows a Senator to utter any falsehoods and insults he pleases, so long as he does not aim them at other Senators.

The privilege achieved in the long English struggle was the privilege of members to be tried and punished by their fellow-members and not by any outside tribunal. It was not a privilege of unlimited slander and vituperation. Therefore, abuses ought to be attacked directly by the legislators who hear and read the abuse. And never, no matter how great the abuses are, should the privilege itself be impaired. For the memorable words of Judge Cuthbert Pound are as true inside Congress as out:[56] "The rights of the best of men are secure only as the rights of the vilest and most abhorrent are protected."

When we are tempted to great impatience over the ability of members of Congress today to abuse private citizens without responsibility in the courts, we should remember that Peter Wentworth and Sir John Eliot died in the Tower of London in order that legislators might engage effectively in their appointed tasks, whether they perform them wisely or not.

The Prohibition of Bills of Attainder

The original Constitution did very little to protect human rights against the states, and the Bill of Rights of 1791 restricted only the national government. We are so accustomed to the Fourteenth Amendment that it is easy to forget how the states could be almost as tyrannical as they pleased before the Civil War, so long as they had a republican form of government. Still, this was only a theoretical danger, for they were restrained by their own constitutions, which safeguarded many human rights. So when the nation began, there did not seem to be much need to impose limitations on the states, except those required by the distribution of powers under the federal system. The members of the Philadelphia Convention were wisely reluctant to multiply obstacles to ratification of the Constitution.

Yet recent events had shown that some state legislatures were very susceptible to certain temptations, like pouring out paper money, cutting down distasteful debts, and confiscating the property of Tories and Englishmen in violation of the Treaty of Peace. Such state laws were making it hard to end the destruction of credit, and to promote friendly relations with foreign countries and the flow of trade across the nation and the Atlantic Ocean. So the framers of the Constitution determined to remove these temptations. The issue of money ought to be made an exclusively federal concern. The most harmful types of revengeful and retroactive legislation should be forbidden. Hence the prohibition in section 10 of Article I, "No State shall . . . pass any Bill of Attainder, *ex post facto* Law, or Law impairing the Obligation of Contracts. . . ." And the first two kinds of law were so objectionable[1] that it was only right for section 9 to put them beyond the reach of Congress too: "No Bill of Attainder or *ex post facto* Law shall be passed."

These are probably the hardest clauses in the Constitution for a non-lawyer to understand. An old story tells how a white man and a Negro, both illiterate, went to register as voters in Georgia. An innocent-looking provision of the state constitution for the benefit of persons unable to read and write allows them to vote if they "can understand and give a reasonable interpretation of any paragraph of the Constitution of the United States . . . that may be read to them by any of the registrars."[2] To the white man the registrar read the paragraph in Article II, section 1, about the qualifications of the President. "Stonewall, what's that mean?" "It means the President has to be born in this country, be thirty-five, and lived here fourteen years." "Good, Stonewall, show up on election day right here." When the Negro's turn came, the registrar read him, "No Bill of Attainder or *ex post facto* Law shall be passed. " "Rastus, what does that mean?" "I guess that means I don't vote."

An ex post facto law can be roughly defined as imposing punishment retroactively. It is well explained in Article 11 of the Universal Declaration of Human Rights, which was unanimously adopted in December, 1948, by the General Assembly of the United Nations:[3] "No one shall be held guilty of any penal offense on account of any act or omission which did not constitute a penal offense, under national or international law, at the time it was committed. Nor shall a heavier penalty be imposed than the one which was applicable at the time the penal offense was committed."

For example, a New Orleans mob in 1891 lynched several Italians. During the ensuing strained relations with Italy, President Harrison urged Congress to pass a statute making it a federal crime for individuals to deprive for-

91

eigners of rights which were protected by a treaty. Suppose that Congress in 1892 had responded to this request by authorizing United States courts to try members of a mob for such violence against aliens, and had put in an express clause to include the 1891 lynchings at New Orleans. This clause would have been unconstitutional as ex post facto, although the statute would be available against future killers of foreigners in breach of a treaty.

The legislature can validly reduce the severity of the penalty for a crime already committed, e.g., by shortening the time in jail. Whatever is left of the former punishment is considered to have been law at the time of the offense. Yet what happens if the new punishment is different, but is commonly regarded as milder than the old? In 1857 James Shepherd set fire to his home in New York City in the middle of the night. His wife burned to death, apparently not deeply mourned by her husband, whose lips, hair and whiskers were singed. Arson of that sort then brought death on the gallows. Next year the legislature substituted life imprisonment at hard labor as the only penalty. So when Shepherd was finally tried and convicted in 1861, he was sentenced to prison. Nowise discouraged, his lawyer persuaded the highest state court to hold the new law to be ex post facto as to Shepherd. The judges refused to say whether it was more merciful to shut a man up for life than to hang him. Since the old law had been repealed, it was too late to hang Shepherd. So he was let off altogether.[4] This is the kind of thing that could only happen in a court. Such a discredited decision[5] does not weaken the principle that retroactive punishments are very unjust.[6]

Although the framers linked bills of attainder with ex post facto laws and the Supreme Court (we shall see) has had some difficulty about deciding into which forbidden class an objectionable statute belongs, they differ in important ways. An ex post facto law usually resembles ordinary criminal laws in operating through the regular courts on people generally. A bill of attainder is a direct condemnation by the legislature without any judicial action. The legislature, all by itself, determines guilt and inflicts punishment upon an individual by name, or more rarely on several specified persons. An example of a blanket bill of attainder, which was familiar to the members of the Philadelphia Convention, was a New York statute of 1779. This enacted that fifty-nine named Loyalists, including all the highest royal officials of the colony and several women, were convicted of the offense of having "voluntarily been adherent" during the present unjust and cruel war to King George III, his fleets and armies, "with Intent to subvert the Government and Liberties of this State." Besides providing for the forfeiture and sale of all their lands and personal property, the legislature declared these fifty-nine persons "to be forever banished from this State; and that each and every one of them, if found in New York at any time thereafter, should 'suffer Death as in Cases of Felony. . . .'"[7] John Jay wrote at the time, "New York is disgraced by injustice too palpable to admit even of palliation."

This New York statute illustrates the important point that a bill of attainder is sometimes also an ex post facto law, and hence doubly objectionable. That is not true of all bills of attainder. For example, a state legislature might enact that John Jones was guilty of murder; and in some of the English bills of attainder, as we shall find, Parliament beheaded a man for treason as it was then defined by law. Contrast the "offense" of adhering to George III for which two former royal Governors, Dunmore and Tryon, had their property forfeited by act of legislature in 1779. When these two men committed the acts here punished, they were carrying out their oath of allegiance

93

to the King who had appointed them and obeying his orders. That was certainly not a crime by any law in New York between 1770 and 1771 while Dunmore was Governor, or after 1771 while Tryon ruled the colony until he took refuge on board ship in New York Harbor in October, 1775. Indeed, before the Declaration of Independence the only legislation in force in New York which had any bearing on the subject was the English Statute of Treasons of Edward III;[8] and this was violated before 1776, not by Dunmore and Tryon, but by many of the very men who voted a few years later that Dunmore and Tryon were guilty of subverting the government. Well might the British soldiers after Cornwallis surrendered march away from Yorktown to the tune of "The World Turned Upside Down."

It is hard to fit old laws into a revolution, as Serjeant Maynard pointed out in 1689.[9] Nevertheless, the Philadelphia Convention believed in the wise principle that when a war is over, it ought to be over. They had seen enough of the bills of attainder in New York and other states to want nothing like them to be enacted again.

The Immediate Background of the Prohibition of Bills of Attainder and Its Relationship to Other Parts of the Constitution

The clauses against bills of attainder and ex post facto laws aroused little opposition in or out of the Convention of 1787. They had the advantage of not being innovations. Both types of laws had already been forbidden by state constitutions in Maryland and Massachusetts, where the language about bills of attainder was admirably clear: "No person ought, in any case, or in any time, to be declared guilty of treason or felony by the legislature." New Hampshire had prohibited ex post facto laws. The New York

94

constitution of 1777 declared that no acts of attainder should be passed by the legislature for crimes "other than those committed before the termination of the present war"—an exception so outrageously put to use in 1779 as to prove the desirability of the rule.

At Philadelphia the prohibition of bills of attainder was accepted without question. Ex post facto laws aroused some discussion on August 22nd as to whether they included retrospective laws in civil cases, which were prohibited by the Continental Congress in the Ordinance it had adopted, about a month previously, for the Government of the Northwest Territory. John Dickinson said that Blackstone's *Commentaries* limited the phrase to criminal cases only, and some further provision for civil cases would be necessary. This led to the clause against impairing the obligation of contracts. Several distinguished delegates opposed the ex post facto clause because, as James Wilson said, "It will proclaim that we are ignorant of the first principles of Legislation." To this Daniel Carroll of Maryland shrewdly replied that "experience overruled all other calculations." In whatever light these laws might be viewed by learned lawyers, "The State Legislatures had passed them, and they had taken effect." Both prohibitions were adopted 7 to 3. On September 14th a motion by George Mason and Elbridge Gerry to reconsider the ex post facto clause so as to extend the prohibition to civil cases was defeated by the votes of eleven states. The only relevant reference I have found in the state ratifying conventions was Randolph's statement in Virginia that "the attention of the [Philadelphia] convention was drawn to criminal matters alone. . . ."

Blackstone, who undoubtedly influenced American thinking about ex post facto laws, treated them quite apart from bills of attainder. He denounces those laws at length as contrary to the basic principle that people ought

95

to be clearly told what acts are wrongful before they do them. They ought to know what they are to obey. Lack of publicity for laws is like Caligula's practice of writing his laws in very small letters and hanging them far up on high pillars where nobody could read them. And it is still more unreasonable to enact laws ex post facto: "After an action (indifferent in itself) is committed, the legislator then for the first time declares it to have been a crime, and inflicts a punishment upon the person who committed it. Here it is impossible that the party could foresee that an action, innocent when it was done, should be afterwards converted to guilt by a subsequent law; he had therefore no cause to abstain from it; and all punishment for not abstaining must of consequence be cruel and unjust."

On the other hand, Blackstone expresses no particular opposition to acts of attainder. He merely mentions them as incidental to his demonstration that the High Court of Parliament is the supreme court in the kingdom.

What is very important in Blackstone for our purposes is his explanation of the word "attainder." This terrible penalty was the immediate consequence of the sentence of death for treason or felony, and it made no difference whether the condemnation was by the legislature or by a court of judges after a normal trial. The consequences of attainder, he wrote, were forfeiture of the guilty person's property to the King and corruption of his blood. This last phrase meant that he could neither inherit lands from his ancestors nor retain those he already possessed, nor transmit them by descent to any heir. He was wiped out as if he had never been born. Thus his wife and children were punished, as well as he, since they could not receive any lands from him or through him. Even if the wealthy father of an attainted man died after his son was beheaded, nothing descended to the orphaned grandchildren. Blackstone admitted that all this might be hard on innocent children and grandchildren. Still, the law was not to blame. It was the fault of the criminal who had "thus knowingly and dishonestly involved others in his own calamities." He ought to have thought of this before he misconducted himself.

Fortunately this indulgent attitude toward the English law was not shared by the Philadelphia Convention. They provided by Article III, section 3, of the Constitution: "No Attainder of Treason shall work Corruption of Blood or Forfeiture except during the Life of the Person attainted."

What has just been said shows that technically bills of attainder were limited to legislative condemnation which put the named person to death. Whenever the punishment was imprisonment or confiscation or banishment, as for the New York Tories, there was strictly no "attainder" and hence the legislation was called an act of pains and penalties. However, nobody has ever doubted that such an act is embraced in the constitutional prohibition of bills of attainder. Indeed, every statute nullified by the Supreme Court under this clause involved some punishment milder than death.

The foregoing discussion has brought out the very important point that freedom is to a large extent indivisible. Just as the habeas corpus clause is intimately connected with many of the provisions about a fair trial in the Sixth Amendment, so the bill of attainder clause is related to several other parts of the Constitution. I have already linked it with the prohibitions of ex post facto laws and corruption of blood. Inasmuch as many of the English acts of attainder were for treason, the limitations in Article III as to the definition and proof of treason are material. Also, there is a rather surprising connection with the clause in Article VI which makes treaties "the supreme Law of the Land." The framers knew that the restoration of commerce with Great Britain was essential to our prosperity. Treaty violations, especially confiscations of Tory property and annihilation of debts to Tories, were bad obstacles to friendly intercourse with the mother country. Consequently, the framers made assurance doubly sure by enabling the national government to strike at such violations both through the clause making treaties supreme and the clause making acts of attainder void. A still more important relationship, which will become obvious later, is with the numerous constitutional clauses about impeachments.

All the attainder and impeachment clauses in our Constitution acquire fuller and sometimes unexpected significance if we look back from 1787 over the long series of beheadings and bitter punishments of individuals by Parliament, which began in the Middle Ages almost as soon as there was a Parliament and had not yet reached its end in England. We would elect two Presidents before Parliament enacted its last bill of attainder in 1798.

Bills of Attainder and Impeachments in the Middle Ages

Instead of delving into the obscure origins of bills of attainder, it will be helpful to take as our starting-point the full text (somewhat modernized) of a bill enacted in 1450, when Parliament had reached considerable maturity and was using standardized phraseology in such legislation.

After Henry VI had lost Normandy and the rest of his French domains through the heroism of Joan of Arc and numerous later disasters, great resentment broke out in Kent, the wealthiest part of England, over this national disgrace, and many domestic wrongs. A Kentish army gathered late in May, 1450, and marched on London. It was led by Jack Cade, a cutter of woolen cloth who had served in the wars and claimed to have Plantagenet blood.

The discontented royal soldiers scattered before him in a single battle. The King fled. All resistance to the rebels was abandoned. On July 1st they entered Southwark, across the Thames from London, where the Common Council voted to receive them into the City.

Yet no lasting success was possible. The gulf between the few in power and the many with genuine grievances was even wider in 1450 than it was in the House of Commons a century later when Peter Wentworth sought to shape the policies of Queen Elizabeth or under James I when the House in 1621 wanted to discuss whether his son ought to marry a Spanish princess. On the one side, during all these conflicts, were the sovereign and his ministers, who, whatever their shortcomings and their unawareness of the need for change, did have long experience in the business of governing a kingdom. On the other side were the mass of people, especially large groups growing in ability and economic strength, who voiced just complaints but lacked the training and capacity to transform these complaints into effective legislation. Their leaders were unfit for the difficult tasks of maintaining order and managing affairs day in and day out. Moreover, there was as yet no peaceful mechanism for turning out corrupt and incompetent ministers, and still less those whose policies, though honest, were much disliked. The only method of transferring power was violence. The choice lay unhappily between misgovernment and anarchy. When that is the case, misgovernment must become very bad indeed before sober citizens will permanently withhold their support from the powers that be and allow them to be replaced by well-meaning amateurs. Even two hundred years after Jack Cade, the Puritans and the Long Parliament proved themselves incompetent to govern England. Nearly two more centuries would go by before the advance of education, economic well-being, and political machinery made it possible for another tailor, Francis Place, to take a prominent part in the bringing about the Reform Bill of 1832, which took the first long step toward a self-governing nation without shedding any blood and at the same time gave the country new rulers who were at least as efficient as the old.

In the light of what has just been said, let us picture the attitude of sober-minded citizens of London toward Cade's Rebellion after the royal government had collapsed. Perhaps Shakespeare's *Henry VI* was unjust to Cade as it was unjust to Joan of Arc, but the words put into the mouth of Cade and his followers probably present their program, not as it really was, but as it was conceived by thoughtful men who saw all the faults of the nobles who had been governing England and yet felt no hope in successors who were believed to talk about their aims like this:[10]

> *Jack Cade.* There shall be in England seven half-penny loaves sold for a penny; the three-hoop'd pot shall have ten hoops; and I will make it a felony to drink small beer: all the realm shall be in common; and in Cheapside shall my palfrey go to grass; and when I am king . . . there shall be no money; all shall eat and drink on my score; and I will apparel them all in one livery, that they may agree like brothers, and worship me their lord.
> *Dick, the butcher.* The first thing we do, let's kill all the lawyers.
> *Jack Cade.* Nay, that I mean to do. . . .
> We will not leave one lord, one gentleman:
> Spare none but such as go in clouted shoon.

After Cade had been occupying London for three days, the better class of citizens became seriously alarmed for the security of property. He went to his quarters at the White Hart in Southwark for the night, was vigorously resisted on London Bridge when he sought to return, and finally gave up the attempt. The King's Council terminated the disorders by a general amnesty, which caused most of his men to disband. A few days later he retreated into Kent with his booty. On July 12th, a proclamation was issued, offering a reward of £1,000 for bringing him to the King alive or dead. Trying to escape, he was taken prisoner the same day by the Sheriff of Kent in Sussex, after a struggle in which Cade received a mortal wound. While his captor was bringing him to London in a cart, he died. His naked body was beheaded and quartered, and the remains were conveyed on a hurdle through the streets. The head was set up on London Bridge, and the four quarters were distributed to Blackheath, Norwich, Salisbury, and Gloucester for public exhibition.

Next year, Parliament passed the following bill of attainder:

Your Commons of this present Parliament pray—

Whereas the false Traitor John Cade, naming himself John Mortimer, late called Captain of Kent, the 8th day of July in the twenty-eighth year of your reign at Southwark in the shire of Surrey, and on the 9th day of July of the year aforesaid at Dartford and Rochester in the shire of Kent, also at Rochester aforesaid and elsewhere on the 10th and 11th day of July then next ensuing, within this your noble Realm of England, falsely and traitorously imagined your death and the destruction and subversion of this your said Realm, by gathering and rearing a great number of your people and stirring them to rise against you falsely and traitorously in the places aforesaid, and the times afore rehearsed, against your Royalty, crown, and dignity, and there and then made and reared war falsely and traitorously against you and your Highness,

And though it be thought he is dead and mischieved, yet by the law of your said land he is not punished,

[your Commons pray you] to consider the premises and to put such Traitors in doubt so to do in time coming, and for the salvation of yourself and your said Realm, by the advice of your Lords Spiritual and Temporal in this your present Parliament assembled, to ordain by authority of the said Parliament, that he be attainted of these Treasons, and by authority

101

aforesaid forfeit to you all his Goods, Lands, Tenements, Rents and Possessions which he had on the said 8th day of July or after, and his blood corrupted and disabled forever, and he be called within your said Realm false Traitor for evermore.

Response: Le Roy le voet.

Since it was too late to execute a dead man, the sole purpose of Cade's attainder, aside from scaring off future rebels, was to forfeit his property and corrupt his blood.

Thomas Haxey, by contrast, was very much alive when he was attainted in 1397. He was a clergyman of parts who persuaded the House of Commons to entertain his petition complaining of extravagance in the King's household, where many bishops and ladies were entertained free of cost. The Speaker incorporated this complaint in his address to the King. Richard II was very angry and demanded to know who was the person responsible. When Haxey's name was revealed, the King presented a bill for his attainder to Parliament. The Commons apologized with great humility and Parliament enacted: "That if anyone, whatsoever his rank or condition, shall move or excite the Commons of Parliament, or any other person, for the purpose of bringing about a remedy or reformation of any matter which pertains to the [royal] person or rule or kingly prerogative, he shall be taken and held for a traitor." Two days later Haxey admitted delivering his petition to the Commons, and the complaisant Parliament accordingly rendered judgment against him as a traitor.

Haxey was not a member of the House, and it is not quite accurate to say that he was condemned for freedom of debate; his offense was really exercising freedom of petition. Still, the whole House had endorsed his complaint, so that their freedom was impaired. To Haxey at the point of death, it did not make much difference which freedom it was. Fortunately Archbishop Arundel intervened on behalf of this clergyman. His life was spared and Richard eventually pardoned him. Like other attainted men and like the Earl of Danby three centuries later, Haxey went down and up with the whirligig of politics. Soon after King Richard had been deposed by Henry IV in 1399, Parliament, after reciting that the attainder of Thomas Haxey two years before was contrary to right and the usage of Parliament, made this petition: "That it may please our very gracious Lord the King . . . to quash & annul that judgment as erroneous; & to restore this same Thomas entirely to his rank, estate, goods & chattels, farms, annuities, pensions, lands, tenements, rents, offices, advowsons, & possessions whatsoever. . . ."

In spite of such occasional mishaps of private offenders like Jack Cade and Haxey, it has become clear to me that most attainders were to solve a different and broad problem—How do you get rid of an undesired high official? This problem arises in any age, and it was frequently presented in medieval England. Sometimes the King himself may have wanted to dispense with a powerful adviser who was getting too big for his boots. More often, probably, royal policies became intensely unpopular and the difficulties of attacking the King made Parliament throw the chief blame on his outstanding advisers. In those times the death of the detested minister seemed by far the safest course. Every great magnate was head of a large armed force and as much ruler in his own domain as a Chinese war-lord a quarter century ago. The King himself was only a little more powerful than his nobles, especially if several of them should combine. Prisons were far less numerous and capacious than in our day. There was no good middle ground between beheading and doing nothing. If the ousted adviser were left at liberty, he could readily turn his resentment into coercion or rebellion and make a magnificent comeback to the utter ruin of those

103

who had driven him from his high place. Therefore, the usual object of Parliamentary proceedings against an important minister was to put him to death.

However, attainder was not the only way to accomplish this object. It was just one of four different methods for getting rid of a powerful official forever:

First, since any accused person was entitled by Magna Charta to "the lawful judgment of his peers," this meant a trial in what is now the House of Lords if he were a noble. This was essentially a regular criminal trial and might be for ordinary crimes. The last instance was twenty years ago, when the House of Lords tried one of its members for manslaughter in a fatal automobile accident and acquitted him.[11] Parliament afterwards abolished this relic of antiquity.[12] The next accused noble will face a judge and twelve jurymen in a criminal court.

Second, the King might summon a great Lord before his Council of magnates and prelates and accuse him.[13] This method fell into disuse, but was revived under Charles I and he tried to use it against the Five Members, as we saw in the preceding chapter.

Third, the House of Commons might impeach the detested adviser of the Crown. Then his guilt would be determined by the House of Lords, sitting as a court. The King, of course, took no part in an impeachment.

Fourth, both Houses might pass an act of attainder, which required the King's consent.

It is easy for the modern historian to distinguish these four methods in the quiet of his study, but, if you will remember what Parliament was like under the early Plantagenets, as sketched in the preceding chapter, you will understand how very hard it is to put any definite label upon a proceeding of that time to condemn a royal minister to death. When the magnates and prelates were summoned without any knights and burgesses, an act of at-

104

tainder was pretty much the same thing as a trial by his peers. Recall the judicial nature of the High Court of Parliament, and you will not be misled into supposing that the determination of guilt had much resemblance to the enactment of a modern statute. Instead, legislation shaded into the decision of particular cases. Hence it is impossible to say when the first attainder really took place. The first impeachment was naturally impossible until the House of Commons attained a recognizable existence. Even then, the fact that almost every act took the form of a petition from the Commons which went up to the King and Council for consideration renders it hard to tell whether a petition for the trial of a chief adviser was a bill for his attainder or a set of charges impeaching him for trial in the House of Lords. A bill of attainder (or of pains and penalties) would mean some sort of trial of the accused person in Parliament down to the very end in 1820, when Queen Caroline escaped condemnation for being unfaithful to her adulterous husband. The trial in such a proceeding may not have been quite so fair as that given by the Lords in an impeachment; but the men who wrote the records did not feel obliged to attach a distinguishing label, and their records are often too uninformative to enable us to attach it several centuries later. To quote Herbert Spencer's characterization of the first stage of evolution, these early Parliamentary attacks on royal advisers seem to us "an indefinite, incoherent homogeneity."

As Parliament developed, however, it becomes possible to distinguish impeachments from acts of attainder, and historians can say with assurance that the last impeachment before 1621 took place in 1459, at the end of the long reign of Henry VI. Attainders were thereafter the recognized method of getting rid of powerful ministers.

Bills of Attainder under Henry VIII

When Henry VIII undertook to rule England with a strong hand and bring under his control the Church, his only real rival, he found the act of attainder to be a very useful weapon. It was not clear until his time whether the law would admit the validity of such an act unless the accused were heard in Parliament in his own defense. However, it was realized in his reign that Acts of Parliament, whether public or private, were always legislation, and the judges felt obliged to admit that these acts must be obeyed, however morally unjust. Sir Edward Coke relates a significant story:[14]

> I had it of Sir Thomas Gawdye knight, a grave and reverend judge of the King's Bench, who lived at that time, that King Henry VIII commanded him to attend the chief Justices and to know whether a man that was forthcoming might be attainted of High Treason by Parliament, and never called to his answer. The Judges answered that it was a dangerous question, and that the High Court of Parliament ought to give examples to inferior Courts for proceeding according to Justice. But beeing by the express commandment of the King, and pressed by [Thomas Cromwell] to give a direct answer: they said that if he be attainted by Parliament, it could not come in question afterwards, whether he were called or not to answer.

The Revival of Impeachments under James I

When the Parliament of 1621 met excited by grievances, as I narrated in the preceding chapter, it was in no mood to spare any individual responsible for those grievances, no matter how lofty his place. The first person to be attacked was one of its own members, Mompesson, who had obtained by royal favor the monopoly of importing and selling gold braid, then in as much demand for gentlemen's clothing as buttons are today. To reach him, the

106

House of Commons pulled out the weapon of impeachment, which had been rusting for 162 years, nearly as
long a time as separates us from the inauguration of
George Washington. Sir Edward Coke produced plenty
of precedents for impeachments, and probably he and
other leaders of the opposition realized their marked advantage over bills of attainder. The King could veto such
bills; but if an influential favorite was impeached, the
Lords could deal with him as they wished and he could
not rely on friends at Court. However, Mompesson found
a less exalted way to escape the punishment he richly deserved. When the messengers arrived to arrest him, Mompesson excused himself to go to his rude bathroom. He
jumped out the bathroom window into the street and
then fled to France.

The House of Commons next sought bigger game in
Francis Bacon, the Lord Chancellor, charging him with
accepting bribes and deciding cases accordingly. It had
long been customary for judges to accept presents from
litigants, and perhaps Bacon had pretty much done the
usual thing. He may have been the victim of an unrealized
change in public opinion about moral standards. At all
events, the line between a present and a bribe, however
blurred, can be crossed. Bacon's chief excuse was that he
took bribes from both sides, so that he was then able to
reach a decision with complete impartiality. When this
defense proved unsatisfactory, he broke down before his
accusers. Luckily he escaped the old-fashioned punishment of death, gave up his office, paid a big fine, and was
banished from London. Thus Parliament not only im-
proved the administration of justice, but also enriched
science and literature with the writings of Bacon's last
years.

A later victim of impeachment was Lord Middlesex,
who as Sir Lionel Cranfield had been the first merchant

107

to receive high office under the Crown and had managed the royal finances with conspicuous ability. His case makes it evident to me that impeachment was getting to be a useful method for driving a disliked minister out of office, and that even the accusers did not really believe that the impeached minister was guilty of treason or high crimes and misdemeanors, whatever they might say about him in their charges.

Proceedings in the House of Commons against the Duke of Buckingham

If any chief minister ever deserved removal from power, it was the Duke of Buckingham. The First Parliament of Charles I, losing confidence in him, contented itself in 1625 with asking the King to decide nothing about hostilities against France without consulting with his Council. The King insisted on being solely advised by Buckingham and dissolved Parliament. His Second Parliament in 1626 went farther and formally impeached Buckingham for high treason, unrolling a long catalogue of offenses. Gardiner puts his finger on the essentially political question at issue:

> It is true that in many respects the charges . . . were exaggerated, or even unsustainable by evidence. Against the underlying ground of complaint—his utter inefficiency for the high positon he occupied—no defence was possible. If Charles had permitted his removal from office, the criminal charges would probably have been dropped. It was because Charles, from motives easily intelligible, rejected the doctrine of ministerial responsibility . . . that the commons persisted in pressing for a judicial sentence. . . . [Even after the impeachment trial had begun] they voted a remonstrance in which they pleaded for the dismissal of the minister simply on the ground that any money they might vote would be misemployed as long as he was trusted with the spending of it.

The King would not listen to such a complaint and ended the impeachment by again dissolving Parliament.

In Charles' Third Parliament, after the Petition of Right, the House of Commons once more considered impeaching Buckingham, but instead voted a new remonstrance declaring his excessive power to be the principal cause of evils under which they suffered, and desiring that he might no longer continue in office. But Charles stood by his favorite, until he was removed by assassination two months afterwards.

The Impeachment and Attainder of Strafford in 1640-41

In the ensuing eleven years, from 1629 to 1640, Sir Thomas Wentworth, Earl of Strafford, of whom much was said earlier, was the chief agent of Charles I in governing without Parliament. Still, the King never gave him the implicit confidence he had bestowed on Buckingham, and the Queen disliked him. The Scottish invasion of England forced the King to summon Parliament at last on April 13, 1640. He got rid of the Short Parliament, but this of course did not solve his difficulties. He had to convene the Long Parliament on November 3, 1640. Strafford was then in Yorkshire with the army which was opposing the Scots. He knew that he would be in great danger in London. The King sent for Strafford because he badly needed his help to deal with the new Parliament. He assured Strafford that, if he came, he "should not suffer in his person, honour, or fortune."

On the evening of November 9th Strafford arrived in London. The Parliamentary leaders had already begun to debate his impeachment. The next day he tried to turn the tables by advising the King to accuse them of treasonable negotiations with the Scottish invaders, and there was plenty of support for such a charge. The King did not follow this advice until a year later when he tried to arrest the Five Members. On the morning of November 11th Strafford took his seat in the House of Lords, but soon left without having said a word. That same morning Pym moved that the doors of the House of Commons should be locked. Then, instead of waiting, as he had originally intended, to make a long investigation of the evidence against Strafford, he got a committee appointed which drew up a resolution for impeachment in a few minutes.

Followed by a crowd of approving members, Pym carried the message of the House of Commons up to the House of Lords. It merely requested Strafford's impeachment, leaving the grounds of the accusation to be disclosed a few days late, and asked that Strafford, being charged with high treason, should be at once committed to prison. While the Lords were discussing this unusual request for imprisonment although the accused was not (to quote the Sixth Amendment) "informed of the nature and cause of the accusation," Strafford got news of the impeachment. "I will go and look my accusers in the face." He strode haughtily up the floor of the House of Lords to his place. Shouts of "Withdraw! withdraw!" rose from every side. As soon as he was gone an order was passed committing him to the custody of the Gentleman Usher. Strafford was then called in and bidden to kneel while the order was read. His request to speak was sternly refused. The Usher of the Black Rod took his sword from him and escorted him out of the House.

On November 25th the formal charges adopted by the Commons were carried up to the Lords and Strafford was immediately committed to the Tower.

The trial of the impeached Strafford began in Westminster Hall on March 22, 1641. The articles of impeachment began with the language which was becoming as commonplace then as advocating the overthrow of the government by force and violence is today. "Thomas, Earl of Strafford, hath traitorously endeavored to subvert the fundamental laws and government of the realms of England and Ireland. . . ." Yet treason, as the crime developed in the Middle Ages, had consisted of acts committed against the person or authority of the King. What the House of Commons really sought to condemn Strafford for, was exactly the opposite of that. He was too close to Charles I to suit them. His heinous fault, as they saw it, lay in his being against the House of Commons and popular sentiment. And what law made this fault into a crime?

Thus a new problem was taking shape, as Holdsworth points out. Should impeachment be limited to prosecuting ministers who had committed a crime defined by law, or could it be used to make the King's ministers follow a line of policy approved by the House of Commons? The second view really swayed the Long Parliament. They urged: "It may often fall out that the Commons may have just cause to take exception at some men for being councillors, and yet not charge these men with crimes, for there be grounds of difference which lie not in proof." Nevertheless, the legal procedure of impeachment obliged them to charge Strafford with the definite crime of treason, although their underlying purpose was not to obtain a judicial determination of his guilt of treason but to get rid of a detested minister whom they regarded as a public enemy. So long as a man of Strafford's commanding personality and intellect walked on earth, they would not end his influence on the King. Shrewdly did a chief opponent brush aside suggestions for a heavy fine or long imprisonment by saying, "Stone dead hath no fellow."

The House of Lords, however, insisted on behaving as judges. On April 10th, after the trial had gone on for three weeks, proof of treason began to break down. Indignant peers cried "Adjourn! adjourn!" and the sitting ended without even fixing a day to resume trial.

The members of the Commons angrily returned to their own House. Instead of any longer trying to establish a definite crime, they brought in a bill of attainder. They were no longer to be mere accusers, with the Lords as judges. They, too, as Gardiner writes, "would be Strafford's judges, and would ask the Peers to join in a sentence which they had first pronounced." Lord George Digby objected—the man who would within a year spur Charles I to arrest the Five Members. Digby was ready to consent to a bill depriving Strafford of all power to do further hurt, but to condemn him as a traitor would be a judicial murder. Such language had little effect. The House of Commons by a vote of 204 to 59 passed a bill which read:[15] "Bee it therefore enacted . . . that the said Earle of Strafford . . . be adjudged attainted of High Treason and shall suffer such pains of Death and incur the Forfeitures of his Goods and Chattells Lands Tenements & Hereditaments. . . ." And then, as if ashamed of the way they had stretched the word "treason" in order to kill their deadliest foe, the Commons added: "Provided That no Judge . . . whatsoever shall adjudge or interpret anie Act or Thing to be Treason . . . in anie other manner than hee . . . ought to have done before the makeing of this Act, and as if this Act had never bin had nor made. . . ."

The House of Lords was resentful at having the matter thus taken out of its control, but was overawed by the clamor of the Commons and a growing excitement in the City of London. Charles might have exerted personal influence upon the Lords or he might have dissolved Parliament, but he was so occupied with thoughts of his own safety and that of his Queen that he did little to interfere. Many Lords hated Strafford because he had wielded the power in which they used to share, and on May 8th the attainder passed in a thin House.

That morning London was a prey to the wildest panic. Rumors spread that a French fleet was coming to the aid of the Queen and a cry was raised to lodge her and the King in the Tower of London. She prepared to fly. Fear reigned in Whitehall through the night. The next morning, Sunday, Charles met his Council who unanimously advised him to yield. All day long the street in front of Whitehall was blocked by a shouting multitude. A vain attempt was made to effect Strafford's escape. At nine in the evening Charles gave way, saying he could not save Strafford's life when his wife and children and all his kingdom were concerned. On Monday, May 10th, the attainder was signed by commissioners on his behalf and became law. Strafford said, "Put not your trust in princes." On Wednesday, May 12, 1641, in the midst of 200,000 spectators, he was beheaded on Tower Hill.

The Impeachment of Danby in 1678-79

While we watched Bacon and Strafford stand trial or (in the preceding chapter) listened to the debates in the Parliaments of James I and Charles I, we could say, "There were giants in the earth in those days." In 1642 the struggle to limit royal power shifted to the battlefields. The King who had sent Strafford to the block suffered the same fate. Cromwell was victorious, but failed to establish a republican form of government which was able to outlast his great abilities. In 1660, after eighteen years of war, dictatorship, and uncertainty, the bulk of the English people turned back with relief to monarchy and put the oldest son of the beheaded Charles I on the throne. Yet there was much that could not be restored with the Restoration. Great changes in thinking had taken place dur-

113

ing the many years of controversy about religion and government.[16] In the reign of Charles II, we find ourselves for the first time among modern politicians. Eloquence has almost vanished and there is far less formulation of inspiring ideas. Instead, we see careful draftsmanship in far-reaching legislation like the Habeas Corpus Act of 1679 and increased skill in supervising finances, in the details of administration, and in the manipulation of men, not unmixed with bribery and corruption.

One of the ablest among this new class of politicians was Sir Thomas Osborne, usually known as the Earl of Danby. The recent biography by Andrew Browning thus sums him up:[17]

> Pride and ambition were his ruling passions through life.
> . . . His ideals never give the impression of being specially high, his knowledge of being specially wide, or his reasoning of being specially profound. He was a man of real ability, but not a genius; a fluent and pointed speaker, but not a great orator; a shrewd and energetic man of business, but not a great financier; an able and efficient man of affairs, but not a great statesman. . . .
> In courage, energy and resolution, the virtues which distinguish the man of action rather than the thinker, [Danby] has been surpassed by few. If he was not one of those who rise superior to the age in which they live, at least he never consciously fell short of the standard it required.

Sir Thomas Osborne was born in 1632, a Yorkshireman like Strafford, to whom Osborne's father rendered valuable services. Afterwards the Royalist father steered his way cautiously through the Civil War until he died and left his son an orphan at fifteen. His widow tried to marry Sir Thomas to his charming cousin, Dorothy Osborne, but she preferred Sir William Temple. Thomas soon found another bride, somewhat older than himself. Dorothy cattily remarked "that nothing tempted my cousin to marry his lady so much as that she was an earl's daughter." The marriage was undoubtedly the first step in advancing the bridegroom's fortunes, but it proved to be fruitful and happy, although her husband's political enemies were quick to use against him her inclination to be penurious and hen-pecking.

Osborne became steadily more influential in Yorkshire, and after the Restoration was appointed High Sheriff of the county. He had six informers in his pay, on whom he relied for intelligence among the old soldiers of Cromwell's disbanded army. When irreconcilable republicans and others who resented the new regime staged an abortive uprising in the North of England, Osborne was active in investigating the ramifications of the conspiracy and getting suspects arrested. "The task was not a pleasant one. The *agent provocateur* had been busy, and it was freely declared that some of the accused had become involved in the plot "not so much from inclination as persuasion of those that evidenced against them."[18] Soon afterward the Member of Parliament for the City of York died. Osborne was chosen to fill the vacancy. He was just under the age of thirty-three.

When he took his seat, a solitary survivor from the Heroic Age was in power among the new politicians. Edward Hyde, Earl of Clarendon, whose advice was ignored by Charles I when he determined to arrest the Five Members, had loyally accompanied the sons of his King into their long exile on the Continent. He directed the policy of Charles II during those unhappy years, and shared his triumph at the Restoration by becoming Lord Chancellor and his chief minister. Within a few months thereafter, he came closer to the Throne by the shotgun marriage of his daughter Anne Hyde to the King's brother, the future James II.

Yet Clarendon had "too magisterial a way" and he soon became very unpopular with Puritans and Cavaliers,

House of Commons and Court. According to a contemporary:[19] "He was always pressing the King to mind his own affairs, but in vain. . . . He was high, and was apt to reject those who addressed themselves to him with too much contempt . . . and disparage the pretensions of others, not without much scorn; which created him many enemies." And Macaulay says of Clarendon that "so great a portion of his life has been passed abroad that he knew less of that world in which he found himself on his return than many who might have been his sons."

In 1667 the Cavalier Parliament fell on Clarendon as furiously as the Long Parliament had fallen on Strafford. Charles II gave way before the storm and dismissed his chief minister, but the House of Commons was not satisfied. Clarendon still had many supporters, his royal son-in-law was working in his favor, and he might well be restored to power or at least be very influential. So his enemies decided to ruin him by an impeachment.

Sir Thomas Osborne took a prominent part in this attack on Clarendon. Even before Parliament opened, he had asserted that "if the Chancellor were not hanged for high treason, he would be hanged himself"—words which it must have been uncomfortable for Osborne to remember eleven years later when he himself was charged with treason and Clarendon had died in bed. In a speech on the motion to impeach, Osborne denounced Clarendon's monopoly of power—"No vessel [can] survive without his hand at the rudder"—and declared that this intolerant persecutor on behalf of the Church of England was "not a true Protestant but a Papist at heart" who "did endeavour to subvert the laws both of Church and State." Bishop Burnet remarked, "Sir Thomas Osborne was a very plausible speaker, but too copious, and could not easily make an end of his discourse."

116

On November 12, 1667, Mr. Seymour formally said at the bar of the House of Lords that Edward, Earl of Clarendon, the faithful servant of two Kings and the grandfather of two future Queens, was impeached by the Commons of high treason and other crimes and misdemeanors. Further particulars were to be given at a convenient time. The Lords refused to repeat what they had done to Strafford and send Clarendon into custody on such a general charge. Osborne regarded this as a plain denial of justice. An altercation between the two Houses went on for many days, until it was suddenly cut short by the arrival of a petition from the Earl. This set forth his defense at length and ended with the statement that he was "withdrawing from so powerful a persecution." In fact, he had prudently fled to France. Both houses then voted: "That the Paper, containing much untruth and scandal and sedition in it, should be publicly burned by the hand of the hangman." And, writes Clarendon in his autobiography, "the poor Paper was accordingly with solemnity executed."

Then, on December 18th, Parliament enacted a bill of pains and penalties that the Earl of Clarendon "shall suffer perpetual Exile, and be forever banished this realm." He was forever disqualified from holding any office. If he returned to England or any of the King's dominions, he was to suffer the pains and penalties of treason without the possibility of a royal pardon. Anybody, except his children, who corresponded with him should suffer the punishment which the law inflicted on those who kept correspondence with traitors. However, this act was to be of no effect if before February 1st next, Clarendon surrendered himself at the Tower of London in order to stand trial on his impeachment.

The Earl did not respond to this kind invitation, but preferred to prolong his life in France, adding seven more years of exile to the fourteen he had spent before restoring the King who now assented to his banishment. There he completed the account of his own times which places him with Sir Winston Churchill; they are the only two Prime Ministers who are also great historians.

The removal of Clarendon and his chief supporters from power left plenty of room for new men. Sir Thomas Osborne rose fast through various offices and titles. When Parliament in 1673 obliged every officeholder, high or low, to partake of the Lord's Supper according to the usage of the Church of England,[20] the King's brother James and several other ministers disclosed their conversion to Roman Catholicism by resigning all their places in the government. Osborne immediately succeeded one of these as Lord High Treasurer and soon became Charles II's chief minister. He showed that he far surpassed any other minister of the time in financial ability; and for this, royal gratitude made him in 1674 Earl of Danby.

Danby can fairly be regarded as the founder of political parties. He did not share Clarendon's confidence that the House of Commons could be caused to support the King through general approval of his policy, but considered this idea to be obviously out-of-date. Instead, Danby sought to form a solid corps of members who would be ready to vote as he directed, rain or shine. He was constantly busy at the task, as Mr. Browning describes it, of "persuading the careless and indifferent to devote regular attention to their parliamentary duties, and of opening the eyes of all to the little recognized fact that nothing could be accomplished unless they would agree to vote solidly together." In the abundant family papers which Danby left behind him, it is significant to find a great many lists of men who might perhaps be counted on to support particular measures. These offer a sharp contrast to the drafts for speeches which loom so large among the papers of political leaders in what I call the Heroic

118

Age. Unfortunately, the process of rallying sure votes led easily into bribery by jobs for those whom it was sought to persuade and their hangers-on.

It was a game at which two could play. Danby's opponents were quick to learn his methods, and his Court Party was soon matched by a tightly knit Country Party. Danby did have the advantage that he had a permanent organization headquarters; he could use the Court itself. The Opposition was mostly obliged to meet in various coffeehouses, where news and politics were sipped with mild beverages. He persuaded the Council to order the suppression of all public coffeehouses, on the ground that they had become the resort of idle and disaffected persons. Vigorous protests from the coffee sellers blocked this measure, but Danby did succeed in getting them put under bond not to allow scandalous papers and reports on their premises. Nevertheless, the Country Party continued. Very soon each party gave its opponents a derogatory nickname—Tories for the Court Party, Whigs for the Country Party. These insulting words became proud titles. So Danby founded the Tories, who are still flourishing under Sir Anthony Eden. And Shaftesbury, Achitophel in Dryden's great satire, started the Whigs, who were transformed into Liberals a century ago and have dwindled into a splinter party since the First World War, obliging British moderates to choose unhappily between two sets of extremists if they want to cast their votes effectively.

A zealous Protestant, Danby opposed the King's flirtations with the English Roman Catholics. His most notable achievement was the marriage of Charles's niece Mary with the Prince of Orange. After this good news, London spent the night in bonfires and ringing bells and the greatest manifestations of joy since the Restoration. Thus Danby paved the way for the Bill of Rights. He also

119

disliked Charles II's long-established practice of getting a substantial part of his revenue in large annual bribes from his cousin, Louis XIV of France, which were kept carefully hidden from Parliament. Yet, in July, 1677, when hard pressed by the continuance of large deficits in spite of his financial reforms, Danby made the fatal mistake of personally participating in these disgraceful transactions. At the King's request, he began sending letters to Ralph Montagu, a speculator in politics and matrimony who was then English Ambassador in Paris. These letters approved Montagu's plan to obtain an increase of the French annual subsidy in return for the adoption of Charles II of various English policies advantageous to France.

Meanwhile, Danby's position at home was none too safe. He had never obtained the confidence of the nation outside the House of Commons. He still had a slim majority there, but few of his party were able speakers or showed any capacity for managing the business of the House. Danby was not the sort of leader whom men follow out of spontaneous enthusiasm. His greed, his submission to a tyrant wife, his pale face and lean person were constantly ridiculed. John Evelyn the diarist wrote that Danby had excellent abilities but nothing generous or grateful. When he was made Treasurer, Charles told him that he had only two friends in England—"The King and his own merits." But he had many formidable enemies, and shortly before 1678 he enlarged their number by causing several officeholders who opposed him to lose their lucrative places, so that hardly anybody except his closest supporters felt secure. A letter at the time said, "Many of our great ones apprehend they hear their bells tolling for them." Besides having Shaftesbury's Country Party in constant opposition, Danby had broken in 1675 with his former associate, the second Duke of

120

Buckingham, who attracted Charles II by the qualities described in Dryden's *Absalom and Achitophel*:

> Stiff in Opinions, always in the wrong;
> Was everything by starts, and Nothing long;
> But in the course of one revolving Moon,
> Was Chymist, Fidler, States-Man, and Buffoon:
> Then all for Women, Painting, Rhiming, Drinking;
> Besides ten thousand Freaks that dy'd in thinking. . . .
> He laughed himself from Court; then sought Relief
> By forming Parties, but could ne'er be Chief. . . .

Although Danby probably imagined that Buckingham was a spent force, "the last expiring flashes of his brilliant intellect were to be devoted almost entirely to accomplishing the Treasurer's ruin."[21] Finally, the intrigues of that period were astonishingly complicated—wheels within wheels. A leader who tried to maintain steady, business-like policies was constantly incurring the dislike of one faction or another, and very likely of several factions at once. As Danby's bigrapher writes:[22] "The King inclined to blame him for the faults of Parliament, and Parliament held him responsible for the faults of the King."

In October, 1678, the troubled waters in which Danby had profitably fished for so long suddenly broke into stormy waves. An ex-Catholic named Titus Oates appeared before legislative investigators and accused prominent Roman Catholics of engaging in a far-flung conspiracy to kill the King and take over the government. There is a familiar ring to the following passage in the old book:[23] "On October 24th [1678], Titus Oates was examined in the House of Commons six or seven hours, at the end of which he was several times, and with great strictness, in-terrogated,*Whether he knew anything more of the plot?* He solemnly answered that he did not. But notwithstand-ing Oates' solemn asseverations of his not knowing any

121

more, he soon began so much to abound with newer discoveries that some began to doubt his veracity."

There was probably a small core of truth amid all the falsehoods about the Popish Plot. A few desperate Roman Catholics appear to have been ready to stop at nothing in order to get rid of the cruel laws[24] which, for over seventy years, had penalized members of their faith and put any priest who conducted mass in peril of death. Yet the real danger was very slight. According to a religious census taken two years earlier under Danby's direction, there were about 15,000 Roman Catholics in all of England, approximately half of 1 per cent of the population.[25] And only 5,000 of these were fit to bear arms. Most of the Roman Catholics were law-abiding members of old country families, esteemed by their neighbors and willing to wait patiently until the rapidly growing spirit of religious toleration gave them freedom to worship God in their own way.

No such calm view of the Plot was taken by the mass of the English people or by their representatives in Parliament. They had been alarmed by the recent conversions to Catholicism in high places, including the heir to the throne. The bribes given by the Catholic King of France to influence English royal policies could not be completely hidden. Englishmen had seen since childhood the lurid pictures of Protestants burning at the stake in the big volume of Foxe's *Book of Martyrs* which was chained in parish churches. The Gunpowder Plot was kept fresh in everybody's memory by bonfires each Fifth of November. Moreover, the Roman Catholic Church was not then regarded as just a religion with which most Englishmen disagreed. To them it was a world-wide conspiracy against England and every other Protestant country. Preachers could produce abundant quotations from former Popes and Catholic dignitaries declaring that it was entirely moral for the subjects of a heretic ruler to depose him, even by assassination. It often happens that the utterances of a few extremists in a group are accepted by outsiders as the cherished opinion of every single member.

Respectable leaders of all political parties, however skeptical about the truth of the Popish Plot, were ready to ally themselves with the informers and those who believed their stories, because these respectable men thought that this would strengthen their own position with Parliament and the electorate. Charles II was almost the only prominent man in England who discountenanced the Plot from start to finish, and never tried to get any personal profit out of it. Danby did not keep his hands clean. Some of his enemies even asserted that he invented the Plot as an excuse for keeping up a large army. Unfortunately for the country and for himself, Danby did get lured by hopes of using the hysteria to his own advantage. It would rally the nation around the King and induce the payment of heavier taxes. "Above all it would turn the hunt away from the Lord Treasurer himself, and provide Parliament, when it met, with something else to occupy its attention."[26] But things did not work out that way at all. Those who sup with the Devil need a long spoon.

As the days went by, more ex-Catholics kept turning up to add new details to the blood-curdling conspiracy. Suddenly all these stories seemed to be proved true by a terrible fact. After a well-known Protestant magistrate had taken the testimony of one of the renegades, he disappeared. Five days later his strangled corpse was found in a ditch, with his own sword driven through from side to side. Who really killed Sir Edmund Berry Godfrey remains a mystery even to this day, but the populace in 1678 had no doubts whatever on this subject. The Papists had done it, and nothing was too bad for them. Right afterwards Parliament reassembled and ordered every Catho-

123

lic in London to go ten miles out of the city within a fort-
night. No Catholic was allowed to sit in either the House
of Commons or the House of Lords. Several Jesuit priests
were seized, tried, and put to death. Five Roman Catholic
nobles were sent to the Tower. One of them died there.
Three stayed imprisoned for five years in fear of trial. The
fifth, a poor old viscount, convicted on the testimony of
Oates and other ex-Catholics, was tried and sentenced to
be hanged, drawn, and quartered; but by the mercy of the
House of Commons he was permitted to die "only by having his head severed from his body."

This hysterical fear of the Catholics was mingled with
more justified suspicions of French influence upon the
government. Danby's troubles did not come singly. As if
Titus Oates were not enough, Ralph Montagu appeared
in Parliament to plague him. A year previously, this sinis-
ter go-between in the French bribes to Charles II had kept
asking Danby to make him a Secretary of State, but Danby
refused to be blackmailed into an undesirable appointment. Then, in the summer of 1678, Montagu was dismissed from the Embassy of Paris because of making love
there to a cast-off mistress of Charles II and afterwards to
her daughter. Determined to avenge his misfortunes on
Danby, he entered into a bargain with the Opposition and
their ally the French Ambassador, that in return for
money he would produce Danby's letters to him about the
subsidies from Louis XIV. Montagu then got himself
elected to the House of Commons and waited for a good
opportunity to carry out the scheme to ruin the Lord
Treasurer.

Danby knew very well what was going on. Learning
that Montagu had been holding secret conferences in
Paris with the Pope's nuncio at the house of an Italian, he
decided to hit first. Early on the morning of Thursday,
December 19th, an extraordinary meeting of the Council

ordered Montagu's papers seized, very likely hoping to get hold of the damaging letters. His home was immediately surrounded by royal messengers. The House of Commons at once resented this action. Seizing a member's papers was almost as much of a breach of privilege as arresting him, unless (as the old law and our Constitution allow) he was charged with treason, felony, or breach of the peace.[27] The Commons were on the point of adjourning when Montagu turned the tables on Danby. Speaking for the first time, he told the House that the whole object of confiscating his papers was to take away from him some letters which incriminated one of the chief ministers. However, he had put these into a special box, which he hoped the King's messengers had not unearthed. The House voted "to have the papers sent for now," and four members were dispatched to find the box.

When they came back with the mysterious box, Montagu pulled out of it two of the letters from Danby to himself. The Speaker read them. They left no doubt of Danby's participation in the bribery negotiations with Louis XIV. The House was all aflame. Member after member moved that the Treasurer be impeached of high treason. One member talked wildly about danger to the King's life from "poisons both liquid and in powders." Danby's supporters did their best. They pointed out that it was "a very ordinary thing" for Kings to get money from each other and that it was not treason. Since Montagu was far more involved in the French negotiations than Danby, they reasonably suggested that Montagu's replies to the letters should also be produced. Yet the House was too excited to reason calmly. The debate continued until ten o'clock of that Thursday night—very late for Parliaments then. Impeachment was resolved by a vote of 179 against 116, and a committee was appointed to draw up articles against Danby.

On Saturday the articles were brought in and adopted after another fierce debate until ten o'clock at night. One article charged Danby, as usual, with having "traitorously endeavored to subvert the ancient and well-established Form of Government." Another linked him with the Popish Plot, despite his zealous Protestantism. Danby had always been doubtful about Titus Oates. So he was accused of being "popishly affected" and having "traitorously concealed (after he had notice) the late horrid and bloody Plot and Conspiracy, contrived by the Papists against his Majesty's Person and government; and [having] suppressed the Evidence, and reproachfully discountenanced the King's Witnesses in the Discovery of it. . . ."

In support of this charge one of the ex-Catholic informers, Bedloe, later told the House of Commons how he went to see Danby on some business:

> His Lordship took him into his Closet, and asked him . . . if he would desist from giving Evidence against the Lords in the tower, &c. To which Bedloe answered, that he had once been an ill Man, but desired to be so no more. To which the Earl replied, you may have a great Sum of Money, and live in another Country, as Geneva, Sweden, or New-England; and should have what Money he would ask to maintain him there. But He, Bedloe, refusing all such Temptations, his Lordship began to threaten him, saying, There was a Boat and a Yacht to carry him far enough from telling of Tales: And after this, the Guards were as Spies upon him, and he was very ill used. . . .

Titus Oates, too, readily took the stand against a new suspect. He declared "That, being one day in the Privy Garden, the Earl of Danby passing by, reflected upon him, and said, 'There goes one of the Saviours of England, but I hope to see him hanged within a month.'"

The House of Lords was incredulous when the charges were formally delivered to it on Monday. Danby at once stood up and defended himself in a convincing speech. He

126

justified his two letters on the French subsidies, which Montagu had disclosed, by showing that the King had annotated the text of each of them with his own hand, "I approve of this letter. C. R."[28] The Lords refused to arrest Danby or even make him withdraw from their deliberations.

The shrewdest remarks in all these debates were made by the Earl of Carnarvon, who had sat in the Lords for years without a word. The Duke of Buckingham played one of his pranks by getting Carnarvon heated with wine and urging him to display his abilities. So the Earl went into the House determined to talk about anything that came up. Accordingly, when the Lords were suddenly asked to impeach Danby whom Buckingham detested, Carnarvon rose to his feet and delivered himself to this effect:

> My Lords, I understand but little of Latin, but a good deal of English, and not a little of the English history, from which I have learnt the mischiefs of such kind of prosecutions as these, and the ill fate of the prosecutors. I shall go no farther back than the latter end of Queen Elizabeth's reign: At which time the Earl of Essex was run down by Sir Walter Raleigh, and your Lordships very well know what became of Sir Walter Raleigh. My Lord Bacon, he ran down Sir Walter Raleigh, and your Lordships know what became of my Lord Bacon. The Duke of Buckingham,[29] he ran down my Lord Bacon, and your Lordships know what happened to the Duke of Buckingham. Sir Thomas Wentworth, afterwards Earl of Strafford, ran down the Duke of Buckingham, and you all know what became of him. Sir Harry Vane, he ran down the Earl of Strafford, and your Lordships know what became of Sir Harry Vane. Chancellor Hyde, he ran down Sir Harry Vane, and your Lordships know what became of the Chancellor. Sir Thomas Osborne, now Earl of Danby, ran down Chancellor Hyde; but what will become of the Earl of Danby, your Lordships best can tell. But let me see that man that dare run the Earl of Danby down, and we shall soon see what will become of him.

This being pronounced with a remarkable humor and tone, the Duke of Buckingham, both surprised and disappointed, cried out after his way, "The man is inspired! and claret has done the business."

Danby was saved for a while when the King unexpectedly prorogued Parliament for a month in order to give everybody a breathing space. The turmoil of the Popish Plot had been raging since October. A politician said of the autumn just past, "I could have lived with more ease in a powder mill."

Then, before Parliament came back, Charles dissolved it without getting the advice of his Council and ordered a general election. The old Parliament had sat off and on since May, 1661, with almost the duration of the Long Parliament, and its House of Commons largely reflected the opinions of the constituencies eighteen years before. Most Englishmen under forty had never had a chance to vote until now. When they did at last go to the polls in February, 1679, they threw out most of Danby's supporters. The house of cards which he had been carefully constructing for years fell apart. The new House of Commons was much more ferocious than the old against the Popish Plot and the Lord Treasurer.

Danby's usefulness as chief minister was plainly ended. He could not get support in Parliament to carry the King's measures. He and Charles hoped that he would be left unharmed if he got out of office. A deal to that effect was made with a group of moderates in the Opposition led by Denzil Holles, whom we have already encountered holding the Speaker in his chair and escaping arrest when the House of Commons was entered by Charles I.[30] Yet this same man helped restore that King's son to the throne in 1660 and was rewarded by a peerage. Such are the queer political upsets of an age of revolution.

In pursuance of the bargain with Holles, the King on March 16th asked the Lord Treasurer to resign. Danby foolishly failed to realize that now his sole object ought to be to keep alive. Instead, he allowed his greed to get the better of him and welcomed the King's offer to make him a marquis with a pension of £5,000 a year for life. This broke up the deal with Holles, and it was more than the Lords could stand. They resolved on March 19th that the dissolution of Parliament had not cut short Danby's impeachment, as he hoped,[31] and ordered him to answer the pending charges against him within a week. The House of Commons was in a fury. It suspected, with good reason, that Danby though out of office would go on advising the King. So it sent a message to remind the Lords that he was impeached of high treason and to ask again that he be put in safe custody.

Danby had an ace up his sleeve. Charles II had given him a blanket pardon on March 1st for all offenses committed before February 27th, two days earlier. When the King asked Lord Chancellor Nottingham, a great judge, to affix the Great Seal to this carefully hushed-up pardon, the Chancellor refused to do more than bring the seal to Charles and let him handle the rest of the dirty work himself. When the King appeared in the House of Lords on March 22nd and summoned the Commons to hear him announce the pardon, Danby's immediate situation became worse. The Lords seemed sure to arrest Danby at last. And the House of Commons, as the old book says, "fell into a violent heat and debate," which ended with a resolution pointing out "the dangerous consequence of granting pardons to any persons that lie under an impeachment of the Commons of England."

Luckily for Danby, the news of the pardon broke on Saturday and Parliament rose for the week-end. The King used this respite to command Danby to go into hiding, if possible overseas. On Sunday night he obeyed by taking refuge in his brother's London house. As soon as the Lords met early Monday morning, they sent the Gentleman Usher of the Black Rod to look for Danby at his own homes, in and near London, but Black Rod came back and reported "that he could not be found." The French ambassador wrote Louis XIV that if Danby had been caught at that moment, he would certainly have lost his head. Both Houses angrily refused to abandon their determination to ruin Danby, but they disagreed on how to go about it. The Lords wanted to banish him forever like Clarendon, if he did not give himself up soon, and the Commons wanted to condemn him to death like Strafford. The bad news traveled fast to Danby in his hiding-place, but he could not make up his mind whether he preferred sure exile or a beheading which might never come off. Standing trial began to seem better than either, if his master would allow it. Eventually both Houses passed a bill of attainder with April 21st as the deadline, and the King was asked to name an early day to have it submitted for his assent. This was never given, for Charles II had no desire to imitate what his father had done to Strafford. Instead, he sent word for the fugitive to give himself up. Late on April 15th, Black Rod had Danby at his door, and next day the former chief minister was brought to the Bar of the Lords and imprisoned in the Tower of London.

A very important question of constitutional law arose as soon as Danby's trial by the Lords began on April 25th. Instead of answering the charges against him in detail, he pleaded his pardon as a bar to the impeachment. He did so because of positive orders by the King, who, besides wanting to help his close adviser, had reasons of his own for such a course. Charles knew that a regular trial with evidence for and against the charges was bound to produce further damaging disclosures about his receipt of French bribes. But if the pardon were accepted as a defense, then no witnesses would be called by either side because the impeachment would stop at once.

The Commons, however, were "not a little disobliged" by Danby's action. They adopted a resolution that the pardon was illegal and void. Still, the Lords were not sure about the point and set it down for argument on May 10th. This "so heated" the House of Commons that on May 9th it resolved that no commoner whatsoever (thus excepting peers) should presume to maintain the validity of the pardon, "and that the persons so doing shall be accounted betrayers of the liberties of the Commons of England." The House ordered this vote to be posted up at the gate of Westminster and at the gates of the various Inns of Court, where all the lawyers congregated.

Danby's lawyers did not know where they stood, under such a vote. If they took part in the argument about the pardon, as the Lords had directed, they might find themselves imprisoned by the Commons. Danby petitioned the Lords for relief on the ground that he was getting deprived of his right to counsel. He said that he durst not appear to argue the validity of his pardon, by reason of the vote of the Commons. "This," the old book says, "only increased the ferment in the lower House; and this indeed proved a hot day. . . ." Thus things dragged along for weeks with the two Houses at loggerheads, which was probably just what the King desired.

All this time the House of Commons was excited over the Popish Plot and considering increasingly drastic legislation against Roman Catholics. On May 11th, though a Sunday, the House sat and ordered a bill brought in to exclude James, Duke of York, from succeeding to the throne. Meanwhile, another bill full of technical language was going through the dull stages of drafting, with very little attention from the contemporary historian of the debates in this Parliament, although it was destined to be a great and enduring contribution to freedom.

May 26, 1679, arrived. The House of Commons adopted a new resolution on Danby's case, which stated incisively how ministerial responsibility would be wiped out if a pardon could protect a bad adviser from being accountable to Parliament: "The Setting up a Pardon to be a Bar of an Impeachment defeats the whole Use and Effect of Impeachments. For, should this point be admitted . . . the chief Institution for the Preservation of the Government would be destroyed and, consequently, the Government itself."

The question was never squarely decided because on that same day Charles II came into the House of Lords in his royal robes and, to save his brother's right to the throne, ended this Parliament, luckily waiting long enough for the Habeas Corpus Act to be passed in its last hours. Yet the contention of the Commons was afterwards regarded as sound, and it is embodied in Article II, section 2, of our Constitution:[32] "The President . . . shall have Power to grant Reprieves and Pardons . . ., except in cases of Impeachments." Plainly this method of legislative redress for official misconduct ought not to be nullified by the chief superior of the officer who is to be removed if guilty.

Two lessons, apart from this important point about pardons, can be drawn from the impeachment of Danby.

First, it demonstrates how unsatisfactorily an impeachment can operate. Frequent disagreements between the two branches of the legislature and constant interruptions by pressing matters destroyed almost all resemblance to an orderly trial in a courtroom before judges. Indeed, this case never did come to any proper conclusion, but merely petered out. The next two Parliaments were too busy about allowing a Catholic heir to succeed and other turmoils to bother to do anything about Danby. Yet he was kept in the Tower for nearly five years awaiting trial, and a new King was on the throne before the Lords in 1685 declared the impeachment to be ended.

Second, we cannot take the charges of treason against Danby very seriously when we find some of his most influential accusers joining with him to bring over the Prince of Orange in 1688 and serving with him among the chief advisers of William III, who made him a marquis at last and then Duke of Leeds. The House of Commons really wanted to get rid of Danby because they did not like his policies. Most of his opponents knew that he was not devoted to Popery or to France, as the charges made out. But they feared with good reason that Charles II and his brother had strong inclinations toward both of these detested causes, and Danby's true offense in the eyes of his accusers was that his vigorous measures were strengthening the royal power and making it easier for Charles and James to do what they wanted.

Danby did resign his high position, but the time had not yet come when that was enough to satisfy the majority in the House of Commons. Punishment for alleged heinous crimes was still the normal device for achieving ministerial accountability to Parliament. Sometimes the chief minister was executed like Strafford. Sometimes he was heavily fined like Bacon or exiled like Clarendon or stayed in prison for years like Danby. In 1945, Churchill, as powerful a personality as Strafford, merely went out in the country and wrote a book.

The Attainder of Sir John Fenwick in 1696

Although proceedings by Parliament against royal ministers like Danby are the most interesting aspect of our subject, bills of attainder, and perhaps impeachments,[33] were not limited to them. A baronet after the Revolution

133

of 1688 was no more exempt from a bill of attainder than Jack Cade and Haxey in the Middle Ages.

Sir John Fenwick had been a devoted supporter of James II, and brought in the attainder of the Duke of Monmouth, which was passed in the Duke's absence right after he made his tragic landing in the West. In 1696 there was a far-flung plot against William III. Some of the conspirators were to assassinate him, and Fenwick was to raise troops who would fight for James when he landed with a French Army. After the plot was discovered, Fenwick stayed in hiding until the other conspirators had undergone trial. Thus he learned that there were only two of his associates whose testimony would inculpate him. Meanwhile, a new statute went into effect requiring two witnesses to prove treason;[34] this greatly influenced the treason clauses in Article III of our Constitution.[35] Fenwick tried to bribe one of his two fellow-conspirators, who took £300 and did nothing except give the government more information. Both accomplices testified against Fenwick before the grand jury which indicted him for high treason. Then he tried to flee to France, but was arrested near the coast. Hoping for a pardon, he offered to reveal everything to the King. Instead, he contrived a confession which omitted the main facts and accused many prominent Whigs of secretly negotiating with the exiled James. The fact that most of these charges were true did not help Fenwick when he was eventually tried in Parliament where several of the men he had named were leaders; but all he thought of at the moment was to avoid being condemned for treason in an ordinary criminal court. Soon afterwards he got good news from his wife that his life was in no danger because there was only one witness against him; she and her friends had succeeded in bribing his other accomplice to vanish into the blue. Fenwick now knew he could defy conviction before a jury.

134

Instead, he was brought to the bar of the House of Commons, which resolved that his confession was false and scandalous. Many members then went home, supposing the affair was over. However, a motion to bring in a bill of attainder was made and overwhelmingly carried. Still, subsequent events disclosed how public opinion was turning against attainders. The act for his execution passed the House of Commons by only a small majority and went through the House of Lords by only seven votes. Much disquietude was caused by the nature of Fenwick's legislative trial in the lower House, which Macaulay thus describes:[36]

> Some hundreds of gentlemen [513], every one of whom had much more than half made up his mind before the case was opened, performed the functions both of judge and jury. They were not restrained, as a judge is restrained, by the sense of responsibility; for who was to punish a Parliament? They were not selected, as a jury is selected, in a manner which enables the culprit to exclude his personal and political enemies.
> The arbiters of his fate came in and went out as they chose. They heard a fragment here and there of what was said against him, and a fragment here and there of what was said in his favour. During the progress of the bill they were exposed to every species of influence. One member was threatened by the electors of his borough with the loss of his seat: another might obtain a frigate for his brother [to command]. . . . In the debates arts were practised and passions excited which are unknown to well constituted tribunals, but from which no great popular assembly divided into parties ever was or ever will be free. The rhetoric of one orator called forth loud cries of "Hear him." Another was coughed and scraped down. A third spoke against time in order that his friends who were supping might come in to divide. If the life of the most worthless man could be sported with thus, was the life of the most virtuous man secure?

Developments in England after 1700

The revulsion caused by Fenwick's trial may have caused bills of attainder to dwindle away. Scotch Jacobites

135

who aided the two Pretenders were condemned in this way but not executed. The last person condemned to death by Act of Parliament was Lord Edward Fitzgerald, leader of the 1798 Rebellion in Ireland, who died in prison while awaiting execution. A bill of pains and penalties was brought to banish Bishop Atterbury, and his friend Swift ridiculed the behavior of the House of Lords in his account of a trial on the island of Lagado in Part III of *Gulliver's Travels*. The last bill of pains and penalties was in 1820, against Queen Caroline, wife of George IV.

The Queen had long been separated from her husband, then Prince Regent, whose infidelities were notorious. Since 1814 she had been leading a nomad life in Italy and Egypt, and had been far from discreet, if not worse, in her relations with her courier and valet, Bergami. When George III died after many years of insanity and her husband became King, she returned to England intending to take part in his Coronation. George IV, who had long desired to get rid of her, resolved that she should never act as Queen. His first step, since Great Britain had a State Church, was to persuade his Cabinet to keep her out of the Book of Common Prayer, so that the congregations in the parish churches each Sunday would not ask God "to bless and preserve our gracious Queen Caroline." The excuse given to the House of Commons was that she was still included in the general prayer for the royal family. Denman replied, "If her Majesty was included in any general prayer, it was in the prayer for all who are desolate and oppressed."

The King was determined to degrade his wife, and his Tory minister lacked the bravery to withstand him. On July 5, 1820, Lord Liverpool, the Prime Minister, introduced a bill in the House of Lords to deprive her of the rights and privileges of Queen Consort and to dissolve the marriage between her and his Majesty.

136

The ensuing legislative trial of Queen Caroline served as a dramatic focus for all the brooding resentment against George IV and his reactionary advisers. The lawyers for the defense saw at once that the form of a public proceeding was used as a cover for what was really a suit for divorce on the charges of adultery, with the vulnerable royal husband kept sedulously out of sight. "Who is your employer or client in this case?" Brougham asked the solicitor for the bill. When the government peers shouted "No! no!" and the witness refused to answer, Brougham went on to the most magnificent use of a poetic quotation in legal history:

"I have never been able to trace the local habitation or the name of the unknown being who is the plaintiff in this proceeding. I know not under what shape it exists—

'If shape it might be called, that shape had none. . . .
What seemed his head
The likeness of a kingly crown had on.'"

Majocchi, the chief witness for the bill, was very damaging at first; but when asked on cross examination about a series of essential matters, he kept replying, "Non mi recordo; non mi recordo"—"I don't remember." The government majority dwindled to nine and the bill was ignominiously dropped. London was illuminated for three successive nights. The Queen went in state to St. Paul's to return thanks for her success amid the acclamations of the mob. Meanwhile the disgust which many felt toward both sides of this travesty of a legal proceedings was expressed with characteristic British humor:

Most gracious Queen, we thee implore
To go away and sin no more;
But, if that effort be too great,
To go away, at any rate.

Never since then has Parliament undertaken to condemn individuals by statute.

137

What is equally impressive is the fading out of impeachments in England. Since 1715 there have been just four. Only two of these took place in the seventy years before the Philadelphia Convention. Lord Chancellor Macclesfield was condemned in 1724 for allowing his clerks to take bribes, and Lord Lovat had the distinction of being the last Englishman to be beheaded because he helped Bonnie Prince Charlie in the '45. Possibly the framers of the Constitution in 1787 were impressed by the impending impeachment of Warren Hastings on charges of misgoverning India, although his trial did not start until February, 1788. It dragged on so long as to be a nuisance and ended in his acquittal after seven years, when over a third of his original judges in the Lords were dead.[37] There was one more impeachment—of Dundas, Lord Melville, in 1805—and he too was acquitted. Contrast these four impeachments in ninety years (1715-1805) with the fifty in the slightly greater span of ninety-four years which preceded it (1621-1715). The proceeding was becoming cumbrous and expensive. Since 1805 Parliament has avoided it entirely for a century and a half.

While bills of attainder and impeachments were thus dying out, something else was happening of great significance. In 1741 under George II, prolonged debates took place in Parliament on the removal of his Prime Minister, Sir Robert Walpole, from office. It was no longer thought essential to accuse and convict a minister of treason in order to get rid of him. Instead, Walpole's opponents asked both Houses to present a humble address to the King "that he will be graciously pleased to remove Sir Robert Walpole from his Majesty's counsellors and counsels for ever." The new attitude was expressed by Lord Carteret in the House of Lords:

> When we proceed by impeachment, by bill of attainder, or by bill of pains and penalties, the design is to punish as well

138

as remove; but there is another way of proceeding in parliament which tends only to remove the minister from the king's counsels without inflicting any real punishment upon him, and that is by an humble address to our sovereign. . . .

When we proceed [by punitive methods] some particular criminal facts must be alleged, and there must be some sort of proof of those facts; but when we proceed [as now] by way of address to the king, a general view of that minister's conduct, a general view of public affairs, may afford just cause for such an address. . . .

This, my Lords, is the difference; and the reason of this difference is very plain. When a man is to be punished . . . some crime or criminal neglect ought to be proved; but as his not being employed in the King's counsels neither affects his person, his freedom, nor his estate, therefore weakness alone or a general bad character may be a good cause for removing him.

Some speakers argued that regardless of Walpole's real merits, he had incurred such unpopularity in many quarters that he was no longer fit to be Chief Minister. Similar reasoning was used not long ago against Dean Acheson. Walpole's supporters made the sound reply, that if this position were to be accepted, a man's political enemies could just spread false rumors about him and then have him put out merely because a good many people happened to believe these lies.

That same day the House of Commons debated a similar resolution, with Walpole listening to his foes. The public expectations had been raised to the utmost pitch, the passages to the visitor's gallery were crowded at a very early hour, the concourse was prodigious. As the hall was too small for all members of the House, several of them secured their seats at six o'clock in the morning, and there was an unusually large attendance of 450 members. At one o'clock the speech introducing the motion was made by Walpole's tireless enemy, Samuel Sandys, of whom Sir Robert's son Horace said that Sandys never laughed but once, and that was when his best friend fell

139

and broke his thigh. The debate went on until four the next morning when, after Walpole's brief and able defense of his conduct, he was sustained by 290 to 106. In the Lords he had already won with a vote of nearly two to one. A year later, however, Walpole realized that the newly elected Parliament would not support his measures and resigned of his own accord.

Again in 1779 in the middle of our Revolution, the Commons conducted a similar debate on the government of Lord North. His opponent, Lord John Cavendish, made a motion for the House to state to George III that "if anything can prevent the consummation of public ruin, it can only be by new counsel and new counsellors without further loss of time. . . ." Another opponent spoke of Lord North's conduct as "treachery." Lord North in replying, said that anybody who accused him of treachery ought to follow this up with specific proof and try to fix the guilt and compel the miscreant to undergo the fate which treachery deserves. Why was not that course pursued if he himself was really charged with crime? If, however, the question was really what he would do when he should find himself deserted by his friends in Parliament, he was prepared to answer, that "he would instantly retire; for whenever the majority of the House should disapprove of a minister's conduct, he must give way."

Lord North like Sir Robert Walpole got his majority vote at the end of the debate, but I have said enough to prove that a new method of obtaining ministerial responsibility was coming into use. It was no longer necessary to punish an unpopular adviser in order to get rid of him. Just vote him down and he would resign.

Look once more at our main problem—How do you get rid of an undesired high official? By the time the Philadelphia Convention met in 1787, Great Britain had gone a long way toward the modern solution of this problem, which has superseded attainders and impeachments. Obtain a majority of the House of Commons against the official on something substantial. Then he will resign, and probably the whole Cabinet will go out of office with him, so that the sovereign will have to appoint all his advisers from another political party. Or else Parliament will be dissolved and a general election will take place. Its outcome will decide whether the old ministry stays in power or immediately gives way to a new Cabinet under a new Prime Minister.

This "Parliamentary system" is the chief way in which the British national government differs from ours, so far as its operation is concerned. The Executive is controlled by the legislature, or at least they must coincide. With us, on the contrary, the Executive and the national legislature are independently chosen. Twice in the last decade the President has belonged to a different political party from the majority in both Houses of Congress.

The British situation is obvious to us, but it was not obvious to the men who framed our Constitution. They are generally supposed to have intended to imitate quite a different conception of the British government. They thought of the King as the Chief Executive and replaced him by the President. Royal governors in the colonies and early state governors may have supplied an added analogy. You cannot get rid of a King or governor by a hostile vote in the legislature, and perhaps their minds stopped there. The importance of a majority vote in Parliament for getting rid of the King's main advisers was overlooked.

This seems a bit odd, because what is now the British constitutional system was strongly indicated before 1787 although it had not fully matured. Still, the way a government actually operates is harder to analyze than its formal structure. For example, the Philadelphia Convention did not foresee American political parties. Perhaps,

141

too, the framers were misled by several contemporaneous facts in British politics which would disappear soon after our Constitution was written. George III had taken a more active part than the first two Georges in managing national affairs. Thus the transfer of leadership from the King to the Prime Minister which had begun with Walpole was temporarily obscured until William Pitt the Younger made it plain during the French Revolution and the wars with Napoleon. Moreover, solid political parties were lacking in most of the eighteenth century; the House of Commons consisted of groups around particular influential persons, as G. O. Trevelyan shows in his delightful *Early History of Charles James Fox*. Cabinet ministers were still the personal choice of the King much more than would be the case when each of two big parties selected its own top men. Therefore, it was not easy for Americans in 1787 to see that the real British counterpart of our President is not the King, but the Prime Minister. Nevertheless, I should have expected the masters of politics in the 1787 Convention to sense the direct responsibility of ministers to Parliament from knowing about the Walpole debates in 1741 and the North debate in 1779.

Not that a better understanding of the actual British situation would have led the men in Philadelphia to copy it by subjecting the President to dismissal by a majority vote in one or both Houses of Congress. This would not have fitted into the kind of Constitution they were planning or into the political experience of Americans for the preceding century and a half.

What I do find rather surprising is that the Convention placed so much reliance on impeachment as the means of getting rid of an undesired official just at the very time when impeachments were shown to be unworkable in England and were dying out. The proceeding which was too cumbrous for the British was made an important feature of our Constitution. The reason, I suppose, was that it had to provide some way to oust a bad officer, and every alternative the Convention could think up seemed undesirable. At all events, the divergence in solving our main problem is very interesting. The House of Commons had been shaping impeachments to make high officials follow a line of policy approved by the legislature, and eventually discovered a quicker and more humane way of accomplishing the same result. The Philadelphia Convention took the opposite course of treating impeachments in accordance with their historical origin and the language of the charges, and making them prosecutions for offenses against the law. At least that is the theory of the impeachment clauses, but I wonder whether we have not tended to some extent toward the English fiction of alleging "high Crimes and Misdemeanors"[38] when we merely want to get rid of the official. It is hard to find any other explanation why the impeachment of President Johnson, on charges which appear very flimsy to us, came within one vote of success. When proposals were made a few years ago to impeach Secretary of State Acheson, did his accusers really believe he was guilty of treason, or did they just want Mr. Truman to appoint a Republican in his place?

The Convention sought to improve considerably the procedure it imported from England.[39] It hoped to make the Senators behave like judges during an impeachment by putting the Senators under a special oath and having the Chief Justice preside when the President was tried. The requirement of a two-thirds vote reduced the danger of unjust and partisan convictions. The most important clause in connection with our subject of bills of attainder is this: "Judgment in cases of Impeachment shall not extend further than to removal from Office, and disqualification to hold and enjoy any Office of honor, Trust, or

143

Profit under the United States; but the Party convicted shall, nevertheless, be liable and subject to Indictment, Trial, Judgment, and Punishment, according to Law." Thus besides wiping out legislative punishments by bills of attainder, the Constitution prevents them from being inflicted through the different method of impeachments. It confines impeachments to their central object of getting the official out of office. Congress is not allowed to impeach a hated man so that it can order him put to death, as the House of Commons impeached Strafford and Danby.

What Falls within the Prohibition of Bills of Attainder?

The preceding historical survey shows the unfitness of legislators, state or national, for the task of determining the guilt of individuals and the task of inflicting punishments. It brings out the soundness of a broad policy that, apart from the special job of excluding men from office by impeachment, the state legislatures and Congress should leave the tasks of trial and punishment to regular criminal courts which have judges trained in such work and a procedure carefully shaped by centuries of experience and the Bill of Rights. The constitutional clauses against bills of attainder are one way of carrying out this broad policy.

Yet it does not necessarily follow that the clauses are as broad as the policy and nullify every violation of it. The Constitution does unquestionably outlaw the most outrageous types of legislative condemnations, those which were familiar to the members of the Philadelphia Convention in Parliamentary Acts of Attainder and the vindictive New York statute against Tories in 1779. The vital question still before us is whether the phrase "bill of attainder" covers only those familiar types of laws which subjected named individuals to the sorts of punishment normally imposed in criminal courts, such as death, imprisonment, and fines; or does it go much farther so as to include attempts of legislators to get men punished in all sorts of ways without trial in a courtroom? This vital question cannot be decisively answered except by the Supreme Court, and we do not yet have enough cases to know just where the Court stands. The best plan is for the rest of this chapter to present a few leading cases and block out important considerations which are likely to shape the pres· ent meaning of "Bill of Attainder" in the Constitution. Morever, some of the reasons against novel types of legislative condemnation ought to make legislators very reluctant to try to penalize the men they dislike without the safeguards of a criminal trial. Even though such action is ultimately upheld as constitutional, it may still be unwise and unjust.

The Constitution has been completely effective in deterring both Congress and the state legislatures from ordering a named individual to be executed or imprisoned or fined. None of the statutes which have come before the Supreme Court under the clauses against bills of attainder resemble the Act of Parliament which sent Strafford to the axe. Nevertheless, crises like the fury of the Long Parliament against Strafford and the hysterical fear of the Popish Plot are not unknown in the United States, and when such a crisis happens legislators are strongly impelled to get rid of the men they hate without the annoying formalities and delays of a jury trial for a clearly defined crime. Knowing that they are clearly forbidden by the bill of attainder clauses to accomplish this purpose by the old-fashioned direct method used against the New York Tories in 1779, legislators are resourceful in discovering other and more roundabout ways for satisfying their passionate desire without, they hope, colliding with the Con-

145

stitution. As Horace wrote, "You may drive out Nature with a pitchfork, yet she will always come back."[40]

American legislatures have not yet seen fit to inflict the death penalty without judicial proceedings. They have, however, indulged considerably in the imposition of other punishments, whose severity was pleasing to themselves if not to the objects of their detestation. Two types of attempts to get around the bill of attainder clauses have come before the Supreme Court. The first type, not often employed, names persons and makes them suffer disagreeable consequences which differ, however, from the punishments imposed by a criminal court after conviction. The second type refrains from giving any names, but seeks to make a considerable group of detested persons lose their jobs by subjecting them to a test oath. This type is much more frequently employed. Indeed, the unending appearance of state test-oath laws nowadays makes me feel like transforming Horace's maxim into the old song of the man with delirium tremens:

Shut the door, they're coming through the window—
Shut the window, they're coming down the chimney—
Caesar's ghost, they're coming through the floor!

The Constitution had been in force for a century and a half before the first attempt was made to get rid of a named man by Act of Congress. In 1940, the immigration officials had decided that Harry Bridges, head of the longshoremen's union on the Pacific coast and then an unnaturalized Australian, was not deportable under existing legislation because he was not at the time a member of the Communist Party. A bill was introduced in the House of Representatives, which read as amended:[41] "That notwithstanding any other provision of law, the Attorney General be, and is hereby, authorized and directed to take into custody forthwith and deport forthwith to Australia

146

. . . the alien, Harry Renton Bridges, whose presence in this country the Congress deems hurtful."

This bill was vigorously opposed by Representative Sam Hobbs of Alabama, though he was always an opponent of Communists and co-author of the Smith Act. He pointed out that Bridges was "not charged with any deportable offense, nor with any offense at all. Far from being denied, this fact is asserted with evident satisfaction. . . ." Hobbs' contention that it was an ex post facto law as well as a bill of attainder was sound unless the bill was saved by the doctrine, often anounced by the Supreme Court, that deportation is not a punishment; "It is simply a refusal by the government to harbor persons whom it does not want."[42] Yet, as Justice Douglas recently said:[43] "Banishment is punishment in the practical sense. It may deprive a man and his family of all that makes life worth while. . . . Their plans for themselves and their hopes for their children all depend on their right to stay. If they are uprooted and sent to lands no longer known to them, no longer hospitable, they become displaced, homeless people condemned to bitterness and despair." Such considerations made little impression on the House of Representatives, which voted to deport Harry Bridges, 330 to 42.

The bill was dropped by the Senate when a general statute of the same year made former members or affiliates of the Communist Party deportable. Congress had hopes, which were later disappointed, that it could thus get rid of Bridges by a law which was ex post facto in a way[44] but was surely not a bill of attainder. So the interesting issue about the constitutionality of the bill to deport a specified individual never reached the courts. The Lovett case indicates that it might have had hard sledding. And if Congress should send a citizen into exile as Parliament banished Clarendon by a bill of pains and penalties, the Constitution would surely be violated.

147

The only Supreme Court decision on a statute subjecting named persons to damaging treatment is *United States* v. *Lovett* in 1946.[45] In order to understand why the law which led to this case was passed, let us recall our main problem—how does a legislature get rid of an official with whose policies it strongly disagrees?—and see whether this problem looks the same to Congress in the middle of the twentieth century as it did to the Philadelphia Convention at the close of the eighteenth.

Only one method for ousting an official is expressly provided by the Constitution—impeachment. However, two serious obstacles to its use have revealed themselves with the passage of time. In the first place, we have come to understand what the English were already realizing before 1787, that impeachment is a very cumbrous and time-consuming procedure. I remember how my uncle, who was a Senator from Rhode Island, complained that the impeachment of a federal judge was disorganizing the work of the Senate while it had ever so much normal business before it. Secondly, the Constitution authorizes removal from office by impeachment only if the disliked officer is convicted of "Treason, Bribery, or other high Crimes and Misdemeanors." Thus the Senate will be violating the Constitution if it sustains the impeachment merely because it has lost confidence in the officer or detests his policies. Something close to this warping of the Constitution did take place in the minds of some Senators who voted to remove Andrew Johnson, but so far as I know the Senate has faithfully adhered to the criminal character of impeachments when trying members of the Cabinet and judges.

Yet Congress has felt the same desire which I showed developing in the English Parliament, to have some way of getting rid of important officials simply because they feel strongly that they ought not to be there. With the enormous multiplication of federal agencies and federal employees and their acquisition of very extensive powers over the behavior of American citizens, this Congressional desire to possess some kind of effective control over the trustworthiness and the policies of officials has gained strength in recent years. Even if Congress were willing to treat the constitutional word "Treason" as a fictitious description of opposition to official policies, just as Parliament did in the case of Danby, still Representatives and Senators would hesitate to disrupt their regular work and spend weeks on an impeachment trial for every official whom they happened to dislike vigorously. Instead, I venture to surmise, they have a considerable longing to be able to do what the opponents of Walpole and Lord North tried to do. They would like it to be possible for the Senate and House by a majority vote to remove a detested official on the basis of conduct falling short of any recognized crime.

Some such attitude seems to me involved in the legislation which led to the Lovett case. In 1943 Martin Dies, the Chairman of the House Committee on Un-American Activities, attacked thirty-nine named government employees in a speech on the floor as "irresponsible crackpot radical bureaucrats" and affiliates of Communist-front organizations. He did not charge them with any crime, but insisted that because of their beliefs and past associations they were unfit to hold a government position. So he urged Congress to refuse to appropriate money for their salaries and thus eliminate these people from public office. A subcommittee of the Committee of Appropriations, with Representative Kerr as chairman, held hearings to investigate all the accused federal employees and give them a chance to prove themselves innocent, not of any established crime but of "subversive activity." This was defined by the subcommittee as follows: "Subversive ac-

149

tivity in this country derives from conduct intentionally destructive of or inimical to the Government of the United States—that which seeks to undermine its institutions, or to distort its functions, or to impede its projects, or to lessen its efforts, the ultimate end being to overturn it all."

Eventually the Kerr Committee found three officials guilty of "subversive activity." Robert Morss Lovett, long professor of English at the University of Chicago and editor of the *New Republic,* was in the Interior Department as Government Secretary of the Virgin Islands. Goodwin B. Watson, for many years professor of Psychology and Education at Columbia University, was chief analyst in the Foreign Intelligence Service of the Federal Communications Commission, which supervises the radio. William E. Dodd, Jr., son of a former Ambassador to Germany, was also on the staff of the FCC. The noncriminal nature of the alleged misconduct of these three officials is indicated by Kerr's statement in his report that the issue before the House was simply "whether or not the people in this country want men who are not in sympathy with the institutions of this country to run it." The issue whether or not these men were in sympathy with the ideas of the House of Representatives may also have played some part in their condemnation.

The House thereupon attached to the long Urgent Deficiency Appropriation Bill of 1943 this amendment by a vote of 318 to 62:[46] "No part of any appropriation ... which is made available under ... this Act, or ... now, or ... hereafter ..., under ... any other Act, shall be used, after November 15, 1943 [five months after enactment] to pay any part of the salary, or other compensation for the personal services, of Goodwin B. Watson, William E. Dodd, Junior, and Robert Morss Lovett. . . ." The men thus named would have to work for nothing or quit unless they got

150

reappointed by the President and confirmed by the Senate for the second time. The Senate and President Roosevelt strongly objected to this rider, but they could not get rid of it without rejecting the entire appropriation bill. That would have been disastrous to thousands of other employees and to the efficient operation of the government.

When the three officials got no more pay, they sued the government in the Court of Claims for services rendered after November 15, 1943, and won. Then, in the Supreme Court, the lawyer for Congress argued that the rider did not provide for the dismissal of the three men, but was a mere appropriation measure. The Constitution, he contended, gave Congress final say about appropriations, and consequently no court could interfere with its decision.

The Supreme Court unanimously rejected this argument, and decided in favor of the officials. However, the Justices divided 6 to 2 about the reasons for blocking the action of Congress.[47]

Justice Black, speaking for the Court, held that the rider was a bill of attainder. The denial of salaries for work which the three named men were lawfully performing was punishment. The rider did more than that—it permanently excluded them from any opportunity to serve the government. That is punishment of the most severe type, which existing law imposes only for special types of odious and dangerous crimes like treason. And this legislative punishing of individuals followed a legislative determination that they were guilty of the crime of engaging in "subversive activities"—a crime here defined for the first time.

The effect was to inflict punishment without the safeguards of a judicial trial and "determined by no previous law or fixed rule." The Constitution declares that this cannot be done. . . .

Those who wrote our Constitution well knew the danger inherent in special legislative acts which take away the life, liberty, or property of particular named persons because the legislature thinks them guilty of conduct which deserves punishment. They intended to safeguard the people of this country from punishment without trial by duly constituted courts. . . . And even the courts to which this important function was entrusted were commanded to stay their hands until and unless certain tested safeguards were observed. . . . [Our] ancestors had ample reason to know that legislative trials and punishments were too dangerous to liberty to exist in the nation of free men they envisioned. And so they proscribed bills of attainder.

And yet, strongly as I agree with what I have just paraphrased and quoted from Justice Black, I find it harder than he did to answer the main question in the Lovett case—Was this rider a bill of attainder? Let me present my difficulties by starting with his statement, elsewhere in the opinion, that the rider "falls *precisely* within the category of congressional actions" which were barred by the prohibition against bills of attainder and ex post facto laws.

My historical survey makes me feel that "precisely" is not quite the right word. The exercise of the spending power of Congress is rather different from the Act of Attainder against Strafford. Justice Frankfurter emphasized this difference and wanted the three officials to recover for their services on another ground, which would not stretch "Bill of Attainder" in the Constitution so as to include a statute forbidding the Treasury to make particular payments out of specifically appropriated moneys. Although (as will soon appear) I now disagree with Justice Frankfurter's interpretation of "Bill of Attainder" I did entertain doubts about the application of that clause while I was considering the Lovett case long before the actual decision. I thought then that the surest reason for invalidating the rider was as follows:

Congress was interfering with the President's right to control his subordinates when it tried to prevent three of

152

them from getting paid. No doubt, Congress can make general regulations for the establishment of agencies and officers and it has to appropriate money for *all* the officials in a given group, but this does not entitle it to say how a single member of that group shall be treated. No doubt, Congress participates in the selection of officials in a way Parliament has never done, because the Senate must approve the appointment of a particular man and can refuse to do so if Senators dislike him. Nevertheless, once a man is confirmed by the Senate, the question whether he is capable of performing his duties so well that he ought to be kept on the job is the concern of his superior officers up to the President, and it is not the business of either House of Congress. The problem somewhat resembles the recent issue about the right of Congressional committees to obtain testimony and documents about consultations inside the Executive organization. Finally, the long controversy which began with the Tenure of Office Act when Andrew Johnson was President was finally settled in 1926 by a Supreme Court decision that Congress cannot force the President to keep an employee whom he wants to dismiss.[48] It is equally objectionable for Congress to force the President to get rid of an employee whom he wants to retain.

Still, I am not surprised that none of the Justices in the Lovett case dealt with this argument against the rider. The Court is always anxious to keep away from the quicksands of the relationship between Congress and the Executive in regard to government officials, if it can possibly do so. With this argument left out of the case, the rider was bound to be upheld unless it was a bill of attainder.[49]

Recall the long series of legislative condemnations of officials and private citizens before the Constitution, from beyond Thomas Haxey through Jack Cade and Strafford and Sir John Fenwick to the New York Tories. Does "No

153

Bill of Attainder . . ." mean "No more of this very thing" as Justice Frankfurter thought, or "No more of this sort of evils" as the Court decided?

Justice Frankfurter reached his conclusion by dividing constitutional issues which come before the Supreme Court into two different types. The larger class concerns broad standards of fairness such as "just compensation" or "due process of law." Such questions "allow a relatively wide play for individual legal judgment." The other class, which includes our problem about bills of attainder, "gives no such scope" (he says) because the issues grow out of "very specific provisions of the Constitution." "These had their source in definite grievances and led the Fathers to proscribe against recurrence of their experience. The specific grievances and the safeguards against their recurrence . . . were defined by history. The meaning was . . . settled by history. . . . Judicial enforcement of the Constitution must respect these historic limits."

At this point I have to part company with my old friend and former colleague. History should be a teacher to enlighten us, not a jailer to shut us up. And I get no sense from the debates that the Convention felt it was making two distinct kinds of clauses. Indeed, the Constitution is not what those men knew about a century and a half ago but the words they gave us for meeting the needs of our own time. The bill of attainder clause is not imprisoned by the past any more than the power to regulate "Commerce." Congress is not obliged to let railroads alone because the only transportation in 1787 was by oxen, horses, and breezes.[50] The Constitution, to vary the metaphor, is the skeleton of a living nation. The bones of a mature man are the bones which came from his mother when he was born, and yet they are not the same bones. All of the Constitution grows while the life of a great community changes.[51]

154

Therefore, despite the fact that fining officials by cutting off their salaries differed considerably from the old bills of attainder, I think that the majority of the Justices in the Lovett case were right when they subjected the constitutional prohibition to "a wide play of judgment" and refused to confine it to one or two old kinds of legislative trials and punishments. Tyranny like fraud is resourceful in discovering new devices to accomplish its detestable purposes. Judges have always been reluctant to give a strict definition of fraud for fear that swindlers would then think up some new sort of cheating outside the definition. The same reasoning applies to the devices of tyranny and of the hysterical desire to suppress heterodox ideas. It is hardly conceivable that Congress would ever pass an old-fashioned bill of attainder. Hence it is futile to stop with nullifying such statutes. The real danger will come from new kinds of legislative determinations of guilt and legislative impositions of punishment upon individuals. Consequently, the Court in the Lovett case did much for freedom when it was willing to regard the attainder clause as directed generally against attempts by Congress or state legislatures to take into their own hands the conviction and sentencing of private citizens and officials, without the safeguards of trial in a courtroom.

At the same time, the obvious unsuitability of impeachments remains. Just as the formalities of treaties have been avoided to some extent by informal executive agreements, I expect that there will be a continued impulse to discover some sort of informal substitute for impeachments. So long as it involves the grossly unfair trials which were held by the Kerr committee, the Supreme Court is unlikely to sanction such a substitute. Whether any more satisfactory substitute can be worked out remains to be seen as the years go by.

The other judicial controversy over bills of attainder comes from frequent legislative attempts to condemn individuals out of their own mouths by the use of test oaths. These differ entirely from the ordinary oath of office which promises faithful performance of duties in the future; instead, each man is obliged to disclaim present or past conduct or opinions. I have already spoken of freedom as to some extent indivisible.[52] Here we find the prohibition of bills of attainder linked with freedom of speech and with the prohibition in the Fifth Amendment: "Nor shall any person . . . be compelled in any criminal case to be a witness against himself. . . ." It is true that the proceedings in which test oaths are now imposed by statute are not strictly criminal, but they do involve the loss of a job and other serious penalties.

In *Cummings* v. *Missouri* and *Ex Parte Garland*[53] after the Civil War, the Supreme Court was just as unwilling as in the Lovett case to confine bills of attainder within the narrow mold of the Act of Parliament against Strafford. The Court struck down test oaths by which priests and lawyers and members of many other professions had to deny that they had shown sympathy with the Confederacy in various ways, or else be excluded from their occupations. The majority of five Justices regarded this as a legislative punishment, although it was inflicted through the participation of the victims and not directly as in the old acts of attainder. The point was that the victim was forced to share in the process without having the safeguards of a determination of his guilt by a court. These two notable decisions made the constitutional prohibition of bills of attainder a powerful declaration of policy against many different kinds of legislative determinations of guilt and legislative inflictions of punishment, including such new types as might be devised by the ingenuity of men whose fears made them anxious to avoid the normal processes of charging recognized crimes and trying them before a judge and jury.

The four dissenting Justices in both cases regarded the test oaths as a method of imposing qualifications on those who sought to pursue a profession. This is a factor which cannot be ignored whenever the validity or the wisdom of a test oath is under consideration. Yet there are really two questions:

(1) Would the fact which the officeholder has to disclaim be a proper ground of ineligibility if it were proved against him by objective testimony in a regular trial, before a court or tribunal of experts?

(2) Is it constitutional or wise to make the officeholder determine his own guilt or innocence of the objectionable fact without any judicial proceeding, especially when much of the relevant evidence is unknown to him and beyond his reach?

These two questions are constantly getting confused, and an affirmative answer to the first question does not dispose of the second, which raises an entirely fresh set of considerations including the possibility that condemnation through self-trial is a bill of attainder.

The whole problem is too complex for further analysis here. It is indeed sad that judges and lawyers are forced to draw fine lines in an area where our governments have no business to be at all.

For test oaths "were an abomination to the founders of this nation," as Justice Black repeatedly points out.[54] They had been used by the Puritans in Cromwell's time to exclude members of the Church of England from holding public office and from teaching in any school or university, and then under Charles II the members of the Church of England enacted them to safeguard the same occupations from Puritans and Roman Catholics. When the New York legislature after the Revolution tried to establish an exculpatory oath to keep Tories out of numerous occupations, Alexander Hamilton wrote:[55]

"This was to invert the order of things; and, instead of obliging the State to prove the guilt, in order to inflict the penalty, it was to oblige the citizen to establish his own innocence to avoid the penalty. It was to excite scruples in the honest and conscientious, and to hold out a bribe to perjury. . . . Nothing can be more repugnant to the true genius of the common law than such an inquisition . . . into the consciences of men."

We had nothing of the sort in our country for seventy-five years after the Cummings and Garland cases stopped the device from being used against adherents of the Confederacy. Yet, since World War II, test oaths have been revived and used with the same enthusiasm as in seventeenth century England and Reconstruction Missouri. In every case except one,[56] the Supreme Court has sustained these oaths by a divided vote, on the ground that the facts they disclaim are a proper ground for ineligibility for the particular office or occupation.[57] The majority, I think, were somewhat inclined to assume that this point settled the matter. They have rather slighted the question raised by the bill of attainder clause, about the validity of throwing a suspected person out of a job without any judicial trial.

In considering the constitutionality or wisdom of a law requiring exculpatory oaths, we should never lose sight of the advantages of a regular trial, which are here denied to the person suspected:[58] "An accused in court must be tried by an impartial jury, has a right to be represented by counsel, he must be clearly informed of the charge against him, the law which he is charged with violating must have been passed before he committed the act charged, he must be confronted by the witnesses against him, he must not be compelled to incriminate himself, he cannot twice be put in jeopardy for the same offense, and even after conviction no cruel and unusual punishment can be inflicted upon him."

So far as actual Communists are involved, their constant subservience to a foreign power does create serious problems, and it is not surprising that the Supreme Court is reluctant to upset the legislative wish to attain safety at the cost of some loss of freedom. Yet the thing never stops with Communists. Test oaths are rapidly becoming a means of punishing all sorts of ideas which happen to diverge from the American party line. The steady encroachment on the policy of the First Amendment is very disturbing. Perhaps the time will come when the stomachs of the Justices will turn.

A third kind of legislative condemnation of individuals has not yet come before the Supreme Court and judicial control of it is perhaps impossible. I refer to the practice of legislative investigating committees, in Congress and many states, of denouncing private individuals for all sorts of behavior constituting no established crime. Yet punishment is inflicted through the loss of jobs or, at any rate, through injury to reputation. Often anybody can see that the committee's purpose in calling a particular witness is not to obtain from him useful information about general conditions or for preparing statutes, but to "get" this man and punish him by ruining his career or jailing him for contempt. Frequently these condemnations by committees are the outcome of a sort of legislative trial which would make the proceeding to attaint Sir John Fenwick a model of propriety.[59] As yet no serious attempt has been made by Congress or state legislatures to set up a decent procedure for investigating committees.

It is no adequate defense to say that what is done by these committees is constitutional. Charles I's levy of ship-money and many more of the actions which eventually cost him his head were firmly upheld by English judges. Legality in the long run will not save governmental measures which are detestable to large numbers of citizens. The committees are increasingly inclined to get the persons who appear before them punished for refusal to answer questions which ought never to have been asked. Respected law-abiding men who have performed useful work for years are to be imprisoned because they decline to betray former associates and make them jobless. Yet every American is brought up from boyhood to regard peaching on his comrades as despicable. The witness who sticks to this time-honored attitude is charged with bringing Congress into contempt, but the men who are really making Congress an object of contempt are the Senators and Representatives who urge the betrayal of friends, who ask a witness "Do you believe in God," who rely implicitly on the testimony of ex-Communist informers just as Parliament during the Popish Plot relied on ex-Catholic informers like Titus Oates.[60]

Congress and the state legislatures during the past decade have disregarded the intimacies of personal conduct and beliefs, fostered poisonous suspicions between fellow-citizens, created constant uneasiness among public and private employees whose minds have hitherto been steadily on their work, and condemned hundreds of individuals to punishment without a fair trial. Does anything we really fear from all the "Communist-front" organizations and "subversive" individuals in the United States justify this wholesale abandonment of the normal processes of a criminal prosecution, this undermining of cherished freedoms and of the American way of life?

There is an admonition by Justice Holmes which is often repeated by judges as a reason for regretfully respecting the numerous recent sedition laws and possible bills of attainder which have been adopted by tremendous majorities in legislatures. For example, Justice Frankfurter quoted it after the rider in the Lovett case had passed the House of Representatives by a vote of 5 to 1:[61] "[It] must be remembered that legislatures are ultimate guardians of the liberties and welfare of the people in quite as great a degree as the courts." Remembered by whom? So far as I can see, this is a maxim which judges constantly remember and legislatures always forget. I wish it were the other way round.

It is all very pleasant to say that the remedy for bad laws lies with the people at the polls, but what Senators or Representatives were ever defeated because they voted for a sedition law? Indeed several have lost their seats by opposing some new law against Communists on account of its threat to constitutional rights.

If legislators are determined not to be guardians of the liberties of the people and if judges refuse to interfere when legislators take those liberties away, what is the use of putting guarantees of fundamental rights into the Constitution except, perhaps, to furnish political orators with noble words to quote while they tell us Americans to thank God that we are not as other men are?

Freedom of Movement

Nothing in the Constitution expressly protects freedom of movement. Hence this chapter cannot follow the example of its two predecessors and use the words of the Philadelphia Convention as our starting-point. Instead, we can take an authoritative statement of this ideal from the Universal Declaration of Human Rights, which was signed by the United States and fifty other governments, and promulgated in December, 1948, by the General Assembly of the United Nations:[1]

"*Article 13.* 1. Everyone has the right to freedom of movement and residence within the borders of each State.

"2. Everyone has the right to leave any country, including his own, and return to his country."

Plainly something is missing here. These words do not cover the whole of freedom of movement conceived geometrically or in terms of what human beings might desire. One can move around in his own country, leave it, and come back to it. One can get out of foreign countries. Yet nothing is said about any right to enter a country not one's own. No land of promise for those who are desolate or oppressed in the nations where they were born —no assurance of a new home and a fresh start. Perhaps the next article holds a little hope—"Everyone has the right to seek and to enjoy in other countries asylum from persecution."[2] Still, nothing here says that they who seek shall find. Before fugitives from justice can enjoy asylum in a foreign country, they have to get into it. And it would be rash to interpret the Declaration as including among "fundamental freedoms of all people" the right to a visa from an American consul.

No doubt, the draftsmen were sensible in not urging the repeal of all immigration laws. It was their task to frame a Declaration which every government would be

162

glad to adopt. So they put into it as much freedom of movement as they could reasonably expect to be granted, and then stopped. They are justified by the fact that the Declaration did become Universal.

"The children of this world are in their generation wiser than the children of light." Still, it is good to listen once in a while to somebody who gives us a vision of a brighter world than seems to us possible. Besides keeping constantly in mind the reasonable definition of freedom of movement in the Declaration, I sometimes like to remember the words of Molly Steimer. After this girl of twenty-one had been sent to prison for fifteen years because she joined the Abrams group in opposing our despatch of troops to Murmansk and Vladivostock in World War I,[3] all the prisoners were pardoned on condition of their going immediately to the Soviet Union at their own expense. Just before the steamer left for Libau, Molly Steimer told the newsmen: "Everybody has the right to live any place in the world he wants, any time." Unpractical indeed, but so are many of the ideals which stir men and women. It was a flaming belief like hers in freedom of movement which brought many of our ancestors to the shores of America.

Lack of Mobility in Seventeenth-Century England

During the period when the American colonies were settled, there was very little freedom of movement for most people in England. Three kinds of laws raised obstacles against the circulation of laborers and skilled workmen from place to place, wherever they might choose.

In the first place, the Statute of Apprenticeship, passed early in Queen Elizabeth's reign, forbade anybody to engage in any trade or craft unless he had been apprenticed to it for seven years. This law kept a man from going to a new place where workmen were badly needed for work which he had not done before. No long training was needed for the new job, and he might dislike his old job and his old home. Nevertheless, the legal barrier made the move impossible.

Next, skilled work was split among ever so many segregated crafts, each of which was under the legal monopoly of its own gild (or corporation). Consequently a worker could not pass from one trade to another even though the operations were so much alike that the change itself would be easy for him. For instance, the arts of weaving plain linen and plain silk were almost the same; and a weaver of either linen or silk could become a tolerable weaver of plain woolen in a few days. Yet both silk weaving and wool weaving were closed to outsiders. If there was no market for linens and a linen weaver was out of work, he could not turn to weaving silk or wool in another town where both were in great demand. Only two choices were left. He could work as a common laborer, perhaps on a farm, for which he was untrained; or he could "come upon the parish," that is, live on poor relief. Usually he chose to let the parish support him. An uncongenial occupation was more disagreeable than salaried idleness, especially as the salary was rather good. Persons receiving relief, one taxpayer complained in 1698, "seldom drink any other than the strongest ale-house beer, or eat any bread save what is made of the finest wheat flour."[4] Still, the taste must have been bitter in the mouth of an ex-weaver with any self-respect.

The last and worst obstacle to mobility arose from this whole business of poor relief. The bulk of the population was frozen into place by the fear of poverty, not so much fear of it by workers who might become poor as fear by the well-to-do of the cost of keeping the poor alive.

164

The abolition of the monasteries by Henry VIII ended their charity to the poor. Somebody had to take over, and a statute of 1601 threw the support of any pauper on the taxes imposed on the lands in his own parish. If a laborer became impoverished in the parish where he was born, his source of support was plain; but if he moved to another parish where work was more abundant or living conditions were pleasanter and afterwards needed relief for himself and his family, both he and the local officials had a deep interest in the problem of what was "his own parish"—Was it the place he lived in now or the place he came from? In order to solve this knotty problem, the general principle was established that he could be returned to his old home at any time until he acquired a "settlement" in his new home. The natural consequence was that the officials at the new home did all they could to prevent him from getting a settlement there. One way to do this was to ship him back long before he became a pauper. If, therefore, a healthy and industrious workman was so rash as to carry his industry to a new place, he could be thrown out at the caprice of any churchwarden or overseer: "Nine tenths of the people of England, all in fact who did not belong to a small class of landowners, were liable to be expelled from any parish save their own, with every circumstance of arrest and ignominy, however good their character and even if they had secured remunerative work."[5]

Nor was this the whole story. Not only did the prospective migrant know that he would be unwelcome in the new place he wanted to work, but also he would find his departure discouraged as much as possible by the officials of the parish he wanted to leave. They did not like to let him go for fear of getting him back later in a worse condition and having to foot all the expense of his return. Being thus faced with impediments at both ends of

165

his intended change of residence, any sensible laborer was likely to give up and stay where he was.

In our times freedom of movement is frequently blocked by the walls of national frontiers. England in the seventeenth and eighteenth centuries was crisscrossed in every direction with thousands of high fences along the boundaries of every parish. Wages differed greatly in places near each other, but the advantages of working elsewhere counted for nothing. A writer on the eve of our Revolution said that the law put it "in the power of a parish officer, to imprison a man as if it were for life." And Adam Smith said of England in the year of the Declaration of Independence:[6]

"[It] is often more difficult for a poor man to pass the artificial boundary of a parish, than an arm of the sea or a ridge of high mountains. . . . To remove a man who has committed no misdemeanor from the parish where he chooses to reside, is an evident violation of natural liberty and justice."

The unhappiness and frustration caused by the various restrictions on freedom of movement in England were strong incentives to go to the great open spaces in her American colonies. There a skilled workman or a laborer would be far away from rigorous trade regulations, gilds, parochialism, and never-ending fear of poverty. He could find plenty of employment, build his own house, and if he wished become the owner of many acres. Yet his desire to go did not necessarily give him the legal right to go. It was hardly logical for the law to prevent a man from moving over the brook to another parish and then allow him to cross 3,000 miles of ocean to a new home.

Of course, the English government needed settlers for its colonial domain, but it did not necessarily follow that anybody who pleased could be a settler, regardless of his station in life or his divergence from the religion of the

166

State. The Kings of Spain and France had possessed great regions in America long before the English sovereigns formed any plans for colonies on the mainland. The Privy Council of Queen Elizabeth and the Stuart Kings might have thought it sensible to get the benefit of the longer experience of the Spanish and French governments in selecting settlers at home and locating them in America. Perhaps Spain and France were worth imitating. So let us see what those two countries did about freedom of movement.

Freedom to Go to America from Spain and France

Spain owned a vast territory from Cape Horn up to a region north of Mexico, in which Brazil was included between 1580 and 1640 because Portugal was then under Spanish kings. Instead of colonizing through corporations of merchants and promoters, as England and France did later, the Spanish government took charge itself. Ten years after Columbus returned from his First Voyage, the Crown set up the House of Trade in Seville to regulate commerce with the new regions. It was ordered that everybody intending to cross to America, whatever his profession or purpose, must come in person to the House of Trade (or its branch-office in Cadiz) to be examined and granted a license. Only Spaniards could be licensed, and not even Germans or Flemings although under the same ruler.

Every emigrant had to be registered in a book kept by the contador of the House of Trade, which recorded his name, parentage, birthplace, whether he was married or single, the ship in which he sailed and his port of destination. This was useful for tracing the heirs of a colonist who died in America; but it was regimentation far beyond what was done by the English, although if they had

167

kept such a register, what a boon it would be now to genealogists in the United States! Any merchant who left his wife in Spain had to have her written consent and post a heavy bond that within three years he would either return or get her over to America to join him. No other emigrant could go without his wife, not even a royal official. Unmarried women, on the other hand, were absolutely forbidden to cross to the colonies unless they were daughters or servants in migrating families. The eastbound voyage was regulated just as strictly. A resident in the Indies who wanted to return to Spain had to get permission from his viceroy, give the reasons for his voyage, and say how long he would be away.

The penalty for crossing the Atlantic without a license was originally ten years' banishment from Spain with a heavy fine, if one was of gentle blood. If not, a hundred lashes were substituted for the fine. The judicial authorities in the colonies were ordered to arrest unlicensed newcomers and ship them back to Spain on the first available vessel. As time went on, the penalties became more severe. In 1560, the offender was to forfeit all the lands and goods he had acquired in America. In 1604, instead of lashes he got four years in the galleys. In 1622 his rowing was doubled to eight years, and the additional ten years of banishment were to be spent in a penal colony in Africa.

The sea captain who carried unlicensed passengers had to pay the same penalty they did at first, but by 1607 he would be put to death. Nevertheless there was much smuggling of emigrants.

Spain had a problem of diverse religions like England; but her state church was Roman Catholic and her nonconformists were Jews, Moors, and heretics. Yet the government made no use of emigration to relieve religious tensions at home while at the same time obtaining energetic though heterodox settlers in America. Heretics, of course, were only fit for burning wherever they were, but Jews would have been able colonists, as was proved by many of them who slipped into Brazil and later got out alive to become leaders in New York and Rhode Island. Moors might have done as well in tropical America as East Indians do in Trinidad today. Nevertheless, nothing was done about Jews and Moors except to treat them badly in Spain, as Cervantes relates with some uneasiness in the Second Part of *Don Quixote.*

The Spanish government always confined the privilege of going to America to persons of unquestioned orthodoxy. As far back as 1501, the regulations of voyages to Hispaniola ordered vessels to carry no Jews, no Moors, no reconciled heretics, no recent converts from Mohammedanism. Soon afterwards these prohibitions were applied to all of New Spain, and expanded: no sons or grandsons of Jews and Moors, or of converts, or of persons who had come into the hands of the Inquisition. Yet these were the people most likely to possess the capital required to develop colonial trade.

Evasions were frequent, especially by Christianized Jews from Portugal. Hence the terrible activity of the Inquisition at Lima for years before 1640 and in Mexico during the next decade.

Freedom of movement between the colonies was allowed to Spaniards after 1548, although for over twenty years before that, migration from the Antilles to the mainland was forbidden on pain of death and forfeiture of property.

The policy of restricting immigration in order to save the Spanish colonies from the contamination of foreigners and heresy made the population grow slowly. The kind of men who were allowed to settle there were unsuited to subdue and colonize the new continent. They sought oc-

169

cupations more lucrative or less laborious than farming and trade. Efforts were concentrated on the search for gold, and agriculture was confined to great estates, especially those held by the Church. The Indians, of course, were serfs. Even toward the settlers from Spain and their American-born descendants, the government exhibited chronic fear and distrust of individual initiative.

"Self-reliance, independence of thought and action, in the colonists was discouraged. Virtually all public matters, great and small, had to be referred to Spain for decision."[7]

The French government also allowed little freedom of movement across the Atlantic. Jacques Cartier was far in advance of systematic English explorers of the North American coast, but Quebec was founded almost simultaneously with Jamestown. Serious colonization began about 1632, when Richelieu formed the Company of New France, which was granted the whole St. Lawrence valley with a complete monopoly of trade. In return it was to take to New France three hundred colonists a year.

In France as in Spain, Catholicism was the state religion; but there was a much more acute conflict of faiths because of the large number of Huguenots who formed a sort of *imperium in imperio* under the Edict of Nantes. Richelieu was struggling with them as James I with the Puritans, but unlike James he imitated the Spanish policy of ignoring the value of his antagonists as settlers in the New World. Only French Catholics were allowed to go to New France, with three priests for every settlement. It was the British colonies whose life was enriched by the Huguenots.

Richelieu's policy was not a success. By 1660, when 85,000 white inhabitants of New England were reaching political and economic maturity, New France had no more than 2,000 and its commercial life was languishing. The Company's charter was revoked and the region be-

170

came a royal province, governed like provinces in France. A new "Company of the West Indies" was organized in 1664 to control French trade and colonization overseas, and the European population of Canada soon doubled. But this company too proved a failure and lost its charter after ten years. There was no more monopoly, but the chief competition thenceforth was between royal governors and the Catholic prelates. By 1690 the English in North America outnumbered the French twenty to one. Under Louis XV, the French still showed little inclination to emigrate to the colonies. There were only 60,000 white settlers in the province of Quebec when it was conquered in 1763. New York alone had more than that, and the thirteen British colonies combined had almost two millions without counting slaves.[8]

Freedom to Go to America from England

Among several causes of the success of the British colonies in North America,[9] both before and after they became independent, their charters were very important.[10] These grants of a large territory to a corporation or named individuals empowered the grantees to dispose of lands and to govern the inhabitants under specified conditions.

The earliest English charter was Queen Elizabeth's Patent to Sir Humphrey Gilbert in 1578, seven years after he provoked the first of Peter Wentworth's outbursts in the House of Commons.[11] Although Sir Humphrey's Patent generously allowed him to settle on any amount of territory anywhere in the world that was not occupied by Christians, he made only one voyage six years later, and never did found a colony. For, after getting beyond Newfoundland and losing the largest of his three vessels with almost all hands when she went aground near Cape Sable Island, he headed homeward for a fresh start. Gilbert was on the frigate "Squirrel" of ten tons, which kept close company with the "Golden Hind" of forty tons. The narrative of Captain Edward Hayes of the "Hind"[12] demonstrates that one of the most influential factors in the development of freedom in British North America was the Atlantic Ocean. If English officials had been able to fly over it instead of having to sail through it, our ancestors would not have been able to shape their own destinies.

> Munday the ninth of September [1584], in the afternoone, the Frigat was neere cast away, oppressed by waves, yet at that time recovered: and giving foorth signes of joy the Generall [Gilbert] sitting abaft with a booke in his hand, cried out unto us in the Hind (so oft as we did approch within hearing) We are as neere to heaven by sea as by land. Reiterating the same speech, well beseeming a souldier, resolute in Jesus Christ, as I can testifie he was.
>
> The same Monday night, about twelve of the clocke, or not long after, the Frigat being ahead of us in the Golden Hinde, suddenly her lights were out, whereof as it were in a moment, we lost the sight, and withall our watch cryed, the Generall was cast away, which was too true. For in that moment, the Frigat was devoured and swallowed up of the Sea. Yet still we looked out all that night, and ever after, until wee arrived upon the coast of England. . . .

So Gilbert like his adversary Peter Wentworth died without accomplishing any of what he set out to do. Yet what is failure and what is success? If Wentworth had been allowed to ask his questions in 1587,[13] the House would not have answered them; but they were asked and answered by the House of Commons of 1621.[14] If Gilbert had started a colony twenty years before Jamestown, it would have faded away like Raleigh's Roanoke; but he did start something else. His Patent of 1578 contained many clauses which were substantially repeated in charter after charter of colonies which endured to become independent states. The pioneer English colonizer was drowned in the ocean which half a million settlers from the British Isles would cross during the seventeenth cen-

172

tury and a million and a half during the eighteenth.[15]
Both Gilbert and Wentworth could have said:
"My dreams have all come true to other men."[16]

Look at the assurance of freedom of movement in Gilbert's Patent:[17]

"And we doe geve full aucthoritie and power to the said Sir Humfrey that he shall and maye at all and every tyme and tymes hereafter have take and leade in the said voyages to travell thetherward or to inhabite there with him such and soe many of our subjects as shall willingely accompany him with sufficient shippinge and furnyture for their transportacions Soe that none of the same parsons be such as hereafter shalbe specially restrayned by us our heirs or successors. . . ."

Contrast this with Spanish and French practice. No examination, no licenses, no mention of religion.

The First Charter of the Virginia Company (1606), which brought about the lasting colony of Jamestown next year, gives a similar assurance in almost the exact words except for modernizing the spelling and adding permission for the emigrants to take with them "Armour, Weapons, Ordinance, Powder, Victual, and all other things necessary for the said Plantations, and for their Use and Defence there." Their equipment is expanded still more by the Patent of the Council for New England, which allowed the Pilgrims to land at Plymouth, so as to include "all Manner of Cloathing, Implements, Furniture, Beasts, Cattle, Horses, Mares. . . ." Freedom of movement went into later charters, with the draftsmen getting more economical of words by 1664, when the future James II was granted by his royal brother New York, Martha's Vineyard, Nantucket, and much more. Now the previous long list of emigrants' possessions is condensed into "cloathing implements furniture, and all other things usually transported. . . ." Yet the Georgia Charter (1732) returns to

173

the verbose list and throws in "merchandise and wares esteemed by the wild people" so as to facilitate the acquisition of furs from the Indians.

A less amusing but more valuable widening of freedom of movement concerned the nationality of settlers in the British colonies. Queen Elizabeth's Patent to Gilbert stopped short at "our Subjects." The same words in the Virginia Charter from James I let in Scotchmen too. In 1620 James liberalized settlement in New England by adding "Strangers that will become our loving Subjects, and live under our Allegiance. . . ." The Georgia Charter modernized "Strangers" into "foreigners." No charter expressly permitted entry by aliens who did not intend to be naturalized, but I do not see how their mental state could have been tested by the free and easy methods of those days. Probably such immigrants to America were rare before the nineteenth century, when we welcomed Garibaldi, Kossuth, and the future Napoleon III, who all wanted to go back triumphantly to their native lands, not to mention the tens of thousands of hard-working Italians who expected to spend their American earnings in a happy old age looking over the Bay of Naples.

The plain truth is that so far as the law was concerned, there was much more freedom of movement between the British Isles and our eastern seaboard at any time between 1607 and 1776 than exists in 1956.

The final aspect of the colonial charters to be discussed here is their treatment of religion. My previous discussion of Spain and France shows that religious intolerance in the home-country tends to cut down freedom of movement to the colonies. When the heterodox are treated as third-class citizens, they are likely to be refused the privilege of a fresh start in the King's overseas dominions. Now, the English government displayed plenty of intolerance between the settlement of Jamestown and the Revolution of 1688. Persecutions run all through my previous chapters. Yet the surprising thing about England is that intolerance and persecution stopped at high-water mark.[18]

It may seem obvious why the greatest migration to New England took place between 1625 and 1640 during the bitter persecutions of the Puritans by Charles I and Archbishop Laud. Naturally, these sufferings made a great many people want to get out of England. But my point is that they were allowed to get out and worship God in their own way when they reached the colonies. Richelieu was persecuting Huguenots in this same period, but he did not let the Huguenots go to Canada. And if he had, they would have been even unhappier there than in France.

The charters went through three stages. James I made some half-hearted attempts to bar religious extremists. Thus his second Charter of the Virginia Company, in 1609, in order to avoid settlers "suspected to affect the superstitions of the Church of Rome," required any person going over to take the Oath of Supremacy. This had been imposed since Elizabeth became sovereign on all state officials, bishops, and clergymen; it forswore the Pope and acknowledged the reigning Queen or King as head of the Church. The Oath of Supremacy was abhorrent to all conscientious Roman Catholics because they reserved this high place for the Pope, and to some conscientious Dissenters who believed that it belonged to no human being but only to God. Still, the Pilgrims although entirely outside the Established Church were not deterred from sailing by the retention of this oath in the 1620 Patent of the New England Council, from whom they received their lands. After that, the Oath of Supremacy dropped out of sight. The Massachusetts Bay Charter in 1629 and the Maryland Charter in 1632 say nothing about the religion of settlers, one way or the other. Finally, with the first Carolina Charter of March 24, 1663, comes the earliest express grant of freedom of worship. Among the migrants, it says, will be those who cannot take the Oath of Supremacy and "cannot, in their private opinions, conform to the publick exercise of religion, according to the liturgy, form and ceremonies of the Church of England." And later on July 18th of the same year, this tolerance was repeated and greatly expanded in the Charter for Rhode Island, whose settlers had declared that "it is much on their hearts (if they may be permitted) to hold forth a livelie experiment, that a most flourishing civill state may stand and best bee maintained with a full libertie in religious concernments."

What astonishes me is that these Carolina and Rhode Island Charters came from Clarendon and other ministers of Charles II who at the same time were vigorously harrying Dissenters in England and Scotland and trying to give the Established Church an ironclad monopoly over the life of the spirit.

Mobility between English Colonies

The earliest settlers from England were likely to stay close to the harbor where they had landed; but as colonies multiplied and the seaboard steadily filled up, there must have been a strong impulse toward intercolonial migration. When most transportation was by water, it was easy to shift to the territory of a different government, and frontiers in the forests were invisible. No doubt, a large number of people were inclined to remain in their own colony where they had political rights and were among friends and familiar ways of life. Still, a craftsman seeking better opportunities in a larger town or a pioneer trudging into a newly opened fertile valley would care little if he had to cross a colonial boundary.

"Americans are always moving on. . . .
I think it must be something in the blood.
Perhaps it's only something in the air."[19]

Since I have done little research on this problem of internal mobility, I shall simply state the impression that freedom of movement inside the colonies flourished in fact without much express sanction in law.

The fundamental documents issued in England by Kings or proprietors said almost nothing on the subject, one way or the other. Occasionally the inhabitants of a colony were forbidden to shut off their coast from other subjects of the King who might wish to come there for trading or fishing.[20] The Rhode Islanders, evidently fore-seeing that they might be unpopular among their neighbors, got a clause inserted in their Charter which gave them the lawful right "to passe and repasse with freedome, into and through the rest of the English Collonies, upon their lawful and civill occasions." A specific restriction on freedom of outward movement, probably intended to stop absconding debtors and fleeing criminals, appears in the Concessions and Agreements for the Province of West Jersey (1677). No shipmaster was to take anybody aboard for a voyage into another country or colony without a certificate from the authorities that such a person was cleared; and the certificate was not to be issued until after three weeks' public notice of the person's intention to go abroad.

Beyond a few scattered provisions of this sort, the charters seem to have taken internal freedom of movement for granted. Certainly, the governmental draftsmen in London knew how to deal with this freedom explicitly when there was any prospect of interference with it. The Treaty of Utrecht in 1713, by which France ceded Nova Scotia, gave the Acadians liberty to remove themselves within a year to any other places, as they saw fit, together

177

with all their movable effects; and it also allowed the Indians full liberty of going or coming on account of trade, and of resorting as they pleased to the British and French colonies without molestation. The absence of any similar specific provisions in the charters indicates to me that no serious barriers were expected to arise along the boundaries between English colonies.

When we look at the legislation enacted by the colonists, we again find little on freedom of movement. The broadest provision was put into the Massachusetts Body of Liberties in 1641: "Every man of or within this Jurisdiction shall have free libertie, not with standing any Civill power, to remove both himselfe and his familie at their pleasure out of the same, provided there be no legall impediment to the contrarie."[21] This liberality to outgoing settlers was followed by hospitality toward some kinds of incoming persons:[22]

> If any people of other Nations professing the true Christian Religion shall flee to us from the Tiranny or oppression of their persecutors, or from famyne, warres, or the like necessary and compulsarie cause, They shall be entertayned and succoured among us, according to that power and prudence god shall give us.
> If any ships . . ., be it freind or enemy, shall suffer shipwrack upon our Coast, there shall be no violence or wrong offered to their persons or goods. But their persons shall be harboured and relieved and their goods preserved in safety, till Authoritie may be certified thereof and shall take further order therein.

Perhaps if a large band of objectionable persons from a neighboring colony had come swarming in within a brief space of time, local prejudice would have produced immigration laws against these unwelcome newcomers. In that event the Privy Council might have had to decide whether freedom of internal movement was one of the rights and privileges of free persons residing in England, which were guaranteed in charter after charter to settlers in the colonies and all their children born there. This would have been an interesting question of law because, as I showed early in this chapter, the bulk of Englishmen at home were greatly restricted when they wished to go from one occupation to another or from one parish to another. However, no such problem seems to have arisen extensively enough to cause significant litigation. Massachusetts did indeed seize Elder Pardon Tillinghast and some other zealous Baptists who had come over from Rhode Island to convert the Puritans, but they were merely warned to stay home.[23] No doubt such border incidents occurred now and then without provoking any bitter intercolonial quarrel.

The almost total silence of the effective charters and colonial legislation with regard to internal freedom of movement can be profitably contrasted with the drastic denials of that freedom in two documents which were intended to govern settlers in New York and the Carolinas, but which fortunately had little effect on colonial life.

First, the Dutch West India Company in 1629 issued a Charter to Patroons in New Netherlands which kept all trading under control of the Company and compelled servants to stay permanently with their own patroon. If they wanted to leave him at the expiration of their indentures, he could send them back to Holland. This attempt to pin settlers to an estate like mediaeval serfs did not outlast the time when New York became an English colony.

The other document was indeed English, but its like was never seen in England or any other free country. All of the present North and South Carolina had been granted by Charles II to a few proprietors. Among these was Anthony Ashley Cooper, Earl of Shaftesbury, whom we have met in earlier chapters. The Ashley and Cooper rivers at Charleston take their names from him. Shaftesbury had a

179

brilliant young secretary, John Locke, and gave him the job of framing a government for the new province. The budding philosopher produced in 1670 the Fundamental Constitutions of Carolina, which owed nothing to Sir Humphrey Gilbert's Patent or any intervening colonial charter. Its purpose, it declared, was to "avoid a numerous democracy." Locke's originality extended even to words like "caziques" for lords of the manor and "leet-men" for the settlers. One of the novel provisions of the Constitutions forbade any leet-man to go off the land of his particular lord and live anywhere else except by license from his lord under seal. "And all the children of leet-men shall be leet-men, and so to all generations." Luckily this document never went into force, but it leaves me with two profound doubts, as to the wisdom of Plato when he wished philosophers were kings and as to the accuracy of recent writers who maintain that Americans think like John Locke.[24] It seems impossible that the man who wrote the Constitutions of Carolina had ever talked with anybody who had lived in the American colonies or with any family which intended to make a new home overseas.

Englishmen, Welshmen, Scotchmen, and Irishmen attained great freedom of movement when they sailed for British North America. They could go whenever they pleased, to any colony they wished, and then, if dissatisfied with their choice, to any other colony they chose. The determining factor in favor of internal mobility was, I think, not legal but practical. When a bark from London made fast to a wharf in Philadelphia alongside a sloop from Annapolis, the passengers who disembarked from both vessels were Englishmen, and no distinction would be made between the two groups by the Englishmen whom they joined in the town or on the farms to the west. Every colony needed strong arms and skilful hands, wherever they came from.

Consequently, as the eighteenth century advanced and the colonies matured, men moved freely across boundaries wherever their work called them. Andrew Hamilton went from Philadelphia to New York to defend Peter Zenger, Dr. William Douglass journeyed from Boston to Rhode Island for a surgical consultation,[25] and Benjamin Franklin left Boston to be a printer in Philadelphia. And when in mid-century waves of pioneers poured through the gaps in the Alleghenies, it must have made little difference to them what particular seaboard government claimed the land where they were battling Indians in order to hunt and trap and raise a family.

The Western Frontier Closed, 1765

Just as freedom to move westward over the long mountain barrier of the Alleghenies was beginning to be important to the colonists, they found it re-enforced by a still more formidable legal barrier. When France gave all of Canada to the British Crown in 1763, George III became ruler of a great unsettled region behind his new French-speaking subjects which adjoined the great unsettled region behind his English-speaking colonists. Large tribes of warlike Indians roamed over both regions without bothering about boundary-lines. The problem was already very troublesome, and it was bound to be made much worse by the entry of quantities of white men. Why not throw both regions into one and handle the whole problem as a unit?

And so the King declared in the Quebec Proclamation of 1765 that, for the sake of leaving the Indians undisturbed, the governors of all the colonies in North America, until further notice, were ordered not to authorize any surveys or grants "beyond the heads or sources of any of the rivers which fall into the Atlantic Ocean from the west

181

or northwest." The King's present plan, it went on, was to reserve for the use of the Indians all territories lying to the westward of the sources of these rivers. Not only was future migration forbidden beyond the crest of the Alleghenies, but also all persons whatsoever who had already settled there must "forthwith remove themselves from such settlements." The end of free land was in sight.

Soon afterwards Parliament turned much of this Proclamation into permanent law by the Quebec Act. Although this reopened everything from Kentucky south for settlement as well as the future site of Pittsburgh, it was a second staggering blow to the hopes of the colonists. For under this Act, the entire region north of the Ohio River from the western boundary of Pennsylvania to the Mississippi was annexed to the Province of Quebec with its own royal governor and no legislature. Even if the pioneers from the Thirteen Colonies were allowed to make new homes beyond the mountains, they would be subjected to different laws from those they had known and merged into a population who mostly spoke a foreign language and cherished the Roman Catholic faith.

Although the Quebec Act was less discussed on the eve of the Revolution than issues of taxation, it was steadily resented. The Continental Congress in 1774 stated as one of the colonists' chief grievances that the limits of the province of Quebec were "extended so as to comprehend those vast regions, that lie adjoining to the northernly and westernly boundaries of these colonies." And the Declaration of Independence denounced George III "for abolishing the free system of English law in a neighboring province, establishing an arbitrary government and enlarging its boundaries. . . ."

Looking back from 1955 over nearly two centuries to the Quebec Act, we can see in it meritorious features which the colonists were unable to recognize. Unification of the western lands was the only workable solution. The vague geography of the charters would have produced bitter and endless boundary-disputes. Imagine the situation if each of several unco-ordinated seaboard legislatures had set up its own scheme for the disposal of land, formed its own policy for dealing with the Indians, used its own militia to fight them, and often provoked them into massacring settlers from some other colony. An overall government had to be able to handle such problems. The Americans themselves reached almost the same solution two decades later when every state ceded its western lands to the United States and Congress organized the whole region into the Northwest Territory by the Ordinance of 1787.

The fatal difficulty in the controversy between the British government and the American colonists, as in the controversy between Charles I and the Long Parliament, was that there were too few peaceful solutions at hand and none of these was workable. The only choice as to who should handle broad American problems lay between thirteen disunited colonial legislatures and the overall government in London. The job plainly had to be done by some overall government, but there was none in America and any attempt by George III to establish one there would have received the same chilly reception Andros got when he tried to unite New England. The concept of Dominion status was a century in the future. The only existing overall government, in London, could not do the job either. The ocean which engulfed Sir Humphrey Gilbert was too wide to permit the colonists any effective control over the few men in London who would determine their destinies, too wide for those few men to understand the wishes and ways of the many whom they would govern. Tom Paine hit the nail on the head in his *Common Sense:*

183

As to government matters, 'tis not in the power of Britain to do this continent justice; the business of it will soon be too weighty and intricate to be managed with any tolerable degree of convenience, by a power so distant from us and so ignorant of us. . . . To be always running three or four thousand miles with a tale or petition . . . will in a few years be looked upon as folly and childishness. There was a time when it was proper and there is a proper time for it to cease. . . .

There is something absurd in supposing a continent to be perpetually governed by an island. It is evident that they [England and America] belong to different systems. England to Europe: America to itself.

The overall government which was essential to solve the problems of the western lands must, Americans felt, be their own overall government. Yet both sides were incapable of creating such a novel institution peacefully. Therefore, the question of regulating freedom of movement to the westward was a strong reason for the Revolution, for Independence, for a permanent Union.

The Articles of Confederation and the Constitution

The individual states took freedom of movement as much for granted as when they were colonies. The only reference to the subject in an early state constitution was after the Philadelphia Convention, when Pennsylvania declared in 1790 "That emigration from the state shall not be prohibited." However, freedom to move across statelines required some sort of general agreement. Hence it was specifically recognized in the Articles of Confederation. Article IV provided:[26]

"The better to secure and perpetuate mutual friendship and intercourse among the people of the different states in this union, the free inhabitants of each of these states[27] . . . [1] shall be entitled to all the privileges and immunities of free citizens in the several states; [2] *and the people of each state shall have free ingress and regress to and from*

any other state, [3] and shall enjoy therein all the privileges of trade and commerce . . . as the inhabitants thereof
respectively . . . [4] [and also the privilege of removing
their property]."

The Philadelphia Convention, as we saw while considering freedom of debate, took care to transfer important parts of the Articles of Confederation into the Constitution, with whatever changes of phrasing seemed appropriate. Article IV called for close study by the Convention
because of the strong need for improving commercial relations among the states. Hence it cannot be an oversight
that the Constitution specifically retains only two out of
the four numbered clauses in that Article. The third
clause about "privileges of trade and commerce" can be
regarded as embraced in the Interstate Commerce Clause.
The Constitution repeats the first clause almost verbatim,
in Article IV, section 2: "The Citizens of each State shall
be entitled to all Privileges and Immunities of Citizens in
the several States." But there is not a trace of the second
clause on "free ingress and regress," which I have italicized.

Two diametrically opposite interpretations are possible
when an important provision in a document is deliberately
omitted by the draftsmen of a later document. *First,* they
left it out in order to get rid of it as objectionable. *Second,*
they wanted to keep the provision operative, but considered that its substance was already embodied elsewhere
and left it out as superfluous. Here, of course, the first interpretation is impossible. The Convention carefully prevented states from passing tariff laws; surely it did not
want state immigration laws. So only the second interpretation is tenable. The reason for not expressly giving "free
ingress and regress" across state lines must be that it is in
the Constitution, somewhere else. But where?

The Debates on Article IV of the Constitution give us
little help. They show that the Privileges and Immunities

185

Clause was taken from the Articles of Confederation by the Pinckney draft, which from the very start omitted the second clause about "free ingress and regress" and the fourth clause about removal of property. The only objections were against leaving out this right to remove property. One delegate wished something said about property in slaves. That was about all, and the Privileges and Immunities Clause was left standing by itself.

One possible explanation of the omission of ingress and egress, though nothing was said in the Debates to that effect, is that freedom of movement was regarded as part of the "Privileges and Immunities of Citizens in the several States," which must also be given to citizens of another state without discrimination. For example, if Rhode Island allows Rhode Islanders to come in and go out as they please, it cannot exclude visitors from Massachusetts. Still, suppose Rhode Island law refuses to readmit any citizen who has been out of the state for over a week. Then there would be no discrimination in keeping out Massachusetts men who have never been in Rhode Island at all. However this may be, the Supreme Court has not relied on Article IV, section 2, to support the right to cross state-lines, and I shall disregard it in the rest of this chapter.

A much more hopeful substitute for the vanished "free ingress and regress to and from any other state" is in Article I, section 8, of the Constitution: "The Congress shall have power . . . To regulate Commerce . . . among the several States. . . ." Here too the Debates give no help. Though much was said about barriers at state-lines against goods, nobody spoke of barriers there against persons. Very likely none had been erected. They would have violated the Articles of Confederation and also what I have assumed to be the long practice in fact during the colonial period. So the silence in the Convention does not seem significant, and the Interstate Commerce Clause will be considered again in this chapter.

No other express clause in the Constitution could affect internal freedom of movement until after the Civil War. In 1868 the Fourteenth Amendment provided: "No State shall make or enforce any law which shall abridge the privileges or immunities of citizens of the United States. . . ." This clause and the familiar Due Process Clause which follows are also relevant to the subject of this chapter.

On external freedom of movement, too, no specific clause was put into the Constitution; but when the United States became a nation, Congress was able to make passage across our frontiers in or out as easy as it might desire. Its express powers over immigration, naturalization, and foreign commerce could serve that purpose.

The problem of migration into the western lands was finally solved by Article IV, section 3, which gave Congress power to govern the territory belonging to the United States. The Ordinance of 1787 had already encouraged mobility in the Northwest Territory by words which may have echoed in Lincoln's mind while he wrote the Emancipation Proclamation: "The navigable Waters leading into the Mississippi and St. Lawrence, and the carrying places between the same shall be common highways, and forever free. . . ."

Freedom of Movement under the Constitution

This chapter has brought out the strong and steadfast desire of the Englishmen who came to America and of the many generations born in the colonies for freedom of movement across frontiers in either direction and inside frontiers. It has shown their bitter resentment when this desire was balked by the faraway government in London which closed the western lands, and how one of the potent causes of Independence was the determination of Americans to be masters of their own freedom of movement.

What have we done with this mastery since we acquired it? I can best answer that question by considering how close we have come to attaining four different aspects of freedom of movement: (1) mobility inside the United States; (2) freedom to go out of the country; (3) freedom to come into it; (4) the right not to be exiled.

1. *Internal mobility*. It will be helpful to state this ideal by repeating the opening words of Article 13 of the Universal Declaration of Human Rights: "Every one has the right to freedom of movement and residence within the borders of each state [meaning 'nation']." Here at least hopes have turned into reality. Everybody agrees that the free passage of American citizens across state-lines is a constitutional right. Yet, as I indicated while speaking of the Philadelphia Convention, there is a queer uncertainty about what clause in the Constitution establishes this right. The question has been before the Supreme Court twice, with an interval of seventy-five years between.[28]

The first decision was *Crandall* v. *Nevada*[29] in 1867. Nevada had imposed a tax of one dollar on each person who left the state. This restriction on freedom of movement was unanimously held unconstitutional. But why?

The Interstate Commerce Clause was invoked against the tax, but only Justice Clifford and Chief Justice Chase upset it on that ground. Justice Miller, speaking for the large majority, was doubtful because the clause merely gives Congress power to regulate and does not expressly forbid the states to do anything. Since Congress had been silent about this tax, why should the clause apply? Miller's position is surely unsound. It runs counter to many solid decisions before and afterwards, that the clause itself deprives the states of power to impose serious burdens on

188

interstate commerce. Therefore, *if* stagecoach passengers are part of interstate commerce, they cannot be subjected to a state export tax. Yet are human beings engaged in commerce when they are not on business trips but traveling from state to state on pleasure bent or in search of new homes? This was the most interesting question in *Crandall* v. *Nevada,* and the Court paid no attention to it.

When the majority threw aside the Interstate Commerce Clause, they had to dig up something else which would get rid of the obnoxious tax. So Justice Miller found that somewhere between the lines of the Constitution there was a right of citizens to leave a state in order to go to the national capital, although there was no evidence in the case that any stagecoach passenger was bound for Washington.

The problem of interstate travel was illuminated more satisfactorily in 1941 by the cross-lights of *Edwards* v. *California.*[30] This time the state was not trying to discourage people from departing; instead, it strove to keep them out. Weary of attracting hordes of unwelcome settlers during the Depression because of its salubrious climate, California made it criminal for any of its citizens to bring in an indigent nonresident, knowing him to be such. A hospitable Californian induced his brother-in-law, who was on federal relief in Texas, to drive to the Land of Sunshine. Twenty dollars, which was all the Texan had, got used up before he joined his relatives. After two weeks of unemployment, he went on federal relief again. Thereupon, the hospitable Californian was sentenced to spend six months in jail. He stayed out because the Supreme Court again unanimously upheld the constitutional right to cross state lines. But again why?

A bare majority of five, through Justice Byrnes, rested entirely on the Interstate Commerce Clause. This, he said, prohibits "attempts of any single State to isolate itself

from difficulties common to all of them by the simple ex-
pedient of shutting its gates to the outside world." Federal
relief supersedes the atomistic theory of the Elizabethan
Poor Law, which I described early in this chapter. Still, I
would remind readers that even the Articles of Confederation denied "free ingress" into other states to paupers.

Out of the four Justices who concurred in nullifying
the California law, but for different reasons than the majority, three spoke through Justice Douglas.[31] He did not
reject the Interstate Commerce Clause; he left it aside
because "The right of persons to move freely from State to
State occupies a more protected position than does the
movement of cattle, fruit, steel and coal across state lines."
Thus Justice Douglas refused to lower the constitutional
principle to the level of Mr. Robert Young's argument for
continuous railroad passenger service from Coast to
Coast—"A hog can cross the Continent, why not a human
being?"

Justice Douglas stood on loftier ground than the Interstate Commerce Clause: "The right of free movement is
a right of national citizenship." To except the poor and
destitute from this right would contravene every conception of national unity. "It would prevent a citizen because
he was poor from seeking new horizons in other States."
On the contrary, "Mobility is basic to any question of freedom of opportunity."

These words breathe the spirit of hundreds of thousands of colonists who crossed the Atlantic in search of new
homes, went elsewhere if dissatisfied with their first
choice, and began opening the West.

"Americans are always moving on."
Yet should a law enacted by a sovereign state be nullified
unless it contravenes a specific clause of the Constitution?

Justice Jackson, concurring separately, put his finger on
such a clause. After agreeing with Justice Douglas that

190

persons desiring to cross state-lines with nothing to sell and no money to buy do not fit easily into the word "Commerce," Jackson preferred to protect them under the clause in the Fourteenth Amendment which forbids any state to abridge "the privileges or immunities of citizens of the United States." It is a privilege of the United States citizenship, he said, "to enter any State of the Union, either for temporary sojourn or the establishment of permanent residence therein." And he linked his decision to the history narrated in this chapter. Any requirement of local approval for a man's choice of his residence is "contrary to the inescapable implications of the westward movement of our civilization."

Despite inspiring statements in all the opinions, *Edwards* v. *California* leaves me somewhat troubled. When five Justices rely on one clause of the Constitution and four on a very different clause, there is no sharp warning to legislators who are eager to put up some new barrier along the borders of their state. Moreover, the needs for protecting freedom of movement across state-lines are not fully met by either of these clauses all by itself.

On one hand, it is risky to lean heavily on the Privileges and Immunities Clause alone. Nobody can be sure that a majority of the Justices in future cases will accept internal mobility as an attribute of United States citizenship. Over and over again, the Court has confined this clause to individual rights with some definite federal purpose like voting for a Congressman or assembling to discuss national issues. For example, it declared almost unanimously that United States citizenship confers no immunity against being run out of Arizona by a mob.[32] How then is a United States citizen entitled to override a state law and get into Arizona? And exclusive reliance on the Fourteenth Amendment leads to the unbelievable result that the Philadelphia Convention did nothing at all to preserve the vital assurance, in the Articles of Confederation, of "free ingress and regress to and from any other state." Unless the Interstate Commerce Clause gave freedom to cross state-lines, there was little or no protection between 1789 and 1868. Justice Miller's fanciful desire to facilitate trips to Washington would not help a Texan driving to California.

On the other hand, although I see no great difficulty in applying the Commerce Clause to the transportation of persons, whatever the purpose of their journeys—the Interstate Commerce Commission has long regulated passenger-fares and the Lindbergh Act punishes kidnappings across state-lines—still I agree with Justices Douglas and Jackson that the Commerce Clause is not enough. Freedom of movement is one of the most cherished of human rights; it ought to be more than an incident of federal-state relations. Together with other fundamental freedoms, it needs to be secured by the Constitution against arbitrary interference by either the states or the national government. And so far as the states are concerned, the Constitution did just this when the Commerce Clause was re-enforced by the Fourteenth Amendment—not in the Privileges and Immunities Clause but in the Due Process Clause.

Here is where I venture to differ from both groups of Justices in *Edwards* v. *California*. Why do we need to struggle through the swamp of the rights of United States citizens when we can walk on solid ground? Already in several decisions the Court has used the Due Process Clause to safeguard the right of the members of any race to reside where they please inside a state, regardless of ordinances and injunctions. Why is not this clause equally available to assure the right to live in any state one desires? And unreasonable restraints by the national government on mobility can be upset by the Due Process Clause in the

Fifth Amendment, if the *Schachtman* case on passports (to be discussed soon)[33] is upheld by the Supreme Court. Thus the "liberty" of all human beings which cannot be taken away without due process of law includes liberty of speech, press, assembly, religion, and also liberty of movement.

2. *Freedom to go out of this country*. Like internal mobility, this ideal is embodied in language signed by the United States in the Universal Declaration on Human Rights: "Everyone has the right to leave any country, including his own. . . ."

Until less than forty years ago this right was completely enjoyed by American citizens. To jump on a steamer in Boston and go to Liverpool was as easy as boarding the night-boat for New York. During the horse and buggy age, in which I was happily brought up, a passport was unknown except for Baedeker's remark that it might help you get permission to look at a private collection of paintings. The only country which required passports was Czarist Russia, and few Americans wanted to visit that despotic domain.

The Czars are dead, but many of their security measures live on. Passports have become obligatory throughout the free world.

The first limitation on outward freedom of movement was imposed by Congress in 1918, when passports were required for the rest of World War I. Although this statute soon expired, the insistence by foreign governments on passports made them a practical necessity between the wars for American travelers overseas. During World War II, the 1918 law was revived and expanded. An American citizen commits a crime when he enters or departs from the United States without a valid passport either in war or during the existence of a national emergency, which the President can proclaim if he finds that the national in-

193

terests require restrictions and prohibitions.[34] Such an emergency has been proclaimed down to date. The President is authorized to make exceptions, and it is still easy to go to Canada and some other neighboring countries. The main point is that a passport is indispensable to visit Europe, which has always been our chief outside source of ideas and inspiration.

Nothing in this legislation expressly allows the State Department to refuse to give a passport to anybody who fills out the necessary blank and pays the fee. The McCarran Act of 1950 does forbid the issue of passports to members of a Communist organization, which according to Congress includes the Communist Party of America;[35] but groups like that raise special questions which need not concern us here. The real problem is whether a hundred and sixty million American citizens who are not Communists have a right to visit the free countries of the world when they wish, or only when it pleases officials in Washington.

Scores of citizens have been denied passports in recent years without any charge that they are Communists. A Presidential Order says, "The Secretary of State is authorized in his discretion to refuse to issue a passport,"[36] and the State Department has behaved as if this discretion were absolute, as if a man had no more right to get a passport than to be appointed Ambassador to the Court of Saint James. Usually the only reason given for interfering with the lawful plans of an American citizen was that his "travel abroad at this time would be contrary to the best interests of the United States."

Let me give two examples. Dr. Martin D. Kamen, professor of radiation physics and biochemistry at Washington University in St. Louis, is an expert on the possibility of synthetic foods and on the use of radioactive tracers in the body for dealing with cancer and other diseases. He

194

was three times refused a passport, when he had been chosen for a visiting professorship in Australia and when he had been invited to scientific conferences in France and England. The State Department said he had dined with a Soviet vice-consul at a public restaurant, and two army intelligence agents at a nearby table had recorded their conversation about the possibility of treating radioactively a Russian consular official who was suffering from leukemia. The Atomic Energy Commission saw no objection to Dr. Kamen's leaving the country. Dr. Kamen's passport was granted in July, 1955, eight years after he first applied for it.

A prominent left-wing writer made a contract with a group of American newspapers to do a series of articles on the land-reform program in Italy and the effect of the Marshall Plan in that country. Then he was refused a passport to go to Italy on the ground that nothing "constructive" could be expected from his writings. The State Department intimated that it might reconsider its decision if he promised to write "constructively." He did so, but his passport was still withheld.

Foreign travel is not just a luxury for wealthy dilettantes. Over 300,000 Americans apply for passports every year. Men may go abroad for a livelihood. Businessmen and performing artists find European journeys lucrative. Foreign correspondents and lecturers on public affairs need first-hand information. Scientists and scholars gain greatly from consultations with colleagues in other countries. Students equip themselves for more fruitful careers in the United States by instruction in foreign universities. Then there are reasons close to the core of personal life— marriage, reuniting families, spending hours with old friends. Finally, travel abroad enables American citizens to understand that people like themselves live in Europe and helps them to be well-informed on public issues. An

American who has crossed the ocean is not obliged to form his opinions about our foreign policy merely from what he is told by officials of our government or by a few correspondents of American newspapers. Moreover, his views on domestic questions are enriched by seeing how foreigners are trying to solve similar problems. In many different ways direct contact with other countries contributes to sounder decisions at home.

In short, freedom to go out of the country has always been a very valuable asset for the United States. It is tragic that this freedom should be curtailed just when the ocean is more easily and rapidly crossed than ever before and at the very time when the lives of all Americans are much more seriously affected than in the past by what is done and thought outside our frontiers. When our government has to send soldiers abroad by the thousands although there is no fighting, it is a grave mistake for it to block the ambassadors of the mind.

And, except for fugitives from justice and perhaps a few plainly dangerous travelers, it is extremely unwise to allow government officials to determine who can go and who cannot go. One of the chief purposes of the First Amendment is to prevent any official from separating good ideas and bad ideas, for, as Jefferson emphasized in the Virginia Statute of Religious Toleration, the official is inclined as a human being to classify as bad the ideas with which he disagrees. Incidents like the denial of a passport for the left-wing writer to report on Italian affairs illustrate one of the worst evils of suppression of freedom of the press. It enables government officials to pursue their own policies by keeping the public from learning facts and ideas which may throw doubt on the soundness of those policies.

Regardless of the importance of a journey abroad to society, it is important to the traveler himself. Government officials in a free society ought to be very reluctant to forbid an individual to do what is dear to his heart, injures nobody else, and creates no clear danger to the safety of the nation, especially when the elected representatives of the people have not expressly made it illegal. Our nation has thrived on the principle that, outside areas of plainly harmful conduct, every American is left to shape his own life as he thinks best, do what he pleases, go where he pleases. Yet the passport policy of the State Department is based on the diametrically opposite principle that the citizen is not to decide whether his journey is desirable—instead, officials will make the decision for him.

Officials were restricting the freedom of movement of American citizens. Congress showed no interest in protecting them. The courts, it was long supposed, were helpless. At last judges began to vindicate this freedom. In 1952 they gave the rejected applicant for a passport the right to a hearing before the officials; he is no longer obliged to accept their say-so.[37] This procedural change did little to alter the policies of the State Department. Thus in 1954, Arthur Miller, who wrote *Death of a Salesman* and won the Pulitzer Prize, was not allowed to go to Brussels to see a performance of his own play *Crucible*. Finally, on June 23, 1955, the United States Court of Appeals for the District of Columbia upset the Department's denial of a passport, because it was based on insufficient reasons.[38] The arbitrary action of the United States government was taking away "liberty" in violation of the Due Process Clause in the Fifth Amendment.

If this decision in *Schachtman* v. *Dulles* is affirmed by the Supreme Court, it will go far to restore the freedom of citizens to cross our frontiers. Of course, most travelers do not plan a European trip far enough ahead to leave time for expensive litigation in Washington, but let us hope that the Department will alter its methods in ac-

197

cordance with judicial attitudes. The proper rule, I venture to think, would be the automatic issue of a passport to any citizen not expressly deprived of one by law, so long as he went through the usual formalities and paid the price. If any exceptions are desirable, the burden should be on the Department of immediately filing specific charges of unfitness against the traveler, and a quick court procedure should be provided because of the traveler's obvious need for a prompt decision.

Especially important in the Schachtman case is Judge Fahy's statement of the importance of this kind of freedom of movement: "The right to travel, to go from place to place as the means of transportation permit, is a natural right subject to the rights of others and to reasonable regulation under law. . . . Freedom to leave a country or a hemisphere is as much a part of liberty as freedom to leave a state."

3. *Freedom to come to this country.* At the time of the Constitution this was the kind of freedom of movement which mattered most. It had brought two million persons to our shores from the British Isles alone and enabled many others to find refuge from oppression on the Continent of Europe. The gates were open to permanent settlers for over a century more. Then they had to be closed. There is no longer enough room. Interesting questions arise about the best method for regulating the trickle of immigrants we still admit, but I shall not discuss them. Freedom to come and live in the United States is at an end.

There is plenty of room, however, for temporary visitors from abroad to land, look around, talk, learn, and let us learn from them. This is an entirely different problem and it does belong in this chapter.

Freedom of foreign travelers to enter the United States is the counterpart of freedom of American travelers to go

198

out of the country, which we have just been considering. Both kinds of freedom serve the same desirable purposes. They make it possible for men and women "to seek, receive and impart information and ideas regardless of frontiers."[39] And road-blocks against either inward or outward traffic produce the harms which President Truman forcibly described in July, 1951: "People who are denied the normal means of communication will not be able to attain that mutual understanding which must form the basis for trust and friendship. We shall never be able to remove suspicion and fear as potential causes of war until communication is permitted to flow, free and open, across international boundaries." Mr. Truman happened to be remonstrating against the refusal of a totalitarian government to allow its citizens to go abroad, but his words are equally applicable to the refusal of a democratic government like ours to allow foreign travelers to come in. What is the use of being able to leave your own country unless you are able to visit other countries?

An American traveler in Western Europe has all the liberty for which Mr. Truman hoped. Recently I entered five countries without a visa. No searching questions were asked about my beliefs or my personal life. I just had to exhibit my passport and open my luggage to show I had nothing dutiable, and on I went.

No similar freedom of movement is enjoyed by a Western European who wants to visit the United States. It may be harder for him to fly over the Atlantic to New York than it was for Marco Polo to go from Venice to the Court of Kubla Khan. A great many distinguished scholars and scientists, including several winners of the Nobel Prize, have been rejected by American officials or failed to get any decision on their applications after months of waiting. Several others whose presence in this country would have contributed much to our national defense and scientific progress have refused invitations to lecture or attend conferences because they would not go through scores of humiliating questions and endless delays.

Since detailed information is accessible about many eminent foreign scholars and scientists who have been kept out without having the remotest tinge of Communism,[40] I shall describe in general terms the three main obstacles which make us fall considerably short of Mr. Truman's ideal that communication should be "permitted to flow, free and open, across international boundaries."

First. The problem of admitting visitors has been scrambled in one law with the very different problem of what kinds of persons we want as permanent settlers. During the twentieth century, Congress has added category after category of aliens who are inadmissible because of objectionable ideologies or membership in objectionable associations. These restrictions apply without regard to the length of intended residence in the United States. Yet they are framed to determine the character of our permanent population. They express the prevailing national policy that when people wish to make new homes here, get steady jobs, and bring up their families, and probably become citizens in due course, they ought not to differ very much from the mass of Americans.

My main point is that for temporary visitors, such considerations are irrelevant. Indeed, differences in outlook may have advantages when our purpose is to build up mutual understanding as a basis for trust and friendship and to increase our knowledge from what foreign travelers tell us. You do not advance your knowledge very much by talking with people whose views are close to yours. Men with original ideas to give the world do not fall into orthodox patterns. If they did, they would probably be unable to tell us anything new. The only real question is—Will this visitor be dangerous as an individual during his brief stay? To put it in legal language, the sole test for a temporary visa might well be, whether the applicant is coming to the United States "for the purpose of engaging in activities which will endanger the public safety." Proof that he has arranged to give lectures or attend conferences here, under the sponsorship of a reputable university or scientific organization, etc., ought to go a long way to satisfy this test. And so should proof that he occupies a distinguished post in an important university in his own country or otherwise has a high reputation there for achievements.

Why are we so afraid? Just what do we really think a single unarmed man could do to us during a few weeks or months spent mostly in tough intellectual work and constant association with American scientists and scholars?

Now balance this risk against what we should gain by making it simple for able foreigners to visit us. Despite our vastly greater wealth, and our bigger and newer laboratories, Europe still goes on producing great and valuable scientific discoveries. American scientists know that they can learn very much from personal discussion with European colleagues. Professor Edward Shils of the University of Chicago points this out:[41] "The real advantage for science of free informal contact, the exchange of impressions and interpretations, the comparison of results and procedures in face-to-face conversations remains as great as it ever was." Holding international conferences in the United States makes it possible for American scientists to engage in these valuable interchanges without needing to spend much time or money. And we profit even more when a distinguished European spends some time at an American university delivering lectures and associating intimately with its members.

201

Yet such great opportunities are lost or seriously hampered by our present legislation and governmental practice, which put the admission of visitors for short periods on the same footing as the admission of immigrants under the quotas who intend to spend their lives in the United States.

It is true that the present law allows the Attorney General to grant dispensations to visitors who fall within the forbidden categories. But this simply prolongs the process of intimate questions and long delays which is involved in learning whether an eminent foreigner is in such a category—and most of those kept out do not in fact belong there. The important thing is to do away with this process which is so humiliating to distinguished scientists, and not merely to supplement it by the possibility of a review higher up.

Second. A feature of the present law which has aroused much indignation among European scholars is the concentration of the power to decide about a visitor's visa in the United States consul in the applicant's country. My suggestion is that, whatever the statutory requirements for temporary visas may be, such a visa should be handled in Washington whenever the foreigner concerned has been invited over to attend a conference or deliver lectures. The institution which has invited him could then arrange for his visa well in advance by conferring with the official who is customarily charged with this problem.

This administrative change would have many advantages. Centralized handling might develop a consistent policy toward eminent foreign visitors instead of the present scattered decisions by scores of consuls. They are diligent and valuable officers of our Foreign Service, but they are chiefly concerned with the legal tangles of American tourists and commercial matters like invoices on imported goods. Consuls cannot fairly be expected to understand the ranking of scientists, the merits of scholarly writing, or the ramifications of European radicalism. Sometimes they receive a leading scholar in his own country in the way a policeman would question a criminal. Often a consul does not take the trouble to look at books written by the applicants. One of them became suspicious of an eminent French mathematician for knowing Russian mathematics. If a single official in Washington made the decisions, he could readily familiarize himself with such matters. He would be helped by information gathered by the consul and by direct contact with American experts in the applicant's field of knowledge.

Third. Long delays in deciding on applications for visitors' visas do more harm than actual rejections in keeping out desirable foreigners and causing ill-will among foreign scholars. In many cases no decision is ever given. In many others, it comes when the conference is over or weeks after the lectures were scheduled to start at the American university. The resulting resentment of the applicants is shared by their colleagues abroad and makes several of them turn down invitations to come to this country. Visits to the United States ought to be as delightful to foreign scholars as visits to Europe are to us. Instead, our government turns the experience into agony before the foreigner reaches our shores. "Hope deferred maketh the heart sick."

Just look at the situation of a distinguished European professor who has been invited to spend several months in the United States and wants to take his family with him. He immediately applies for a visa and answers many disagreeable questions. He makes elaborate arrangements for the conduct of his laboratory during his absence, and somebody is engaged to teach his courses. Very likely he sublets his house or apartment to provide money for some of the traveling expenses. All this has to be settled well

203

in advance of sailing for the United States. Then he waits for the visa. And he waits. His wife is frantic. He takes her and the children to the port of departure. At last he gets news—his visa is rejected. Or still nothing happens. The American trip is called off with everything at home in a mess. Although action by Congress would be necessary to relax the restrictions on temporary visitors and to end the autocratic power of consuls, only the officials are to blame for this exasperating slowness.

4. *Freedom from exile.* Few experiences can be bitterer for a man than being torn from his home and forced to start all over again among strangers in a strange land. Think what it would mean to you to be banished forever from the country where you have lived since childhood, gone to school, spent all your active career; to be deprived of congenial well-done work for which you were trained; to be cut off from all your friends and from your wife and children too unless you ask them to leave the place where they were born and go among foreigners to share your isolation and struggles to keep alive.

The point I want most to stress is that the hardships of exile have no necessary connection with the nationality of the banished person. Exile is leaving the place where a man really lives, where he has his roots down, even if the law there classifies him as an alien. Suppose an unnaturalized Italian whose parents brought him to Brooklyn at the age of two, who has lived in Brooklyn ever since, worked on Flatbush Avenue, married a Brooklyn girl, had three boys born in Brooklyn, and cheered for the Dodgers at dozens of games. Suppose he is deported to Italy where he knows nobody and cannot speak a word of the language. The law calls him an Italian, but he is far more of an exile in Italy than Bernard Berenson, an American citizen and art critic who has spent years at

204

his beautiful villa in Settignano within easy reach of the Uffizzi Galleries.

I urge Americans when they consider the desirability of our deportation policies to look at the facts of particular situations. Do not let them be hidden by words in law-books. Suffering comes from facts, not words. Ask yourselves what is happening to human beings.

Individuals were sporadically banished in ancient times. The Athenians ostracized Aristides, weary of hearing him called "the Just," and Thucydides wrote his great history in exile. Cicero's enemies marooned him in Asia Minor and the Emperor Augustus sent Ovid to the Black Sea. Sad to relate, it was religious zeal which first brought about deportations on a large scale. Edward I drove 15,000 Jews out of England; the Spanish Kings harried Jews and Moors out of Spain. Then crime came to be systematically punished by exile. The British government transported thousands of convicts to the American colonies and later to Australia, but this practice ended about 1850. Meanwhile, political activities were only an occasional cause for banishment from England as in the bills of pains and penalties against Clarendon and Atterbury.[42] In the nineteenth century, the Czars began mass deportations to Siberia for political beliefs and activities, and subsequent totalitarian rulers have been merciless in moving populations around. Finally, as civilization advanced, the wholesale removal of people from their homes became the concluding horror of almost any war. In times of peace, however, most of the free world is now preserving the right to stay where you live. The only nation on our side of the Iron Curtain which inflicts extensive deportations by its ordinary laws is the United States of America.

The Constitution says nothing about the power of Congress to enact deportation laws. I surmise that the idea of such laws would have been repulsive to men of that

205

time. Banishments were a thing of the remote past when the Puritans ejected Roger Williams and Anne Hutchinson from Massachusetts. Even the detested Alien Law of 1798 merely interned foreigners on the eve of an expected war, but did not deport them. Genêt the French Minister, who behaved about as subversively as any alien in our midst ever did, merely lost his official status; he was allowed to remain here and become an American citizen. Very likely the Constitution would have failed of ratification if the members of the state conventions had been told that the proposed national government would be able to throw people out of this country.

For many decades freedom from exile stayed unimpaired. Then dislike for Chinese laborers and the shocking assassination of President McKinley by a violent anarchist impelled Congress to start passing deportation statutes. Its power to do so was upheld by the Supreme Court a century after the Constitution was adopted, as an unmentioned incident of national sovereignty.[43] During the past fifty years Congress has ordered more and more classes of aliens to be deported, no matter how long they have been here, if officials find forbidden beliefs or membership in an organization which is held to further such beliefs, even though the alien does not agree with them and joined the group because of his interest in some of its legitimate purposes.

Virtually every kind of alien who can be excluded for his ideas or associations when he applies for admission can also be thrown out of the country. Thus the law scrambles two kinds of proceedings which often have very different consequences in causing hardship. Exclusion merely sends the alien back to the home he has just left. Prompt deportation may not be much more severe. Suppose he is let in when he ought not to have been; the government soon discovers its mistake and rectifies it by getting him to his old home only a little later than if he had not been admitted. The situation wholly changes when the alien has been in the United States for years. His old home has been submerged, his old friends are scattered. He has a new home here, a permanent job, a family with all but himself American citizens. Nevertheless, his freedom to stay where he lives never becomes established so far as his intellectual and social life is concerned. The Deportation Laws have had a time-limit for insanity, but there is no time-limit against exile for radical ideas.

The proscribed categories of course include violent anarchists and conspiratorial Communists, but the authorities are also required to deport radicals with much milder views. For instance, they have expelled philosophical anarchists who follow Kropotkin in wanting to substitute friendly co-operation for the use of force by the government or anybody else and never acted on their beliefs, as Thoreau did when he refused to pay taxes, but have always been law-abiding members of the community.[44] Mere membership in the Communist Party of America is a ground for deportation, although the McCarran Act of 1950 declares that it is not a crime. Some of the deportable groups are so vaguely defined as to violate Blackstone's basic principle that a law ought to tell people clearly what acts are wrongful before they do them and incur severe penalties.[45]

In its eagerness to get Harry Bridges back to Australia, Congress made the Deportation Laws as retroactive as possible.[46] An alien is deportable who "has been at any time" in one of the forbidden classes, before or after he entered the United States, no matter how long ago. Radical beliefs may have been replaced by hardshell conservatism and business success. Or he may have joined a leftish group while in college and repented before graduating. Membership in this group may not have been a cause for

deportation when he belonged to it. It makes no difference. Out he goes.

About the only right the alien has, except not being
forced to cross the Atlantic in a sailing-vessel of ten tons
like Sir Humphrey Gilbert, is that he must be given a
hearing. This is not before a judge or a jury. What happens is that officials from the same Department which
filed deportation charges against him decide whether
those charges have been sustained. It used to be the Department of Labor, which was concerned with many aspects of welfare, so that the alien had some chance of being
judged by officials with a humanitarian outlook. Now it
is the Department of Justice, which is largely composed
of policemen and prosecutors.

When officials in this Department think that an alien
is possibly deportable, they can put him in jail and keep
him imprisoned until the charges against him are found
to be true. Although a person awaiting trial for a crime
can go home on bail until he is convicted, except in cases
of very serious offenses like murder, nevertheless an alien
accused of some ground for deportation has no right to
bail even when this ground is not a crime at all. It is
enough for the Attorney General or some subordinate to
find that public safety requires the man's incarceration.
Then no court can let him out.[47] This practice runs directly counter to the principle that a man is presumed innocent until he is proved guilty. Ever since the Petition
of Right prevented Charles I from shutting men up on
his own say-so,[48] it has been one of the great tradi-
tions of English-speaking freedom that, as Judge Edgerton
said in the *Schachtman* passport case:[49] "Those who inflict
a deprivation of liberty are not the final arbiters of its
legality."

Congress began by curtailing freedom to stay in the
United States and ended by curtailing the still more pre-

cious right of liberty of the person inside the United States. It has enabled government officials, without a jury verdict or a court order or a charge of crime, to put men and women into prison for months or even years on American soil.

By now it is evident that the present chapter fits much more imperfectly than my other two chapters into a book on Human Rights in the Constitution. Freedom of Movement is a valuable human right, but is it in the Constitution? Only part way. Freedom to live where one pleases inside the United States is in it somewhere, as the Supreme Court has established, and the freedom of a citizen to leave this country has at last been recognized by a lower court. However, the freedom of foreigners to come into this country is inevitably outside the Constitution, and their freedom to stay in the homes they have made here is almost equally unprotected. Since deportation is not regarded as a punishment, although it is more painful than the punishments visited upon fairly serious crimes, it is not subject to the prohibition against ex post facto laws or to the safeguards which the Bill of Rights ensures in criminal prosecutions. There is no right to bail, as we have just seen. The First Amendment has never been held to impose any restriction whatever on deportations for what an alien believes, speaks, or publishes, or for his part in assemblies. At all events, many men and women have been torn from their homes by immigration officials for beliefs, utterances, and conduct which Supreme Court decisions have held to be immune from criminal prosecutions and other forms of governmental interference. The upshot of all this is that, where it is a question of deportations, aliens, no matter how long they have lived in the United States, are at the mercy of Congress.

Congress has thus far shown very little mercy. It does not follow, however, that this will always be the case. As was true of freedom of debate, its possession of almost unlimited power over freedom to stay in the United States puts on Congress a solemn responsibility to be sure that its power is used justly. Perhaps Congress and the public to which it is accountable will reconsider in calmer times the Deportation Laws which were enacted in periods of great strain like the Fall of France and the fighting in Korea.

Looking forward to such a reconsideration of the problems of freedom from exile, I shall say no more about law but urge that we Americans look at three kinds of facts. The first is, what harm do we really think most of the radical aliens in our midst could do to us, leaving out violent revolutionaries and perhaps those who would be worth prosecuting under the Smith Act? The second fact is the human suffering which deportation will inflict on a great many of the persons who are described by the existing laws. The third fact is that radical aliens are men and women, most of whose days and nights are not concerned with the opinions which we detest, but are filled with normal occupations and emotions and family ties just like our own lives. Some people do not see why we should bother about what is suffered by aliens who have long been here—it's their own fault that they didn't become American citizens. Yet there is nothing wicked about being an unnaturalized alien. Herbert Hoover had that status in China and England for decades before he became Secretary of Commerce and President. The same is true of hundreds of American businessmen abroad. A good many aliens here who have long been law-abiding and completely orthodox are reluctant to apply for naturalization because of some youthful indiscretion, which would have to be disclosed and might cause them great trouble. Finally, American citizenship ought to be sought as a proud privilege. We cheapen it greatly if we tell every alien to become a citizen as a prudent precaution against being deported, just as religious faith is degraded when men are forced to profess it in order to avoid drastic persecution.

What is happening to human beings? Look at two women and a man in recent deportation cases in the Supreme Court.

Mrs. Dora Coleman came to the United States from Russia at the age of thirteen. She married an American citizen and has three citizen-children. She became a member of the Communist Party three times because of some injustice the Party was fighting, and quit after a year or two each time. She first joined at eighteen and last got out in 1938, when she was about thirty-five. She held no office; her activities were not significant. Eleven years after she finally left the Party, she was arrested and held deportable. In 1952 the Supreme Court decided that she could not stay in the country where she had spent thirty-five years—half a lifetime.[50]

John Zydok was fifty-six years old when his case was decided. He came from Poland to the United States at seventeen, and lived here ever since. He owned his home, had violated no law, had a wife, two sons, a daughter, and five grandchildren, all born in this country and American citizens. Both sons were in the armed forces in World War II. Zydok, who was then a waiter, sold $50,000 in war bonds to customers and friends, and donated blood to the Red Cross for the army seven times.

During 1949 Zydok became a member of the Communist Party and was financial secretary of a local unit. Perhaps there was also some minor participation in Communist affairs. The lower court expressly found that he was "not likely to engage in any subversive activities." Zydok was soon arrested, and put in prison to protect the public safety until the officials could decide whether to ship him to Poland after thirty-nine years of absence. He tried to get out on bail, but the majority of the Supreme Court Justices felt obliged to accept the Attorney General's judgment that Zydok was too dangerous to be at large,[51] although the eleven top-string Communist leaders were then at home on bail after getting convicted under the Smith Act.[52]

Mrs. Miriam Stevenson was born in England in 1907 and at twelve migrated to Canada with her family. She came to the United States in 1923 at sixteen and settled in Los Angeles. After her marriage to an American citizen during a few hours' visit to Mexico in 1938, she sought naturalization but was discouraged because of some question as to the legality of her entry, either from Canada or Mexico. She had a son, an American citizen. In 1949, when her son was afflicted with undulant fever, she was arrested for deportation on the charge of currently being a member of the Communist Party. She had been a Unit Organizer and a member of the Hollywood Subsection Committee in 1936, and secretary of a unit in 1938. The evidence of subsequent affiliations was her participation in a Lenin celebration at Los Angeles and her admission in 1948 of attending Communist meetings and also of membership in the American League for Peace and Democracy and being a correspondent of the People's Education Center. Both these organizations had been listed as Communist by the Attorney General. On the basis of this proof, she was imprisoned without bail. The boy needed her nursing. Her seventy-year-old mother needed her help at home. So did her husband. The district judge tried to get the immigration authorities to agree to bail, but they refused, insisting that she must be detained in jail as "dangerous" to our national security. And there a majority of 5 to 4 in the Supreme Court left her.[53]

I do not say that these imprisonments were unlawful, as the dissenters contended. I do not say that they were

212

undesirable, although that is not the same thing. What is lawful may be detestable. It was lawful to behead Strafford by Act of Parliament. It was lawful to imprison John Bunyan for years.

What I do say is that we have wandered a long way from the kind of country we loved; and it is time to stop and look over the distance which separates us from what we once were. It is time to ponder whether it is worth while to do all we have done to men and women such as I have been describing, whether freedom should be sacrificed so much as this to fear.

I have been asking what is happening to the aliens we deport. Now I ask what is happening to ourselves. Why are we doing this? Why are we so afraid? What kind of country is it that does not dare let a mother go home to nurse a boy with undulant fever and has to lock up a man who gave his blood seven times to the Red Cross?

Notes

INTRODUCTION

1. See Chafee, *How Human Rights Got into the Constitution* (1952), for a fuller exposition of the scope of my inquiry. Chaps. I and II, after rapidly pointing out the various human rights in the Constitution, discuss at length the general background of these rights in America and England, viz., proceedings in Congress before and after the Declaration of Independence, the Articles of Confederation, early state constitutions, colonial charters, and English history.

2. (Boston University Press, 1952), chap. 3.

3. Learned Hand, J., in United States v. Kirschenblatt, 16 F. 2d 202 at 203 (C.C.A. 2d, 1926).

4. Robert Frost, "The Wood-pile."

5. Since the present book is, to some extent, a continuation of *How Human Rights Got into the Constitution,* I have thought it appropriate to repeat some sentences (from p. 74) which state the principal theme of both books.

FREEDOM OF DEBATE IN CONGRESS

1. For the reader's convenience, footnotes in this book have been kept fewer than would be possible if references were given to the sources for every statement. Instead, I have placed at the close of the book a long "Note on Sources."

2. Md. Decln. of Rights, Art. VIII (1776); Mass. Decln. of Rights, Art. XXI (1780); N.H. Bill of Rights, Art. XXX (1784). N.Y. Cons. Art IX (1777): "That the assembly . . . shall enjoy the same privileges . . . as the assemblies of the colony of New-York formerly did." New York adopted on January 26, 1787, a legislative Bill of Rights expressly recognizing freedom of debate. See 2 *Laws of the State of New York,* 1785-88 (republished by the Secy. of State, 1886) 345. Perhaps New Jersey and South Carolina can be added to these four states. Their 1776 constitutions declare that the common law of England should still remain in force; and it is arguable that freedom of debate was part of the common law. On the recognition of freedom of debate by other states before and after the Constitution, see Frankfurter, J., in Tenney v. Brandhove, 341 *United States Reports* 367 (1951) at 373-376.

3. Strictly, Halifax was only Viscount at this time; but he was made Marquis soon afterwards, and it is the title by which he is commonly known.

4. Charles II received the last rites from a Benedictine monk; but, whenever this secret conversion took place, it was not disclosed until after his death and had no effect upon the public attitude toward him or upon his constitutional position.

5. 1 James II, chap. 2 (1685); 5 New Parliamentary History 1362-1365 (1808).

6. Macaulay, *History of England,* chap. 4.

7. W. S. Lilly, article on "England" in 5 *Catholic Encyclopaedia* at 451-452 (1909). See also Edwin Burton's account of the Revolution of 1688, 13 *id.* 7; and Michael Ott on Innocent XI, 8 *id.* 22.

8. See the concluding chapter of W. K. Jordan, *The Development of Religious Toleration in England,* 1640-1660 (1940).

9. Luttrell, *A Brief Historical Relation of State Affairs* 442, 448 (1857).

10. Compare Article I, section 8, clause 12 of the Constitution with the Mutiny Act (1689); Article III, section 1, with the Act of Settlement (1701); Article III, section 3, with the Trials for Treason Act (1696); and the First Amendment with the Toleration Act (1689). These English statutes are re-

printed in Stephenson & Marcham, 605-612 *passim.* The Trials for Treason Act affected the case of Sir John Fenwick, discussed in chap. II.

11. Macaulay, *History of England,* chap. 10. I have made some omissions without indicating them.

12. See the case of Sir John Coventry in 1670, in Macaulay's *History,* chap. 2; 12 *Dictionary of National Biography* 358.

13. *Infra,* pp. 81-83.

14. D. Pasquet, *An Essay on the Origins of the House of Commons* (translated by R. G. D. Laffan) 115-116 (1925).

15. *Infra,* pp. 102-103.

16. 4 Henry VIII, chap. 8 (1512).

17. Strictly in Oxfordshire, but the manor of Lillingstone Lovell was like an island surrounded by Buckinghamshire, into which it was later absorbed. Compare Brookline, Massachusetts, an isolated portion of Norfolk County.

18. Over the portal of Langdell Hall at Harvard Law School are inscribed in the original Latin, these words of Henry de Bracton, who in the thirteenth century wrote on the law of England, *"Non sub homine sed sub deo et lege."*

19. Some omissions in the ensuing quotations from this pamphlet are not indicated.

20. See 4 Holdsworth, *History of English Law* 88-97 (1924).

21. S. T. C. #8668, in the Houghton Library, Harvard. On the earlier proclamation of December 24, 1620, S. T. C. #8649, see 4 Gardiner, *History of England* 117-118.

22. See J. M. Landis, "Constitutional Limits on the Congressional Power of Investigation," 40 *Harvard Law Review* 153 (1926), at 189-190.

23. *Supra,* pp. 30-31.

24. Thomas Crewe of Northampton, 1 New Parliamentary History 1359-1360. I have slightly modernized the punctuation and sentence-structure.

25. The words *"de arduis et urgentibus negotiis regni"* in the Writ of Summons have been translated, and I have slightly expanded this head so as to bring out its meaning.

26. For the sake of easier reading, I have broken the Protestation into separate paragraphs.

27. There was a quiet last sitting next morning (December 19th), when the King adjourned this Parliament until February. It never met again.

28. On the same day his horse threw him into a small river, so that "nothing but his boots were seen." His riding companion jumped into the water and pulled him out.

29. The Five Knights' Case and the Petition of Right are discussed at length in Chafee, *How Human Rights Got into the Constitution* 64-72 (1952).

30. S. R. Gardiner, *History of England in the Reigns of James I and Charles I,* at the close of chap. 68. I have not indicated several omissions from this passage.

31. Clarendon's account, in volume 1 of his *History of the Rebellion and Civil Wars* of events in late December of 1641 and January of 1642 is reprinted in large part in 3 Chafee, *Documents on Fundamental Human Rights* 867-885. Omissions from Clarendon's text are not always indicated in the quotations from him in the present chapter, and his punctuation is occasionally altered.

32. Under our Constitution, it seems impossible to impeach a member of either House of Congress. He is not holding a "civil office" (Art. I, sec. 6, cl. 2); and only "civil officers" are removable by impeachment (Art. II, sec. 4). In 1797 the Senate refused to let Senator Blount of Tennessee be impeached, and then expelled him by a two-thirds vote.

33. *Infra,* p. 104.

34. The Earl of Bristol's Case is in 2 Howell's *State Trials* 1267 (1626). Charles accused Bristol in order to head him off from giving deadly testimony in the pending impeachment of Buckingham. The dissolution of Parliament broke off the proceedings against both these nobles. See also the life of Bristol in 15 *Dictionary of National Biography* 56.

35. The brother of Pride was also in the Massachusetts Bay Colony and gave his name to Pride's Crossing.

36. 12 *Lords Journals* 164-166.

37. See *supra*, pp. 64-69. Sir George Croke's *Reports of the Reign of Charles I* in Norman-French were translated into English by his son-in-law, Sir Harbottle Grimston. Eliot's Case is at p. 181.

38. *Infra*, pp. 116-118.

39. *Supra*, pp. 27-28.

40. See the life of Vaughan (1603-1674) by J. M. Rigg in 58 *Dictionary of National Biography* 167 (1899). Bushell's Case, 6 Howell's *State Trials* 951 (1670) concerned one of the jurors who were imprisoned for acquitting William Penn when he preached in the London streets. The cases of both Penn and Bushell are reprinted in 2 Chafee, *Documents on Fundamental Human Rights* 306 ff.

41. 12 *Commons Journals* 166. Capitalization and punctuation have been slightly altered.

42. 3 Howell's *State Trials* 332-333 (April 15, 1668).

43. 6 *Diary of Samuel Pepys* (Wheatley ed.) 199.

44. Justice Miller in Kilbourn v. Thompson, 103 *United States Reports* 168, at 204-205 (1881).

45. Cochran v. Couzens, 42 *Federal Reporter*, 2nd Series, 783 (District of Columbia Court of Appeals, 1930).

46. Coffin v. Coffin, 4 *Massachusetts Reports* 1, at 32-33 (1808). See Sir Erskine May's *Parliamentary Practice* (15th ed., 1950) 63-64.

47. See the colloquy between Chief Justice Parsons and Attorney General Bidwell, 4 Mass. at 10-11.

48. Justice Miller in Kilbourn v. Thompson, *supra*, note 44, at 203-204.

49. This question was presented by the facts in a libel suit by General Samuel T. Ansell against Senator Huey P. Long of Louisiana; but it was not put in issue by the defendant or considered by either appellate court. All that was decided was that a Senator has no constitutional privilege not to be sued during the session. Long v. Ansell, 69 *Federal Reporter*, 2nd Series, 386 (District of Columbia Court of Appeals, 1934) affirmed in 293 *United States Reports* 76 (1934).

50. Quoted by Justice Frankfurter in Tenney v. Brandhove, 341 *United States Reports* 367, at 373 (1951). To the same effect was Chief Justice Parsons of Massachusetts in the case cited *supra*, note 46; he was quoted with approval in the case cited *supra*, note 44.

51. Justice Prettyman in Barsky v. United States, 167 *Federal Reporter*, 2nd Series, 241, at 250 (District of Columbia Court of Appeals, 1948).

52. American Law Institute, 3 *Restatement of the Law of Torts* §611.

53. Both these pieces of research are listed in the "Note on Sources."

54. This recommendation was signed by all the members of the committee. Later, one Senator changed his mind for reasons which may have convinced himself.

55. 100 *Congressional Record* 16360-16381 (Dec. 2, 1954).

56. Dissenting in People v. Gitlow, 234 *New York Reports* 132, at 158 (1922).

THE PROHIBITION OF BILLS OF ATTAINDER

1. Observe that the Convention trusted Congress, but not the state legislatures, to act wisely about impairing the obligation of contracts. See Home Bldg. & Loan Assn. v. Blaisdell, 290 *United States Reports* 398, at 427-429 and 453-465 (1934). Subsequently, the Fifth Amendment took some of this power away when it prohibited Congress from arbitrarily depriving any person of "property." Lynch v. United States, 292 *id.* 571 (1934).

2. Georgia Constitution of 1877, as amended in 1908, § 2-604(4); Georgia Constitution of 1945, § 2-704.

3. The Universal Declaration of Human Rights is reprinted in 3 Chafee, *Documents on Fundamental Human Rights* 956 (1952).

4. Shepherd v. People, 25 *New York Reports* 406 (1862). Some facts are taken from the opinion in an earlier appeal, 19 *id.* 537 (1859).

5. In New York thirty years later, doubts were cast on the Shepherd case by Judge Rufus Peckham, who said "if the change be of that nature which no sane man could by any possibility regard in any other light than that of a mitigation of punishment," it can validly apply to previous offenses. People v. Hayes, 140 *id.* 484, at 492 (1894). In the United States Supreme Court, Justice Harlan remarked that "the court must assume that every rational person desires to live as long as he may." Rooney v. North Dakota, 196 *United States Reports* 319, at 326 (1905). See also Justice Holmes in Biddle v. Perovich, 274 *id.* 480 (1927). Changes from death to life imprisonment, after the offense, were held valid in Massachusetts and Mississippi.

6. Some German opinions to the contrary under the National Socialist regime are discussed by Jerome Hall, *General Principles of Criminal Law* 30 (1947).

7. New York Laws, 1777-1783, chap. 25, pp. 85-91 (Oct. 22, 1779); reprinted in 3 Chafee, *op cit. supra*, note 3, at 713, with references to bills of attainder in other states during the Revolution.

8. (1352), reprinted in Stephenson & Marcham, *Sources of English Constitutional History* 227 (1937).

9. *Supra*, p. 17.

10. *Henry VI*, Part II, Act IV, scene 2.

11. Trial of Lord de Clifford, [1936] Weekly Notes 4, gives an interesting account of the ceremonial on the preceding December 12th.

12. Criminal Justice Act, 1948. 11 & 12 George VI, chap. 58, §30.

13. See Roger de Mortimer's case in 1330, 3 Chafee, *Documents on Fundamental Human Rights* 646 (1952).

14. 4 Coke, Institutes 37-38.

15. Act of 16 Charles I, chap. 38; reprinted in 3 Chafee, *Documents on Fundamental Human Rights* 654 (1952).

16. See Buckle's stimulating account of the intellectual achievements during the reign of Charles II in chap. 7 of his *History of Civilization in England* (1857).

17. 1 Browning, *Thomas Osborne: Earl of Danby and Duke of Leeds* 567-568 (1951).

18. *Op. cit. supra*, note 17, at 27-28.

19. 1 Bishop Burnet, *History of His Own Time* 94-95.

20. The First Test Act is 25 Charles II, chap. 2 (1673); reprinted in Stephenson & Marcham, *op. cit. supra*, note 8, at 555.

21. 1 Browning *op. cit. supra*, note 17, at 218.

22. *Id.*, 270.

23. 1 *A Collection of Parliamentary Debates in England from the Year 1668*, 225 (Dublin, 1741). Some immaterial omissions are not indicated.

24. See, for example, two Acts of 1605, after the Gunpowder Plot: 3 James I, chaps. 4, 5.

25. 1 Browning, *op. cit. supra*, note 17, at 197-198.

26. *Id.*, 291.

27. U.S. Constitution, Art. I, sec. 6. For the English law, see the Case of John Wilkes, 19 Howell's *State Trials* 981 (1763); reprinted in 2 Chafee, *Documents on Fundamental Human Rights* 341 (1951). See also *supra*, p. 30.

28. It is commonly stated that Charles put these words on Danby's original letters before they were sent to Montagu. Browning, *op. cit. supra*, at 309 note, gives strong reasons for thinking that the King wrote on the two drafts kept by Danby, and did so on the Sunday which intervened between the adoption of the charges in the Commons on Saturday and their delivery to the Lords on Monday. Thus Charles acted just in time to solidify Danby's defense. The words written by Charles are reported differently in the Parliamentary Debates, but I follow Browning's version with its royal misspelling.

29. Carnarvon was, of course, not referring to the second Duke, who had filled him with wine, but to his father, the first Duke, who (as hitherto narrated) was impeached in 1626 and assassinated in 1629.

30. *Supra*, pp. 64-68, 73-78.

31. This decision was formally reversed by the House of Lords in 1685 when Danby was finally released from the impeachment. The question whether an impeachment carries over into a new session of Congress has not, I think, been decided. An affirmative answer is suggested by the fact that the Senate is a continuous body.

32. The records of the Philadelphia Convention indicate that the exclusion of impeachments from the pardoning power was suggested by John Rutledge (2 Farrand 146 and 171-172). Perhaps Rutledge can be shown to have read about the Danby case. The debates dealt only with the wording of this clause (2 *id.* 411, 419-420). An interesting suggestion was made and immediately dropped, that a pardon could not be granted until "after conviction" (2 *id.* 422). This would annul any pardon which came before trial as Danby's did. Yet President Wilson did grant an anticipatory pardon, though for specified offenses and not in blanket form like Charles II. Burdick v. United States, 236 *United States Reports* 79 (1915).

33. The article on "Impeachment" by Lewis Mayers in 7 *Encyclopaedia of Social Sciences* 600 (1932) says: "In England impeachment will in theory lie against all crimes and misdemeanors, even though wholly unrelated to the public service and against offenders of all ranks." However, the Lords in 1681 refused to entertain the impeachment for high treason of Fitzharris, an informer against the Popish Plot after men had become skeptical about it. The Lords thought that this commoner belonged in a common-law court, where he was subsequently convicted and then hanged, drawn, and quartered. 8 Howell's *State Trials* 223, at 231. The famous impeachment of Dr. Sacheverell in 1710 for preaching seditious sermons at St. Paul's in London can perhaps be regarded as directed against a public servant, since he was a minister of the Established Church (15 *id.* 1). Private persons may have come to be exempt from impeachments in England as in the United States, where their purpose is only to remove men from office and disqualify them for the future. The Constitution (Art. II, sec. 4) makes impeachments lie only against the President, the Vice-President, "and all civil officers of the United States."

34. Trials for Treason Act (1696), 7 & 8 William III, chap. 3; reprinted in Stephenson & Marcham, *op. cit. supra,* note 8, at 609: ". . . no person . . . whatsoever shall be indicted, tried, or attainted of high treason . . . but by and upon the oaths and testimony of two lawful witnesses . . ., unless the party . . . shall willingly, without violence, in open court confess the same, or shall stand mute or refuse to plead." If the word "attainted" refers to bills of attainder, this statute was repealed *ad hoc* by Parliament in the Act of Attainder against Fenwick.

35. Constitution, Art. III, sec. 3: "No Person shall be convicted of Treason unless on the Testimony of two Witnesses *to the same overt Act* or on Confession in open Court." The italicized phrase is not in the English statute of 1695. See Cramer v. United States, 325 *United States Reports* 1 (1945); Willard Hurst, "Treason in the United States," 58 *Harvard Law Review* 226, 395, 806 (1944).

36. Macaulay, *History of England* (1st ed., 1855), chap. 22. The same ideas are rephrased in a passage in chap. 23, but less vividly.

37. See Macaulay's essay on Hastings, which despite some inaccuracies remains a magnificent achievement.

38. Constitution, Art. II, sec. 4.

39. Constitution, Art. I, sec. 3. See also Alexander Hamilton in *The Federalist,* Nos. 65, 66.

40. "Naturam expellas furca, tamen usque recurret."—Horace, Epistles, Bk. I, ep. 10, line 24.

41. 86 *Congressional Record* 8203 (June 13, 1940). The debate runs from p. 8181 to p. 8214, where the vote is recorded. The speech of Mr. Hobbs against the bill is on 8201-8202.

42. Justice Holmes in Bagajewitz v. Adams, 228 *United States Reports* 585, at 591 (1913), holding a statute not to be an ex post facto law which made prior conduct a cause for deportation. A recent decision to the same effect is Harisiades v. Shaughnessy, 342 *id.* 580 (1952); Justices Black and Douglas dissented on the ground that an alien has the right to be immune from arbitrary banishment.

43. Dissenting in the last case cited in note 42.

44. The general law, combined with the Smith Act in a single statute, was held to be valid in the Harisiades case cited in note 42. It did not succeed against Bridges because proof of past Communist connections was held insufficient by the Supreme Court in 1945. Bridges v. Wixon, 326 *id.* 135 (1945). For ten years more, the government tried in vain to establish that Bridges was a Communist. In 1955 it gave up. *New York Times,* October 1, 1955, p. 22. It took no appeal from United States v. Bridges, 135 *Federal Supplement* 638 (Cal. 1955).

45. 328 *United States Reports* 303 (1946); reprinted in 3 Chafee, *Documents on Fundamental Human Rights* 752 (1952).

46. 89 *Congressional Record* 4605 (May 18, 1943).

47. Only eight Justices sat in this case; Justice Jackson took no part. The majority comprised Chief Justice Stone and Justice Black, Douglas, Murphy, Rutledge, and Burton. The concurring opinion by Justice Frankfurter was joined in by Justice Reed.

48. Myers v. United States, 272 *United States Reports* 52 (1926).

49. I have not discussed Justice Frankfurter's reasons for letting the three officials recover judgments against the government for their salaries, even if the rider was constitutional. It raises technical questions remote from the subject of this chapter.

Even after the Supreme Court had held the rider to be a bill of attainder, the House of Representatives almost refused to appropriate money to pay these judgments. Mr. Sam Hobbs got the item passed by a margin of only one vote (99-98). 93 *Congressional Record* 2991 (April 1, 1947). Probably judgments based on any other theory would not have been paid by Congress.

50. The argument here regarded as absurd was actually advanced a half century ago by a New York lawyer, who was subsequently a resourceful breeder of dairy cattle. E. Parmalee Prentice, "Congress, and the Regulation of Corporations," 19 *Harvard Law Review* 168, at 173-174 (1906).

51. See Chafee, "The Disorderly Conduct of Words," 41 *Columbia Law Review* 381, at 398-404 (1941).

52. *Supra,* pp. 97-98.

53. 4 *Wallace Reports* 277 and 333 (U.S. 1867); both reprinted in 3 Chafee, *Documents on Fundamental Human Rights* 717 and 734 (1952).

54. Dissenting opinions in *In re* Summers, 325 *United States Reports* 561, at 576 (1945); American Communications Assn. v. Douds, 339 *id*. 382, 447-448 (1950), giving many examples of the uses of such oaths in England and persecutions of Protestants on the Continent. See also his concurring opinion in Wieman v. Updegraff, *infra,* note 56.

55. Quoted by Justice Field in Cummings v. Missouri, *supra,* note 53.

56. Wieman v. Updegraff, 344 *United States Reports* 183 (1952).

57. American Communications Assn. v. Douds, 339 *id*. 382 (1950); Gerende v. Board of Supervisors, 341 *id*. 56 (1951); Garner v. Board of Public Works, 341 *id*. 716 (1951); all reprinted in 3 Chafee, *Documents on Fundamental Human Rights* 772-809 (1952).

58. Justice Black for the Court, in United States v. Lovett, *supra,* note 45.

59. *Supra,* p. 135.

60. *Supra,* pp. 121-126.

61. United States v. Lovett, *supra,* note 45, quoting from Holmes in Missouri, Kansas & Texas Ry. Co. v. May, 194 *United States Reports* 267, at 270 (1904).

FREEDOM OF MOVEMENT

1. The Universal Declaration is reprinted in 3 Chafee, *Documents on Fundamental Human Rights* 956.

2. Article 14 (1) of the Universal Declaration of Human Rights.

3. Abrams v. United States, 250 *United States Reports* 616 (1919), in which Justice Holmes made his most famous dissent. The case is narrated in chap. 3 of Chafee, *Free Speech in the United States* (1941).

4. G. M. Trevelyan, *English Social History* 278 (1943).

5. *Ibid.*

6. Smith, *Wealth of Nations,* Book I, near close of chap. 10.

7. Clarence H. Haring, *Trade and Navigation between Spain and the Indies in the Time of the Hapsburgs* 133 (1918). An omission has not been indicated.

8. Useful population figures at various dates for the American colonies of Spain, France, and Britain are given by Ferenczi in 10 *Encyclopaedia of the Social Sciences* 430-433.

9. See Adam Smith's interesting views about these causes just before the Declaration of Independence. *Wealth of Nations,* Book IV, chap. 7, part 2.

10. Several aspects of the colonial charters are discussed in Chafee, *How Human Rights Got into the Constitution* 26-42 (1952).

11. *Supra,* p. 35.

12. D. B. Quinn, *The Voyages and Colonising Enterprises of Sir Humphrey Gilbert*, 417-420 (1940), from Hakluyt's *Voyages*. The narrative of Gilbert's last days is reprinted in 1 Chafee, *Documents on Fundamental Human Rights* 40 ff.

13. *Supra,* pp. 39-40.

14. *Supra,* pp. 57-59.

15. Ferenczi, *loc. cit. supra,* note 8.

16. Edwin Arlington Robinson, "Old Trails."

17. Quinn, *op. cit. supra,* note 12, vol. I, pp. 188-194 (1940); reprinted in 1 Chafee, *Documents on Fundamental Human Rights* 33. Several omissions are not indicated.

18. This point is developed in Chafee, *How Human Rights Got into the Constitution* 40-42.

19. Stephen Vincent Benet, *Western Star* 3, 4 (1943).

20. See Patent to the New England Council (1620), trading; Massachusetts Bay Charter (1629), fishing; Connecticut Charter (1662), fishing; Massachusetts Province Charter (1691), fishing.

21. Body of Liberties, paragraph 17. The "impediment to the contrarie" probably refers to a pending criminal prosecution or lawsuit.

22. *Id.,* paragraphs 89, 90.

23. *Suffolk County Court Records,* 1671-1680, p. 519 (29 *Publications of the Colonial Society of Massachusetts,* 1933).

24. See, for example, F. C. S. Northrop, *The Meeting of the East and the West* (1946).

25. Chafee, "The Rhode Island Court of Equity," 35 *Publications of the Colonial Society of Massachusetts* 105-107 (1944).

26. Emphasis supplied. Bracketed numbers have been inserted to distinguish the interstate privileges.

27. Paupers, vagabonds, and fugitives from justice are excepted.

28. Mention should also be made of United States v. Wheeler, 254 *United States Reports* 281 (1920), which held that it was not a federal crime under existing legislation to deport men out of a state by force.

29. 6 *Wallace Reports* (U.S.) 35 (1867).

30. 314 *United States Reports* 160 (1941).

31. Justices Black and Murphy joined in this opinion.

32. United States v. Wheeler, *supra,* note 28. Only one Justice dissented.

33. *Infra,* note 38.

34. 8 United States Code § 1185. See also 22 *id.* §§ 211A, 212, which provide that the State Department, consuls, etc., "may grant and issue passports," but only to American citizens.

35. 50 *id.* (1951) §§782(5), 785, 794(c); 50 *id.* (1955 Cumulative Pocket Part), § 843.

36. 22 *Code of Federal Regulations* § 51.75.

37. Bauer v. Acheson, 106 *Federal Supplement* 445 (District of Columbia, 1952), decision by three judges. See also Nathan v. Dulles, 129 *id.* 951 (same court, 1955).

38. Schachtman v. Dulles, 225 *Federal Reporter,* 2nd Series, 938 (D. C. Appeals, June 23, 1955).

39. Universal Declaration on Human Rights, Article 19.

40. "American Visa Policy and Foreign Scientists," 8 *Bulletin of the Atomic Scientists* 209 (Oct., 1952); reviewed by the author in 101 *University of Pennsylvania Law Review* 703 (1953).

41. *Id.,* 212.

42. *Supra,* pp. 116-118, 136.
43. See Chafee, *Free Speech in the United States* 232-240 (1941); Harisiades v. Shaughnessy, 342 *United States Reports* 580, at 587-588 (1952).
44. See Lopez v. Howe, 259 *Federal Reporter* 401 (2nd Circuit, 1919); and other cases in Chafee, *op. cit. supra,* note 43 at 228-231.
45. *Supra,* pp. 95-96.
46. *Supra,* pp. 146-147.
47. Carlson v. Landon, 342 *United States Reports* 524 (1952); 8 *United States Code Annotated* (1953) § 1252.

The majority opinion in the Carlson case did say (at 541) that the discretion of the officials ordering detention could be overridden "where it is clearly shown that it is without a reasonable foundation." This exception seems practically unimportant. A Court which regarded the imprisonment of Zydok and Mrs. Stevenson (in text, *infra*) as having a reasonable foundation is unlikely to upset any immigration order for the detention of an alien on the ground of his opinions or affiliations.

48. See Chafee, *How Human Rights Got into the Constitution,* chap. III.
49. Schachtman v. Dulles (1955), *supra,* note 38.
50. Justice Jackson for the Court, in Harisiades v. Shaughnessy, 342 *United States Reports* 580, at 583 (1952).
51. The facts are taken from a statement adopted by the Supreme Court in Carlson v. Landon, 342 *id.* 524 (1952), at 532 note.
52. See the valuable opinion by Justice Jackson, Williamson v. United States, 184 *Federal Reporter,* 2nd series, 280 (C. C. A. 2nd, 1950).
53. The facts from the Record before the Supreme Court are summarized by Justice Black, dissenting, in Carlson v. Landon, 342 *id.* at 549-550. The details of her Communist activities are taken from the same case below, 187 *Federal Reporter,* New Series, 991 (9th Circuit, 1951), at 997-999.

Note on Sources

Documents and Decisions: Many relevant extracts from documents, cases, etc., which are mentioned in the text, are reprinted in Chafee, *Documents on Fundamental Human Rights,* 3 pamphlets (Harvard University Press, 1951, 1952). This is cited in this Note as Chafee, *Documents.*

Constitutional Debates: The best edition of the debates in the Philadelphia Convention during the drafting of the Constitution is by Farrand, *The Records of the Federal Convention,* 4 vols. (1911, 1937). For debates in the state ratifying conventions, see Elliot's *Debates,* 4 vols. (2d ed.. 1836). For debates in the House of Representatives on the Bill of Rights, see 1 *Annals of Congress* (ed. Gales, 1834) 424 ff., 660 ff., 703 ff., 766 ff., 779; debates in the Senate were unrecorded at that time. A convenient one-volume edition of *The Debates in the Federal Convention* . . ., edited by Hunt & Scott (1920), collects in an appendix, 651 ff., the requests for amendments which were submitted by the ratifying conventions in several states.

The Continental Congress: Documents both before and after Independence, including the Articles of Confederation, are in *Journals of the Continental Congress,* 1774-89, 34 vols., published by the Library of Congress (Washington, Govt. Printing Office, beginning in 1904).

Early State Constitutions: These can readily be consulted in Thorpe, *Federal and State Constitutions, Colonial Charters and Other Organic Documents,* 7 vols. (1909). The arrangement is by states, alphabetically. A valuable book on thought and activities in the states, which affected their early constitutions, is Nevins, *The American States during and after the Revolution, 1775-1789* (1924).

United States Supreme Court Decisions: These are contained in over 300 volumes of the *United States Reports.* These reports are accessible in county bar libraries, university libraries, and large public libraries.

English History: For the text of the main documents mentioned in this book, see (in addition to Chafee, *Documents*) Stephenson & Marcham, *Sources of English Constitutional History: A Selection of Documents from A.D. 600 to the Present* (1937). This contains many other documents bearing on the development of basic liberties in England. It is cited in this Note as Stephenson & Marcham. There are several other valuable collections of English documents for specific periods. Parliamentary debates are reported at length, with added information of interest, in two series: (1) *The Parliamentary or Constitutional History of England,* 24 vols. (1751), known as the Old Parliamentary History. (2) *The Parliamentary History of England . . . to the Year 1803,* 36 vols. (1806-1820), edited by Wm. Cobbett, printed for Hansard, and known as the New Parliamentary History. I have also used *A Collection of the Parliamentary Debates in England from the Year MDCLXVIII . . .,* 21 vols. (1741). Political and other famous trials are reported in that most entertaining of law-books, Howell's *State Trials,* 34 vols., another of Cobbett's projects.

FREEDOM OF DEBATE IN CONGRESS

General: References in 3 Chafee, *Documents* 8-11. Much use was made of A. F. Pollard, *The Evolution of Parliament* (1920); this contains interesting pictures of the House of Lords at various periods and a plan of the Houses of Parliament in 1833 before their destruction by fire. See Carl Wittke, *The*

NOTE ON SOURCES

History of English Parliamentary Privilege (Ohio State University Bulletin, vol. 26, No. 2, 1921).

English Bill of Rights of 1688/9: The official text is 1 Wm. & Mary, st. 2, chap. 2; reprinted in 1 Chafee, *Documents* 264, and in Stephenson & Marcham. For a vivid narrative of the Revolution of 1688 and the deliberations of the Convention, see Macaulay, *History of England,* chaps. 9-11. Macaulay has also been used for earlier events. Because of his Whig sympathies, his statements have been checked by use of other sources, e.g., J. R. Green, *History of England*; H. D. Traill, *William the Third*; A. W. Ward's life of James II, 29 *Dict. Nat. Biog.* 181; and articles in the *Catholic Encyclopedia.* Lucile Pinkham, *William III and the Respectable Revolution* (1954), though the conclusions do not convince me, gives the facts fully, with new material from the Dutch archives.

British Colonies: Carl Wittke, "Parliamentary Privilege in the Empire," in *Essays in History and Political Theory: In Honor of Charles Howard McIlwain* 320 (1936).

The Medieval House of Commons: In addition to Pollard, see Pasquet, *An Essay on the Origins of the House of Commons* (1920); McIlwain, *The High Court of Parliament and Its Supremacy* (1910); White, *Self-government at the King's Command* (1933); and several documents in Stephenson & Marcham. Frank M. Stenton's recent article on "The History of Parliament," in the (London) *Times Literary Supplement,* January 6, 1956, p. xii, cites other valuable studies and shows that my account of this period is oversimplified.

The Speaker's Requests: A long extract from the Journals of Sir Simonds D'Ewes, reprinted in Stephenson & Marcham, narrates the opening of Parliament in 1559.

Queen Elizabeth and Peter Wentworth: J. E. Neale, *Elizabeth I and her Parliaments, 1559-1581* (1953); Neale, "The Commons' Privilege of Free Speech in Parliament," in *Tudor Studies, Presented . . . to A. F. Pollard* (1924) 257; Neale, "Parliament and the Succession Question in 1562/3 and 1566," 36 *English Historical Review* 497 (1921); Neale, "Peter Wentworth," 39 *id.* 36, 175 (1924). Several extracts from the Parliamentary debates are in 3 Chafee, *Documents* 821-851, and in Stephenson & Marcham. See also the life of Wentworth by Sir Charles Dilke in 60 *Dict. Nat. Biog.* 261 (1899).

James I and the Parliament of 1621: 1 *Journals of the Commons;* Sir Edward Nicholas, *Proceedings and Debates in the House of Commons in 1620 and 1621* (1766); *Commons Debates, 1621,* edited by Notestein, Relf, and Simpson (1935), an admirable collection of diaries kept by members. Much use has been made of S. R. Gardiner, *History of England under James I and Charles I.* The chief papers and narratives of important proceedings are reprinted in 3 Chafee, *Documents* 852-866; Stephenson & Marcham.

Charles I and the Five Members: Again Gardiner is my chief source. Clarendon's reprinted in 1 Chafee, *Documents* 250. For the session of 1629, I have relied mainly on Gardiner. Eliot's resolutions are reprinted in Stephenson & Marcham.

Charles I and the Five Members: Again Gardiner is my chief source. Clarendon's account in his *History of the Rebellion* is reprinted in 3 Chafee, *Documents* 867. See Mary F. Keller, *The Long Parliament, 1640-1641: A Biographical Study of its Members* (1954); D. Brunton & D. H. Pennington, *Members of the Long Parliament* (1954).

NOTE ON SOURCES

Freedom of Debate under the Constitution: Judicial decisions are collected in 3 Chafee, *Documents* 887-897. On the history of censure of members of Congress by either House, see an unpublished thesis in the Harvard Law School Library by Avram J. Goldberg, "The Power of Each House of Congress to Punish and to Expel its Members" (1954); Claude M. Fuess, "Hot Words on Capitol Hill," 34 *Saturday Review* 13 (Oct. 6, 1951). A longer paper by Mr. Fuess on the same subject will soon be published in *Proceedings of the Massachusetts Historical Society.*

THE PROHIBITION OF BILLS OF ATTAINDER

General: C. H. McIlwain, "Attainder," 2 *Enclopaedia of the Social Sciences* 304 (1930); Lewis Mayers, "Impeachment," 7 *id.* 600 (1932); Holdsworth, *History of English Law* (4th ed., 1927), passages cited in Chafee, *infra;* Jerome Hall, *General Principles of Criminal Law,* chap. 2 (1947); and other references in 3 Chafee, *Documents* 644. Many documents and cases are reprinted in 3 *id.* 646-809.

The Immediate Background: 1 Blackstone, Commentaries *45-46, 2 *id.* *251-261, 4 *id.* *380-389, Some passages are reprinted in 3 Chafee, *Documents* 705-712.

Attainders and Impeachments in the Middle Ages: The cases of Cade and Mortimer are in 3 Chafee, *Documents* 646-653, and that of Haxey in *id.* 813. All three are in Stephenson & Marcham.

The Revival of Impeachments under James I: See references in chapter I to James I and Parliament of 1621. Gardiner is a valuable source, as usual.

Impeachment and Attainder of Strafford: The act of attainder, 16 Chas. I, chap. 38, is reprinted in 3 Chafee, *Documents* 654; and in Stephenson & Marcham. See Gardiner; C. V. Wedgwood, *The King's Peace, 1637-1641* (1955); and the life of Strafford by Gardiner in 60 *Dict. Nat. Biog.* 268 (1899).

Impeachment of Danby: My chief source was 1 Browning, *Thomas Osborne: Earl of Danby and Duke of Leeds* (1951). The Old Parliamentary History was much used, and the New Parliamentary History somewhat. Macaulay, *History of England,* chap. 2, was helpful. Several papers and narratives of proceedings are reprinted in 3 Chafee, *Documents* 657-681; and in Stephenson & Marcham. See also the lives by P. C. Yorke in 16 *Encyclopaedia Britannica* (11th ed., 1911) 366; and by Sidney Lee, 42 *Dict. Nat. Biog.* 295 (1895).

Attainder of Sir John Fenwick: The case is reported in 13 Howell's *State Trials* 538. See Macaulay, *History of England,* chaps. 22, 23; the life of Fenwick by T. F. Henderson in 18 *Dict. Nat. Biog.* 329 (1889); unpublished thesis in Harvard Law School Library by Thomas D. Mantel, "The History and Legal Background of the Proceedings against Sir John Fenwick in Parliament . . . " (1953). As to witnesses in treason cases, see Willard Hurst, "Treason in the United States," 58 *Harvard Law Review* 226, 395, 806 (1944); Cramer v. United States, 325 *United States Reports* 1 (1945).

Developments in England in Subsequent Centuries: For the trial of Queen Caroline, I used 2 Spencer Walpole, *History of England from 1815.* On the impeachment of Warren Hastings, see Macaulay's *Essays.* The debates on the removal of Sir Robert Walpole are in 11 New Parliamentary History 1047-1066, 1085-86, 1098-1185, 1215; they are reprinted in 3 Chafee, *Documents* 682-704, and in Stephenson & Marcham. See Walpole's life by I. S. Leadam in 59 *Dict. Nat. Biog.* 178 (1899). The 1779 debates on the removal of Lord North are in 20 New Parliamentary History 1096-1150; extracts are reprinted in Stephenson & Marcham.

NOTE ON SOURCES

The Prohibition in the Constitution: All the important decisions here discussed are reprinted in 3 Chafee, *Documents* 717-809. See "The Constitutional Prohibition of Bills of Attainder: A Waning Guaranty of Judicial Trial," 63 *Yale Law Journal* 844 (1954).

FREEDOM OF MOVEMENT

Mobility in Seventeenth-century England: Adam Smith, *The Wealth of Nations,* chap. 10; G. M. Trevelyan, *English Social History* (1943).

Freedom to Go to America from Spain and France: Clarence H. Haring, *Trade and Navigation between Spain and the Indies in the Time of the Hapsburgs* (1918); George M. Wrong, "Canada," 5 *Encyclopaedia Britannica* (11th ed., 1911) 156-158; H. L. Osgood, "United States," 27 *id.* 672; Imre Ferenczi, "Migrations," 10 *Encyclopaedia of the Social Sciences* 429 (1933).

Freedom to Go to America from England: D. B. Quinn, *The Voyages and Colonising Enterprises of Sir Humphrey Gilbert,* 2 vols. (1940). The Gilbert patent, his last voyage, and extracts from colonial charters are in 1 Chafee, *Documents* 33-143. See also Wm. Macdonald, *Select Charters and Other Documents* (1904).

The Western Frontier Closed, 1765: The Quebec Proclamation of 1763 is in 1 Chafee, *Documents* 145; Macdonald, *Select Charters* 267. The Quebec Act of 1774, 14 Geo. III, chap. 83, is in 1 Chafee, *Documents* 162; Stephenson & Marcham. The Memorial to the Inhabitants of the British Colonies in 1774 is in 1 *Journals of the Continental Congress* 98, and in 1 Chafee, *Documents* 163.

Freedom of Movement under the Constitution: On freedom to go out of the country and passports, see, in addition to decisions, "Passport Refusals for Political Reasons. Constitutional Issues and Judicial Review," 61 *Yale Law Journal* 171 (1952); Reginald Parker, "The Right to Go Abroad: To Have and to Hold a Passport," 40 *Virginia Law Review* 853 (1954); Linus Pauling (Nobel prize-winner), "My Efforts to Obtain a Passport," in first item in next paragraph.

On freedom to come to this country and our visa policy, see the valuable collection of facts in "American Visa Policy and Foreign Scientists," 8 *Bulletin of Atomic Scientists* 209 (Oct., 1952), reviewed by Chafee, 101 *University of Pennsylvania Law Review* 703 (1953).

Some information relating to the last two paragraphs was taken from Maurice I. Goldbloom, "Civil Liberties" in *Civic and Political Status,* a pamphlet reprinted from *The American Jewish Year Book* (1954).

227

Tables of Constitutions and Laws

1. UNITED STATES CONSTITUTION

[Abbreviations: Hist. bckgd., historical background of the particular item in events, documents, etc., in England and this country before the Constitution; Interp., interpretation of the particular item in the Convention, courts, and discussion, including situations which fall within the policy of the clause if not its legal scope.]

GENERAL TOPICS:

Framing by Philadelphia Convention, 1-3, 90, 94

Ratification by states, 90

Constitution considered as a whole, 4

Suggested classification of clauses into broad standards and specific safeguards, 154-155

Preëmption by Congress, 188-189

Judicial review of unconstitutional statutes, 152, 154, 159, 160-161

Political rights in general, 1, 4

Human rights provisions in general, 1-3, 90, 160-161, 213

Freedom of movement: not specific right in Cons., 162, 209; hist. bckgd., 117-118, 130, 166, 173-174, 176-181, 184-185 and n. 27, 187-188, 190, 191, 198, 205-206. Interp., 185-187, 188; internal mobility, 188-192; fdm. to go out of this country, 193-198; fdm. to come into this country, 198-204; fdm. from exile, 204-209; implied right of citizens to go to national capital or cross state lines, 189, 190; fdm. inside a state, 192; due process clauses best basis for fdm. of movement, 192-193

PREAMBLE, 1, 3

ARTICLE I, SEC. 1

Legislative powers vested in Congress, 18, 83

Establishment of Congress, 1, 4

ARTICLE I, SEC. 2

Impeachments by House: hist. bckgd., 48, 72, 73-74 and n. 34, 81, 104-105, 108-112, 116-117, 125-127, 131, 138, 140-144; interp., 98, 140-144; 216, n. 32

ARTICLE I, SEC. 3

Impeachment trials in Senate: hist. bckgd., 48, 73-74, 98, 104-105, 106-108, 110-112, 116-117, 126-128, 130-133, 138, 142-143; interp., 98, 143-144 and n. 39, 148-149, 153, 155, 216 n. 32

Question whether impeachment ends with session of Congress, 129 and n. 31

Consequences of impeachment: hist. bckgd., 98, 103-105, 130, 133, 138, 144, 219 n. 33; interp., 98, 139, 143-144

ARTICLE I, SEC. 4

Frequent meetings of Congress, 18, 44

ARTICLE I, SEC. 5

Punishing members: hist. bckgd., 7, 20; interp., 5-6, 88-89, 209-210 and n. 54, 216 n. 32

ARTICLE I, SEC. 6

Privilege from arrest: hist. bckgd., 30, 75, 125 and n. 27; interp., 30, 125, 217 n. 49

229

231

EIGHTH AMENDMENT
Bail: hist. bckgd., 18, 208 and n. 48; interp., 208-209 and nn. 47, 48, 209, 211-213 and nn. 51-53
No cruel and unusual punishments: hist. bckgd., 18, 96-97, 101, 117-118, 124, 205-206, 219 n. 33; interp., 18, 97, 147, 159, 204-207, 211-213
FOURTEENTH AMENDMENT, new restrictions on states
In general, 90
Privileges and immunities of U.S. citizens: interp., 187, 189, 190-192 and n. 32
Due process (and police power), 186, 187, 192
Equal protection of the laws, 91, 186
FIFTEENTH AMENDMENT
Votes for negroes, 91

2. PROCEEDINGS OF THE CONTINENTAL CONGRESS, 1774-1789

Memorial to the Inhabitants of the British Colonies (Oct. 21, 1774), 182
Declaration of Independence (1776), 94, 166, 182
Articles of Confederation (1778-1781), 6, 184-187 and n. 27, 190, 191-192
Resolutions urging states to cede western lands to nation (1780), 183
Ordinance for the Northwest Territory (1787), 95, 183, 187

3. ACTS OF CONGRESS, PRESIDENTIAL ORDERS, ETC.

Emancipation Proclamation (1862, 1863), 187
Test oath legislation (1862, 1865), 156-159
Tenure of Office Act (1867), 153 and n. 48
Interstate Commerce Commission Act (1887), passenger fares, 192
Espionage Act (1917), punishing wartime sedition, 60
Lindbergh Act (1934), interstate kidnapping, 192
Bill to deport Harry Bridges (1940), 146-147 and n. 41
Smith Act (1940), punishing peacetime sedition, 147, 210, 212, 220 n. 44
Urgent Deficiency Appropriation Act (1943), cutting off salaries of specified persons, 150-155, 161
Labor Management Relations Act, or Taft-Hartley Act (1947), test oaths for union officers, 158 and n. 57, 221 n. 54
Subversive Activities Control Act, or McCarran Act (1950): mere membership in Communist Party not crime, 207; passports forbidden, 194 and n. 35; aliens imprisoned without bail, 208-209 and n. 47, 211-213
Sedition laws in general, 161
Passport laws, 193-198
Immigration and visa laws, 162-163, 174, 187, 198-204
Naturalization laws, 210-211, 212
Deportation laws, 146-147 and nn. 42-44, 187, 200-213

4. COLONIAL AND STATE CHARTERS, CONSTITUTIONS, AND LEGISLATION

Colonial charters in general, 170 and n. 10, 172-179 *passim*
Sir Humphrey Gilbert's Patent (1578), 171-173, 174, 180
New England Council Patent (1620), *see* Massachusetts
State constitutions in general, 90
State bills of attainder in Revolution, 94, 98, 218 n. 7
State test-oath laws in general, 158-159, 161
State investigating committees in general, 159-161

5. ENGLISH STATUTES AND LAWS, AND OTHER ACTIONS BY PARLIAMENT

235

Index of Cases and Persons

[Cases in italics are decisions on questions of law. Criminal trials, impeachments, and attainders are indexed under the names of the persons involved. Writers are entered when their views appear in the text or footnotes, but not for compilations of documents. The Note on Sources is not indexed.]